Contents

Medicine as Culture

Illness, Disease and the Body in Western Societies

Second Edition

Deborah Lupton

SAGE Publications
London • Thousand Oaks • New Delhi

First edition published 1994. Reprinted 1995, 1996, 1998, 2000, 2001, 2002
Second edition published 2003

SAGE Publications Ltd
6 Bonhill Street
London EC2A 4PU

SAGE Publications Inc.
2455 Teller Road
Thousand Oaks, California 91320

SAGE Publications India Pvt Ltd
B-42, Panchsheel Enclave
Post Box 4109
New Delhi 100 017

British Library Cataloguing in Publication data

A catalogue record for this book is available from the British Library

ISBN 0 7619 4029 4
ISBN 0 7619 4030 8 (pbk)

Library of Congress Control Number: 2003103977

Typeset by C&M Digitals (P) Ltd., Chennai, India
Printed in Great Britain by TJ International Ltd, Padstow, Cornwall

Western societies in the early twenty-first century are characterized by people's increasing disillusionment with scientific medicine. Paradoxically, there is also an increasing dependence upon biomedicine to provide the answers to social as well as medical problems, and the mythology of the beneficent, god-like physician remains dominant. On the one hand, doctors are criticized for abusing their medical power by controlling or oppressing their patients, for malpractice and indulging in avarice; on the other, in most western societies, access to medical care is widely regarded as a social good and the inalienable right of every person. Medical views on health, illness, disease and the body dominate public and private discussions.

Some critics would argue that the medical profession has too much power and too high a social status, that people are placing too much trust in medical practitioners and the treatment they offer, that the resources devoted to medical technology are disproportionate. In the past two centuries, a range of behaviours from homosexuality to alcoholism have come under the rubric of medicine. With the current obsession for locating the genetic precursor of illnesses, diseases and behaviours, the knowledge base of scientific medicine has encroached even further into defining the limits of normality and the proper functioning and deportment of the human body. Yet it cannot be denied that illness and disease are debilitating states, and that the populations of western societies are vastly longer-lived and more free of pain and discomfort now than at any other time.

The increasing secularization of western societies, the dependence on rationality and individualism which are legacies of the Enlightenment, the increase in average life expectancies and decrease in numbers of deaths from infectious diseases, the turn to biomedicine and science as the ultimate weapons against illness, disease and premature death have generated ideas and practices which tend to deny the fragility and mortality of the human body. For the populations of western societies, serious illness and death are strange, mysterious, frightening and *unexpected* events, except perhaps for the very old. Medicine, or faith in medicine, is a creed. There is a set of expectations surrounding health and the body prevailing in western societies: we expect to feel well, without pain or disability, long after middle-age; we expect all children to survive birth and infancy, all women to give birth with no complications, all surgery and medical treatment to be successful. And for the majority of people, these expectations are indeed met, serving to reinforce them even more strongly.

However, although medical authority may confer an image of reassuring competence and control of the situation, the construction of the medical practitioner as omnipotent inevitably leads to disappointment and dis-illusionment when things go wrong, resulting sometimes in legal action against doctors. When the unexpected happens – when early death inter-venes, when surgery or medical treatment fails, or produces even worse health, when infants and children die, when illness remains chronic and debilitating – there are few explanations that can provide meaning to the experience. Furthermore, while we continue to look to medicine to provide help when we are ill, we also express resentment at the feelings of power-lessness we experience in the medical encounter.

As its title suggests, this book examines the socio-cultural dimensions of medicine in western societies, seeking to cast light upon the reasons why medicine is characterized by such strong paradoxes, why issues of health and illness are surrounded with controversy, conflict and emotion. The book draws upon scholarship and research published predominantly in the sub-disciplines of medical sociology/sociology of health and ill-ness, the history of medicine and medical anthropology, but also makes excursions into the insights offered by feminism, cultural studies and dis-course analysis.

An interdisciplinary perspective, while exciting and stimulating in its breadth, poses its own problems. When one is integrating research and scholarship from a number of disciplines, it can be very difficult to know where to draw the boundaries. One response to this dilemma is the deci-sion to focus this book mainly upon developments in scholarship and research published since 1980. In addition, this book largely avoids dis-cussion of the individual psychological dimension of illness, including the psychoanalytic explanations which have flourished in media and cul-tural studies and feminist scholarship. Related to this is the decision to omit detailed discussion of mental illness, an area which could itself fill the pages of a book such as this and hence could not be given justice in the space allowed.

This book is an attempt to link cogently the different theoretical per-spectives informing scholarship and research directed towards under-standing the socio-cultural dimension of medicine, illness and the body at the beginning of the twenty-first century. This discussion is supported with pertinent examples from research studies which have attempted to provide empirical evidence of the lived experience of these phenomena, and gives due recognition to the macro-political processes which frame, shape and constrain such experiences and knowledges. This book adopts the field of cultural studies' interest in mass media and elite cultural arte-facts as the sites of the reproduction of meaning, and the poststructuralist concern with discourses (ways of representing and talking about phenom-ena) and their role in the construction of practices and concepts of reality.

Chapter 1 is an overview of the major theoretical perspectives brought to bear on medicine and society. The chapter reviews developments and paradigmatic changes in medical sociology and the sociology of health and illness since the 1950s, including discussion of functionalism, the political economy perspective, social constructionism and Foucauldian theory. The contributions of medical anthropology and the history of medicine to scholarship are then discussed, as are those offered by the newer interdisciplinary fields of cultural studies and discourse analysis. The chapter discusses the extent to which these sub-disciplines and inter-disciplines have merged in the wake of the poststructuralist and postmodernist movements and demonstrates how a broad appreciation of their differences and similarities assists the understanding of the socio-cultural dimensions of medicine, health care and the doctor–patient relationship.

The remaining chapters build on this theoretical basis to examine more specific dimensions of medicine as culture. Chapter 2 is devoted to examining the body in western medicine, incorporating the insights of prominent contemporary scholars in the humanities and social sciences to understand the construction of the sexual and gendered body, the disciplined body, the clean body, the commodified body and the dead body in the context of medico-scientific and public health discourses. Chapter 3 moves to a focus on language and visual imagery in examining dominant discursive and iconographic representations of medicine, illness and disease. Particular attention is paid in this chapter to the portrayal of illness, disease and death in literature and popular culture and changes in metaphors of the body and illness since medieval times, including the currently dominant machinery and military metaphorical systems, metaphors of the immune system and cancer, and metaphor and gender. Chapter 3 also discusses visual images of people living with AIDS, the iconography of the interior of the body, and the use of the cultural analysis of representation as a strategy for political activism.

Chapters 4 and 5 are highly interrelated. Chapter 4 is devoted to examining the lay perspective on health and illness. The chapter traces the notion of the 'patient' in the context of changes in the modes of medical treatment over the centuries and then focuses on the effect of the emergence of scientific medicine upon patients' experiences of health care. The chapter also looks at the 'sick role', the moral dimension of illness, the contemporary experience of illness, particularly in the clinical or hospital setting, the effect of medical technology upon subjectivity and beliefs about illness causation from the lay perspective. Chapter 5 covers in detail issues surrounding power relations in the medical encounter, and is centred around contemporary theoretical debates and research surrounding medical dominance, the doctor–patient relationship, patient dependency and resistance, the nurse's position in medicine and the doctor's perspective on the medical encounter. The chapter also examines the claims of alternative (holistic) therapies and self-help groups that they offer valid alternatives to the alleged problems inherent in the orthodox doctor–patient encounter.

The last substantive chapter, Chapter 6, reviews feminist scholarship as it has been applied to the socio-cultural analysis of biomedicine and health care. In so doing, the chapter picks up some of the issues and debates canvassed in earlier chapters. It discusses the development of the medical specialization of gynaecology and its implications for the ways in which the female body has been constructed historically, and then examines in detail power struggles, discursive definitions and theoretical debates around contraception and abortion, menstruation and menopause, childbirth, prenatal screening technologies and the assisted reproduction technologies. The brief conclusion following Chapter 6 serves to bring the dominant themes and arguments of the book together and looks at ways in which a sophisticated socio-cultural awareness of the discourses and imagery relating to medicine, health and illness may contribute to the expansion of alternative 'ways of seeing'.

1
Theoretical Perspectives on Medicine and Society

Over the past two decades or so there has been an increasing propensity for the boundaries between disciplines to blur, particularly among the humanities and social sciences. As a result, it is becoming more and more difficult to ascribe labels to scholarly endeavours. Literary studies, psychoanalytic theory, philosophy, social psychology, cultural studies, linguistics, history, sociology and anthropology have all experienced changes which bring them closer together in their projects. Of particular note is the emergence of the 'linguistic turn', or the increasing attention paid to language and discursive processes in the production and maintenance of social life and subjectivity.

In line with these developments, the scholarly activities which may loosely be gathered under the rubric of the sociology of health and illness have altered focus. There have been several major impetuses fuelling this change. One is the emergence of a growing disillusionment with scientific medicine on the part of both intellectuals and some consumers in the late twentieth century. As the effectiveness and benevolence of medicine began to be challenged, so too was its claim to inaccessible and arcane knowledge based on objectivity and political neutrality. The other is the impact of poststructuralist and postmodernist theories, including the release in the anglophone world of the translated works of the French philosopher-historian Michel Foucault, and the growing concern of feminist scholarship with gender and the body. In response to these impetuses, anthropologists and sociologists of health and illness, particularly in continental Europe and Britain, but increasingly so in North America and Australia, began to call into question the claims to 'truth' and political neutrality of biomedical knowledge (that which is founded upon scientific principles and understandings).

In this chapter, the major fields of scholarship and research in the humanities and social sciences that have examined the social role of medicine in western societies are reviewed for the theoretical developments which have occurred over the past fifty years or so. Particular attention is paid to the emergence of social constructionism as a dominant perspective appropriate for engaging in inquiries into the socio-cultural dimensions of medicine, health and illness. There is also greater discussion of the sociological tradition compared with those of anthropology, history and cultural studies, as this book is written from and principally positioned within the sociological discipline. For the purposes of this chapter and for clarity's sake, distinctions have been drawn in the time-honoured way concerning perspectives and paradigms between and within disciplines. However, the caveat is made that such distinctions are, in many cases, no longer as valid or appropriate as once they were. Indeed, one of the strongest points I seek to make in this chapter is that sociologies, anthropologies, histories and cultural studies of medicine, health and illness share an intellectual tradition and trajectory based on the same trends and developments in social theory.

The sociology of health and illness

As it first developed in the anglophone world, medical sociology (as the sub-discipline was first named and which term is still preferred in the United States) or the sociology of health and illness (the term preferred in Britain and Australia) was primarily concerned with systematic empiricism using the measurement of objective variables deemed quantifiable. Early in its development, in order to be accepted as a quasi-scientific discipline applied to a scientific discipline (that is, medicine), medical sociology adopted largely positivist values which to some extent are still evident, although more so in the United States than Britain and Australia. As a result, often medical sociology could best have been described as a derivative of social medicine rather than as a sub-discipline of critical sociology (Jordanova, 1983; Scambler, 1987; Mechanic, 1993). Accordingly, in line with the assumptions of the model of scientific medicine itself, for much of the history and development of medical sociology and the sociology of health and illness the biological, human anatomy conception of the body has remained unchallenged (Armstrong, 1987a: 651). That is, until social constructionism, in train with the impact of poststructuralism and postmodernism and the ascendancy of feminist and Foucauldian critiques of medicine, began to reassert itself as an influential approach in the early 1980s.

There have been three dominant theoretical perspectives in the history of medical sociology/sociology of health and illness: functionalism, the political economy approach and social constructionism. Variants of all three are currently in circulation in scholarship in the sociology of health and illness. However, it is clear that since the 1970s functionalism and, to a lesser extent, the political economy approach have been on the wane, while the social constructionist perspective continues to prosper.

Functionalism

The functionalist approach to medical sociology views social relations in the health care setting as products of a consensualist society, in which social order and harmony are preserved by people acting in certain defined roles and performing certain functions. It is interested in the processes by which doctors and other health care professionals carry out their everyday work, and how people cope with illness and disease. The classic functionalist position is to view illness as a potential state of social 'deviance'; that is, failure to conform to societal expectations and norms in some way. Illness is considered an unnatural state of the human body, causing both physical and social dysfunction, and therefore a state which must be alleviated as soon as possible.

Functionalists argue that the feelings of stigma, shame and vulnerability accompany many illnesses. Therefore the role of the medical profession is to act as a necessary institution of social control, or a moral guardian of society, using its power to distinguish between normality and 'deviance' as the Church once did. The maintenance of social order is thus the basis of the functionalist theorizing on the nature of illness and the medical encounter, with medicine being viewed as an important mechanism to control the potentially disruptive nature of illness.

The leading scholar in the application of functionalist theory to medicine was the American sociologist Talcott Parsons. His explanations of the demands and function of the 'sick role' and its implications for the doctor–patient relationship and discussion of the social aspects of the institution of medicine as a profession were influential in medical sociology in the 1950s and 1960s. According to Parsons and his followers, a person afflicted with serious illness is physically disabled and thereby forced to rely upon others, and hence is deviating from the expectations of social roles. Parsons argued that conforming to the norms of the sick role legitimates such deviance. He described four major components of the sick role: ill persons are exempted from the performance of social obligations which they are normally expected to fulfil; they are not blamed for their condition, and need not feel guilty when they do not fulfil their normal obligations; however, ill people must want to try and get well – if they do not, they can be accused of malingering; and being sick is defined as being in need of medical help to return to 'normality' – the sick must put themselves into the hands of medical practitioners to help them get well again (Parsons, 1987/1951: 151–2).

The patient is therefore placed in the role of the socially vulnerable supplicant, seeking official verification from the doctor that she or he is not 'malingering'. The role of the doctor is seen as socially beneficent, and the doctor–patient relationship as inherently harmonious and consensual even though it is characterized by an unequal power relationship. Parsons argues that patients often unconsciously view doctors as parental figures, investing their need for support and help in doctors and reverting back to the dependence of childhood. The sick role and the power differential between patients and doctors works to deal with this dependency productively and in ways that allow patients to cast off their dependency and eventually re-enter the world of the well. They are therefore mechanisms by which society deals with the potential threat of people harbouring a motivation to avoid responsibility by allowing themselves to become and remain ill (Lupton, 1997a).

While Parsons' work was ground-breaking in elucidating the social dimension of the medical encounter, the functionalist perspective has been subject to criticism based on its neglect of the potential for conflict inherent in the medical encounter. There appears to be a streak of implicit moralism in Parsons' ideas relating to the potential of people to become 'malingerers' by claiming illness (Lupton, 1997a). Critics argue that the functionalist position typifies patients as compliant, passive and grateful, while doctors are represented as universally beneficent, competent and altruistic (Turner, 1995). On the contrary, critics assert, the conflict of interest between patient and doctor is expressed over a struggle for power, which may be explicit or implicit, and involves negotiation and manoeuvre at every step in the encounter (Gerson, 1976; Strong, 1979: 7). It should be taken into account that doctors and patients have different, and often conflicting, interests: doctors, to perform their duties of the professional in the medical workplace, seeking to earn a living and progress in their career; patients, to alleviate the physical pain or discomfort that is disrupting their lives. Furthermore, it is argued, there are organizational constraints in the medical setting and external factors influencing the behaviour of doctors and patients when they meet in the medical encounter which go beyond the dynamics of the sick role model. Both the doctor and the patient have relationships outside the medical encounter which affect their approach to the encounter.

As I noted earlier, the functionalist approach has become unfashionable in medical sociology and the sociology of health and illness, largely because of the critiques outlined above. Despite this, it still has important things to say about the emotional relationship between the doctor and the patient, and the needs and drives, both conscious and unconscious, that underpin it (Lupton, 1997a).

The political economy perspective

The political economy approach developed as a critical response to functionalism in the context of larger changes in social thought occurring in the 1970s, particularly Marxist views on the capitalist economic system. Also known as critical structuralism, the approach was a dominant intellectual movement in the 1970s and early 1980s, and remains influential in the sociology of health and illness. Under this perspective, good health is defined in political terms not only as a state of physical or emotional well-being but as 'access to and control over the basic material and non-material resources that sustain and promote life at a high level of satisfaction', meaning that 'a key component of health is struggle' (Baer et al., 1986: 95). For political economists, ill, ageing or physically disabled people are marginalized by society because they do not contribute to the production and consumption of commodities. Other marginalized groups, such as women, people from non-English-speaking backgrounds, non-whites, the aged, the unemployed and members of the working class, tend to endure greater social and economic disadvantage than those from privileged groups, have restricted access to health care services and suffer poorer health as a result (see, for example, recent critiques by Ahmad and Jones, 1998; Manderson, 1998; Estes and Linkins, 2000).

From this perspective the institution of medicine exists to attempt to ensure that the population remains healthy enough to contribute to the economic system as workers and consumers, but is unwilling to devote resources for those who do not respond to treatment and are unable to return to the labour market. Medicine thus serves to perpetuate social inequalities, the divide between the privileged and the underprivileged, rather than ameliorate them.

Political economy writers comment on the 'cultural crisis of modern medicine', in which health care under capitalism is perceived as largely ineffective, overly expensive, under-regulated and vastly inequitable. For writers such as Freidson (1970), the high status of the medical profession and the faith that is invested in its members' abilities to perform miracles have resulted in other social problems being inappropriately redefined as illness. He contended that as a result of the widening of medical jurisdiction, more social resources have become directed towards illness, and the medical profession's power and influence increased markedly in the twentieth century, with little scope to question its activities or use of resources.

This 'medicalization' thesis was adopted by other political economic critics, including Zola (1981) who saw medicine as becoming a major institution of social control, superseding the influence of religion and law as a 'repository of truth'. Illich (1976) argued that modern medicine was both physically and socially harmful due to the impact of professional control over medicine, leading to dependence upon medicine as a panacea, obscuring the political conditions which cause ill health and removing autonomy from people to control their own health: 'Such medicine is but a device to convince those who are sick and tired of society that it is they who are ill, impotent, and in need of technical repair' (1976: 9).

Like the functionalists, political economists see medicine as a moral exercise, used to define normality, punish deviance and maintain social order. Where the two approaches differ is that the latter school of thought believes that this power is harmful rather than benevolent and is abused by the medical profession. The political economic critique questions the values of biomedicine and focuses on the identification of the political, economic and historical factors that shape health, disease and treatment issues. Scholars claim that the capitalist economic system has promoted a view of health care as a commodity, in which the seeking of profit is a major influencing factor, and that therefore the relationship between doctor and patient is characterized by conflict and the clash of differing interests and priorities. They argue that biomedicine attempts to narrow the cause of ill health to a single physical factor, upon which treatment is then focused. Medical care thus tends to be oriented towards the treatment of acute symptoms using drugs and medical technology rather than prevention or the maintenance of good health. Political economists suggest, however, that the causes of ill health are more diffuse and are related to socio-economic factors which are themselves the result of capitalist production: for example, over-processed foods treated with chemicals, pollution, stress, alienation and occupational hazards (McKee, 1988: 776).

Political economy commentators have written extensively about the state's failure to acknowledge the role of environmental toxins resulting from industry in causing illness, to regulate the activities of multinational corporations to create healthier environments, or to take steps to control the production, marketing and advertising of unhealthy commodities such as alcohol and tobacco (for example, Epstein, 1978, 1990; Breslow, 1982; Syme and Alcalay, 1982; Doyal, 1983; Russell and Schofield, 1986: Ch. 2). They see a symbiotic relationship therefore existing between capitalism and health care: capitalism produces health needs which are treated in such a way as to obscure their origins and demands the consumption of commodities to secure the healing process, which in turn supports the capitalist system of production (Navarro, 1976; Renaud, 1978). The proposed alternative is a socialized system of health care, in which the state provides care for all free-of-charge and alternative, non-biomedical methods of health care delivery such as natural therapies are accepted as valuable.

There are thus two major facets to the political economy approach. The first largely accepts that biomedicine is a politically neutral 'good' and seeks to provide more and better medical services to the underprivileged, while the second, more radical critique has questioned the value of biomedicine itself and highlighted its role as an institution of social control, reinforcing racism and patriarchy (Ehrenreich, 1978). However, both approaches conform to the 'use/abuse' model of medical knowledge, which tends to accept the neutrality and objective validity of medical knowledge itself, but questions the use to which it is put in the interests of doctors and the wider capitalist system, often retreating into 'doctor-bashing' (Jordanova, 1983: 91). Political economists have traditionally been concerned with medical knowledge as serving the interests of the ruling classes concealed behind an apparent political neutrality, rather than engaging in a philosophical analysis of such knowledge (1983: 86). Their critique sometimes seems contradictory: for example, medicine is typically criticized for being both overly expansionist and exclusionist (of the underprivileged), and illness is seen as being caused by both deprivation and medical domination (Gerhardt, 1989: 318–22).

The political economy perspective has been criticized for ignoring the micro-social aspects of the doctor–patient relationship (Ehrenreich, 1978). For many writers from this perspective, the doctor–patient relationship is represented as the equivalent of the capitalist–worker relationship, in which the former exploits the latter. In this conceptualization, an individual who is ill may be reduced to 'a specimen of societal processes', his or her suffering not acknowledged as the focus of the doctor's wish to help, and emphasis upon structural societal change may detract from the plight of current cases needing immediate attention (Gerhardt, 1989: 350–1). Furthermore, the political economy perspective calls for a mass social movement to change dependency upon medical technology, decommodify medicine, challenge the vested interests of drug companies, insurance companies and the medical profession, and redirect resources towards ameliorating the social and environmental causes of ill health (Ehrenreich, 1978: 25–6; Gerhardt, 1989: 323). For some sociologists, such a call may seem idealistic and unrealistic, particularly given the symbiotic relationship between capitalism and medicine (see, for example, Renaud, 1978).

The political economy approach has also been criticized for its unrelenting nihilism; its tendency to fail to recognize that advances in health status and increased life expectancy which have occurred over the past century, associated with improvements in the human diet, reforms in sanitation and the supply of clean water, a rise in standards of housing, better contraceptive technologies and progress in medical treatment and drug therapies, are intrinsically linked to the requirements and demands of the capitalist economic system (Hart, 1982). It has been further argued that while political economists tend to be highly critical of patterns of health status and inequality in capitalist societies, they fail to fully recognize that socialist states are no more successful in reducing inequalities, and indeed that the overall health status and access to health care of the populations of such societies have historically been worse than that of populations of capitalist societies (Turner, 1995).

Nonetheless, this approach remains an important perspective on the social aspects of health and illness, especially in its focus on highlighting the political and economic dimension of health states. Without this perspective, the social structural reasons for disparities in patterns of ill health across populations would not be identified and challenged. Continuing problems of access to health care and the larger environmental and political issues surrounding the question of why certain social groups are more prone to ill health remain important points of discussion for the political economy approach.

Social constructionism

The perspective of social constructionism began to receive increased expression in the sociology of health and illness and the history of medicine in the 1980s, and it remains a dominant approach in the early years of the twenty-first century. In the 1980s and 1990s, poststructuralist and post-modernist approaches were important in building upon earlier writings adopting a constructionist approach. Foucault's works were most influential during this time, and have now stimulated a large body of research (see, for example, Armstrong, 1983, 2002; Lupton, 1995; Turner, 1995; the essays in Petersen and Bunton, 1997). Postmodern scholars such as Kristeva, Derrida, Cixous and Deleuze and Guattari have also been employed to theorize relevant issues (see particularly the work of Fox, 1993, 1997, 1998, 2002).

Social constructionism is an approach which questions claims to the existence of essential truths. What is asserted to be 'truth' should be considered the product of power relations, and as such is never neutral but always acting in the interests of someone. The social constructionist perspective argues, therefore, that all knowledges are inevitably the products of social relations, and are subject to change rather than fixed. Knowledge is seen not as a universal, independent reality but as a participant in the construction of reality. Human subjects are viewed as being constituted in and through discourses and social practices which have complex histories. Thus the examination of the ways in which the 'common-sense knowledge' which sustains and constitutes a society or culture is generated and reproduced is a central interest.

While this approach is certainly not new in the history of sociological theory (see, for example, scholars in the sociology of knowledge field such as Berger and Luckmann, 1967), the growing predominance of poststructuralist and postmodernist analyses of issues surrounding concepts of reality and bodily experiences in the humanities and social sciences has given renewed vigour and intellectual interest in its application to the area of the sociology of health and illness after a long period of marginalization. These new areas of interest have also brought into the social constructionist perspective the somewhat previously neglected consideration of issues of power relations at the macro-level, thus incorporating some of the concerns of the political economy perspective. It is predominantly this modified version of social constructionism that this book adopts to illuminate medicine as culture.

The primary focus of social constructionists is examining the social aspects of biomedicine, the development of medico-scientific and lay medical knowledges and practices. The social constructionist approach does not necessarily call into question the reality of disease or illness states or bodily experiences. It merely emphasizes that these states and experiences are known and interpreted via social activity and therefore should be examined using cultural and social analysis. According to this perspective, medical knowledge is regarded not as an incremental progression towards a more refined and better knowledge, but as a series of relative constructions which are dependent upon the socio-historical settings in which they occur and are constantly renegotiated.

In so doing, the approach allows alternative ways of thinking about the truth claims of biomedicine, showing them to be as much social products as lay knowledges of medicine. Such a project has brought together sociologists, anthropologists, philosophers and social historians interested in the cultural assumptions in which biomedicine is grounded and the practices that sustain it. The feminist movement has led the way in devoting attention to the ways in which medical and scientific knowledges are used to privilege the position of powerful groups over others. It has developed a trenchant critique of the 'biology as destiny' ideology which has frequently been adopted in the medical context to deny women full participation in the public sphere (see Chapter 6 for a detailed discussion of feminist scholarship as applied to medicine).

There are a range of political positions taken by scholars adopting the social constructionist approach (Bury, 1986). Some view medical knowledge as neutral, while others emphasize the social control function of discourses, arguing that such knowledge and its attendant practices reinforce the position of powerful interests to the exclusion of others. However, social constructionist scholars generally avoid viewing power as being wielded from above and shaped entirely by the forces of capitalism, recognizing instead a multiplicity of interests and sites of power. The notion that medicine acts as an important institution of social control has remained, but the emphasis has moved from examining medical power as an oppressive, highly visible, sovereign-based power, to a conceptualization of medicine as *producing* knowledges which change in time and space. Those adopting the social constructionist perspective argue that medical power not only resides in institutions or elite individuals, but is deployed by every individual by way of socialization to accept certain values and norms of behaviour.

While the social constructionist perspective is currently rather fashionable, particularly in Britain, Australia and continental Europe, it is not a universally accepted perspective in sociology, a discipline that has traditionally been characterized by antipathy between competing paradigms (the Marxist/conflict perspective versus the functionalist/consensus school, for example). Constructionist analyses have been criticized for concentrating upon medical discourse at the macro-level, for making broad generalizations and avoiding a detailed examination of the micro-context in which discursive processes take place (such as the everyday experiences of people) for their insistence that discourses have general social effects, regardless of social class, gender or ethnicity and for not recognizing human agency and the opportunity for resistance (Outram, 1989; Shilling, 1991; Turner, 1996).

Critics of the social constructionist approach have argued that the approach, like all others influenced by the poststructuralist movement, can descend into relativism and nihilism if taken to its logical conclusion, that all knowledges are social products, and that therefore the insights of social constructionist analyses are themselves to be questioned. How are the claims of social constructionist analyses to be justified, if they themselves are contributing to discourses that provide certain ways of seeing the world which are not necessarily any more valid or reasonable than other ways (Bury, 1986; Williams, 2001)? These kinds of objections have dogged the relativist constructionist project since its emergence in sociology. So too, critics have argued that social constructionism tends to ignore the material reality of embodiment in its focus on the discursive construction of illness, disease and other bodily ills (Williams, 2001).

However, in response it may be argued that the intellectual purpose of social constructionist scholarship is to highlight these very difficulties, and that therefore their own analyses should not be regarded as attempts to define 'truth' but as alternative versions of events which may be placed against other versions and perspectives for comparison, and judged on their fruitfulness for insight rather than their verisimilitude (Nicolson and McLaughlin, 1987). All researchers need to be aware of the assumptions upon which their analysis is founded; in this poststructuralist age, such reflexivity is almost mandatory. As Nicolson and McLaughlin (1987: 117) argue: 'Far from relativism being an "abyss" to be avoided, proper standards of sociological scholarship imply and demand that sociologists of knowledge be methodologist relativists. Anything less unnecessarily detracts from the scope and power of sociological inquiry.'

The social constructionist approach need not be uncompromisingly relativist. Indeed, despite the contentions of their critics, very rarely is it claimed by those adopting the constructionist perspective that fleshly experiences are simply 'social constructs' without a reality based in physical experience. Most social constructionists acknowledge that experiences such as illness, disease and pain exist as biological realities, but also emphasize that such experiences are always inevitably given meaning and therefore understood and experienced through cultural and social processes. Furthermore, social constructionism is not nihilistic if it is recognized that exposing the social bases of medicine, health care and illness states renders these phenomena amenable to change, negotiation and resistance. As I noted above, at their most political, social constructionist perspectives may be brought to bear to challenge the inequalities that exist in health care provision and health states.

Medical anthropology

Like many other disciplines and sub-disciplines in the humanities and social sciences, over the past two decades the projects of medical anthropology and medical sociology/sociology of health and illness have come closer together, to the extent that it is difficult to identify the boundaries separating them. Anthropological research aids a cross-cultural understanding of orientations to health care which may differ from the traditional biomedical model, including the lay health beliefs of ethnic minorities living in a western culture (Kleinman et al., 1978; Littlewood, 1991), and provides a comparative perspective against which the western medical system may be examined. Due to its tradition of participant-observation ethnographic research in small-scale societies, anthropology has developed sophisticated analytic tools to document and understand the meanings of communicative processes in the medical setting (Lazarus, 1988; Leslie, 2001).

Medical anthropologists have traditionally been concerned with the interpretation and lived experience of illness. They recognize that the culture within which a patient is operating influences the illness experience, although 'culture' when used by anthropologists in this context often refers to ethnicity or race. This approach views disease and illness as 'a form of communication – the language of the organs – through which nature, society, and culture speak simultaneously' (Scheper-Hughes and Lock, 1987: 31). Although the major focus of western anthropologists has been upon studying small-scale, rural, underdeveloped cultures rather than the large, urban, late-capitalist cultures in which they themselves have been encultured, recent scholarship in medical anthropology has begun to examine the health beliefs of western society. DiGiacomo (1992: 132) has termed this process 'Anthropologizing the West'.

However, the work of scholars and researchers in medical anthropology has sometimes suffered from their close links with biomedical practice and their need to appear institutionally 'useful'. In their avoidance of the social criticism perspective for fear of losing access to the health arena, medical anthropologists have often supported hegemonic ideologies supporting medical assumptions and neglected the macro, socio-economic perspective for a more politically neutral micro-level of analysis. Clinical anthropologists have sometimes been expected to act as cultural translators or public relations personnel in health care settings rather than as analysts and critics of the social and political structures in which biomedicine is embedded. While going well beyond the biomedical model of understanding illness, and questioning notions of medical epistemology in relying upon empirical evidence in which symptoms are regarded as the objective expression of bodily disorders, medical anthropologists' project of exploring the cultural construction of illness has often been positioned as a tool of doctors for the better diagnosis of patients' ills and enhanced understanding of their experiences of illness. Non-western culture's medical beliefs have sometimes been viewed as 'superstitions' and anthropologists have sought to encourage compliance of these cultures with biomedical practices (Gordon, 1988a; Leslie, 2001).

As a result, medical anthropology scholarship and research sometimes portrayed the patient as a constellation of 'unknown' meanings, which it was up to the doctor to 'decode', using the elicitation of patients' narratives as the method of inquiry as opposed to the use of tests. Biology was considered essentially universal, while culture was considered as external to disease and biology (Gordon, 1988a: 28). While placing emphasis upon the socio-cultural nature of illness, such an approach also tended to imply that 'folk illness' was an inferior version of 'real' biomedical illness as diagnosed and treated by doctors and described in medical textbooks and journals. An example is the comment of Stoeckle and Barsky (1981: 233, emphasis added) that '[f]olk and *primitive* beliefs persist today, even in the attributions offered by the modern "well-educated" patient, not only in those of the less educated, ethnic minorities'.

Since the 1960s, however, the political economy approach and social constructionism have begun to influence medical anthropology research and scholarship in the anglophone world. A perspective drawing upon both approaches, entitled 'critical' or 'interpretive' medical anthropology, began to receive expression and challenge old ways of research and thinking (Baer et al., 1986; Leslie, 2001). Singer (1990) has identified several areas of research interest for critical medical anthropologists which are also relevant to medical sociologists and historians. These include the following: the social production of medical knowledge; the functions of medicine and public health in social control; the importance of consciousness and agency in health-related behaviours and beliefs; the relation of health and medical language to power; the identification and labelling of disease; the contestable nature of medicine and disease as biomedical realities; and the meaning of the illness experience.

As this list demonstrates, recent critical approaches are interdisciplinary, incorporating political economy concerns with the structural economic features of society and how they impinge upon health status, with a social constructionist interest in epistemology and language use, as well as an interest in the experiential aspects of the medical encounter. From this perspective, the human body is understood both as a product of biology and of social and cultural processes; simultaneously totally biological and totally cultural (Guarnaccia, 2001). These concerns are identical with sociological and historical approaches that adopt a social constructionist perspective.

The historical dimension

Until some four decades ago, in the attempt to maintain some semblance of legitimacy for medicine and public health, the history of medicine tended more toward the hagiography of medicine in viewing scientific medicine as enlightened, ever progressing and triumphant (Wright and Treacher, 1982; Brandt, 1991). However, as in the sociology and anthropology of medicine, recent social histories of the ways in which society has responded to disease and illness have taken a more critical constructionist approach. The history of medicine has therefore moved towards medical sociology and anthropology, and vice versa, for one of the most important features of social constructionism as adopted in medical sociology and anthropology is its recognition of the historical nature of medical knowledges.

History provides a perspective which is able to show, as does the cross-cultural perspective offered by anthropology, that the conventions of western biomedicine are no more 'scientific' or 'objective' than medical systems in other cultures or in other times. The historical perspective provides a chronological approach, a sense of continuity as well as change, and an ability to interweave different levels of interpretation in its analysis of medical and public health issues and events (Berridge and Strong, 1991). It also allows an insight into social issues which, by highlighting their historicity, demonstrates that the taken-for-granted features of the present should be challenged: 'We use the past to shake confidence in the "obvious" appearance of medicine today; not in order to sanctify it as has so often happened in histories of medicine' (Wright and Treacher, 1982: 2).

Without the historical perspective, the beliefs and behaviours of people in response to health issues often appear inexplicable, irrational and self-defeating. Such accounts are valuable in providing an important perspective upon contemporary western society's responses to health threats and diseases. They are particularly useful for casting light upon the reasons why certain responses occur; why, for example, some diseases are stigmatized and provoke widespread fear and moralistic judgements; why certain kinds of imagery and rhetorical devices continue to enjoy resonance in the mass media's coverage of medical matters; why current health policies succeed or fail. As Brandt, in a review of the history of medicine, concluded:

> History offers us an avenue to better understand critical aspects of human motivation, organization, and relationships. In the crucible of sickness, these relationships are thrown into sometimes stark and dramatic relief, enhancing our ability to see and perhaps understand them. Ultimately, then, in studying the history of medicine we learn about the constraints and prospects of the human condition across time and cultures. (1991: 211)

The historical writings of Foucault have been a major impetus to the reshaping of histories of medicine. Such classics as *Madness and Civilization* (1967), *The Birth of the Clinic* (1975) and the three volumes of *The History of Sexuality* (1979, 1986, 1988) have called into question the 'truths' of historical interpretations and shown how networks of power produce medical knowledges and medical experiences. Thus, for example, in *Madness and Civilization* Foucault argued the definitional and diagnostic processes developed in psychiatry as it emerged as a system of medical knowledge in the seventeenth and eighteenth centuries produced mental illnesses by labelling some behaviours as normal and others as abnormal, requiring treatment. Mental illness was therefore presented by Foucault as socially constructed, while he portrayed psychiatry as a system of knowledge exerting disciplinary power upon the bodies and minds of those who were defined as 'mad'. This was a perspective considered radical for its time, but it was taken up by members of the anti-psychiatry movement in the 1970s as part of their critique of contemporary ways of dealing with mental illness (Armstrong, 1997).

As noted above, Foucault's writings have proved highly influential and iconoclastic not only for historians but also for writers and researchers in sociology and anthropology. The Foucauldian perspective has inspired radically different ways of viewing the role played by medicine, in particular seeking to identify the discourses that shape ways of thinking about and acting upon the human body and the relations of power that are inextricably part of the medical experience. It is a perspective that is vital to the concerns of this book.

Cultural studies

The fields of the sociology of culture and cultural studies are primarily concerned with documenting and explaining the processes of producing and circulating meaning through the channels of the artefacts and practices of culture. The emphasis is upon deconstructing the apparent 'naturalness' of the way culture is understood. Scholars interested in the rules which govern contemporary western activities such as food preparation and consumption, table manners, dress, notions of style and taste and the consumption of commodities have gone beyond the traditional sociological concern with organizations, the economy and public life to examine the rules, norms and symbolic meanings underlying social interaction in the domestic sphere and the reproduction of daily habits in everyday life (see, for example, the work of Douglas, 1974, 1984; Murcott, 1983, 1993; Bourdieu, 1984; Mennell, 1985; Fischler, 1986, 1988).

Lately, the hitherto-neglected human body has become a focal point of sociological investigation, led by the work of Bryan Turner (1992, 1995, 1996) (this area of interest as applied to medicine is reviewed in detail in Chapter 2). Such studies bring together the concerns of the sociology of knowledge and the sociology of culture in ways which provide fascinating explanations of how such seemingly individual characteristics as a person's physical appearance, style, taste, manners and bodily deportment are not merely personal idiosyncrasies but are highly influenced by socio-cultural norms linked to social class, gender and ethnicity.

The theoretical base and empirical research produced by the field of cultural studies offer important insights into the socio-cultural aspects of medicine. Cultural studies is an interdisciplinary area that originally developed from the sociology of culture (Williams, 1976) and has incorporated literary theory, film studies, Marxist, linguistic and psychoanalytic theory to examine not only the products of elite cultural endeavours, such as the opera, fine art, theatre and literature, but mass-produced commodities and the products of the popular mass media (see Turner, 1990, and Fiske, 1992, for introductions to and histories of cultural studies). The process of revealing the structures which allow audiences to make sense of the signs represented in the products and practices of the mass media and other social institutions is the unifying area of interest for all the different approaches utilized in cultural studies. The field takes an explicitly critical approach in examining the ways in which the mass media and other institutions are used to support the position of powerful interests and social groups under capitalism (Turner, 1990: 5).

Because most social scientists have tended not to view medicine as a product or part of culture, but as an objective body of scientific knowledge external to culture (where 'science' is seen as the antithesis of 'culture'), until recently the cultural studies approach had rarely been adopted to analyse biomedicine or public health institutions and practices (although in Europe and the anglophone world there currently exist strong programmes in the analysis of science as culture and the history and philosophy of science). Yet people construct their understandings of the world, including their beliefs about medicine and disease, from their interaction with cultural products as well as personal experience and discussions with others. The mass media are important in portraying medicine, health care, disease, illness and health risks in certain ways, from the soap opera's kindly doctor to the news bulletin's account of medical miracles, contributing to people's understandings of these phenomena, especially when they have little or no direct experience of them.

It is clear that medicine, health care, illness and the doctor–patient relationship are cultural activities and experiences, and as such are appropriate areas of study for sociologists of culture and scholars in the field of cultural studies. Furthermore, the study of the ways in which medical practices and institutions are represented in the mass media and the reception of such representations by audiences is integral to interpretive scholarship attempting to understand the socio-cultural aspects of medicine and health-related knowledges and practices (Lupton, 1992, 1994a; Lupton and McLean, 1998; Gwyn, 2002).

Discourse and the 'linguistic turn'

As noted previously, all areas of the humanities and social sciences, including cultural studies, have experienced a heightened interest in language and discourse in the past two decades, with an increasing preoccupation with recognizing and understanding the role of language in constituting and maintaining social order and notions of reality (Atkinson, 1990; Jensen, 1991; Howarth, 2000; Lehtonen, 2000). The linguist de Saussure was the first to develop semiotics, or the science of signs, and apply it to the explanation of the structure of language. Barthes' (1973) application of the methodology of semiotics to popular culture in the 1960s was a major step in the analysis of the meaning produced in

such hitherto neglected cultural texts. Subsequent approaches to the critical scrutiny of the products of mass and elite media either have grown out of, or have been strongly influenced by, the insights into language and culture provided by early semiotic theory. The breakthrough in theoretical approach was the fact that semioticians thought of people as 'spoken by, as well as speaking, their culture: spoken through its codes and systems' (Hall, 1980: 30).

The poststructuralist concept of *discourse* marries the structuralist semiotic concern with the form and structure of language and the ways in which meaning is established with an understanding that language does not exist in a social vacuum but is embedded in social and political settings and used for certain purposes. Discourse, in this usage, can be described as a pattern of words, figures of speech, concepts, values and symbols. A discourse is a coherent way of describing and categorizing the social and physical worlds. Discourses gather around an object, person, social group or event of interest, providing a means of 'making sense' of that object, person, and so on (Parker, 1992; Parker and the Bolton Discourse Network, 1999). All discourses are textual, or expressed in texts, inter-textual, drawing upon other texts and their discourses to achieve meaning, and contextual, embedded in historical, political and cultural settings. Common to most strands of discourse analysis is a concern with the way in which discourse is organized in terms of abstract principles, the view that discourse is an active means of communication used purposively and strategically to achieve desired ends, and an interest in the perspective of the actual communicators.

It is recognized that an integral and intertwined relationship exists between discourses – the way we speak or visually represent phenomena – and practices – the actions and activities surrounding these phenomena. For example, the ways in which the maternal body and the foetus are described, visually represented and treated in western societies tend to make an explicit separation between woman and foetus which is not evident in some other cultures. Debates over abortion in popular and legal settings, accusations made against women for smoking or drinking alcohol while pregnant, the training of medical students in obstetrics and gynaecology, the use of ultrasound that represents the foetus as an image separate from the maternal body, colour photographs in books and popular science magazines that show the foetus in the womb, seemingly floating in space, the way that people speak of the foetus as having a potential gender and name before birth, all serve to reinforce this division between mother and foetus. Practices constitute and reinforce existing discourses, and vice versa.

The examination of texts is central to discourse analysis and other forms of interpretive research. Indeed, it is becoming recognized in all areas of social research that texts are important items of analysis as sensitive barometers of social process and change (Potter and Wetherell, 1987; Jensen, 1991; Fairclough, 1992; Lehtonen, 2000). Any communication which is verbal is considered a text worthy of study for the identification of discourses. For scholars interested in medical discourses, texts to examine may include medical textbooks, hospital records and admission forms, popular self-help manuals, novels, television programmes about health issues, articles in medical and public health journals and popular newspaper or magazine articles, as well as the transcripts of conversations between doctors and patients or interviews between researcher and subject. When applied to socio-cultural analyses of medicine, the analysis of discourse has the potential to demonstrate the process by which biology and culture interact in the social construction of disease, and the ways in which western culture uses disease to define social boundaries (Brandt, 1988; Lupton, 1992, 1994a; Gwyn, 2002).

Conclusion: a merging of perspectives

While there are important differences in the manner in which different disciplines, sub-disciplines and interdisciplinary fields approach the analysis of medicine as culture, what is common amongst all the perspectives discussed above is the acceptance that in modern western societies the institution of medicine has an important part to play in social control, in shaping the regulation of human action, the deportment of human bodies and the construction of subjectivity. As such, medicine is eminently worthy of attention on the part of scholars in the humanities and interpretive social sciences. There is much to be gained from an eclectic perspective that approaches the same research problem from different theoretical and methodological angles, while at the same time maintaining an awareness of the disciplinary traditions and rationale of the different approaches. As the following chapters demonstrate, analysing medical phenomena can now be approached from a number of disciplines and perspectives at different levels of inquiry. The potential exists for the different theoretical approaches and research methodologies to incorporate elements from each other to meet their own deficiencies, and perhaps, in the process, to weaken the boundaries that tend rather artificially to separate them.

2

The Body in Medicine

The human body, in either explicit or latent ways, is ultimately the subject of all research and scholarship directed towards analysing the social dimension of medicine, health and illness. This chapter provides a review of recent theories of the body emerging from scholarship in the humanities and social sciences. Discussion includes the gendered body, the sexual body, the clean body, the disciplined body, the sporting body, the commodified body and the dead body. In doing so, the chapter examines notions of health as a secular religion, anxieties over the maintenance of body boundaries, the ideology of rationality and bodily control in public health discourse, the discourse of diet, and above all, the concept of the body as a social construction, vulnerable to ideological shifts, discursive processes and power struggles. Central to such inquiries is an analysis of the body in medicine, for in contemporary western societies, 'our capacity to experience the body directly, or theorize it indirectly, is inextricably medicalized' (Frank, 1990: 136).

Social theory and the body

It is easy to ignore the existence and importance of bodies, simply because they are so taken-for-granted as parts of ourselves: 'We have bodies, but we are also, in a specific sense, bodies; our embodiment is a necessary requirement of our social identification so that it would be ludicrous to say "I have arrived and I have brought my body with me"' (Turner, 1996: 42). When pain, sickness or discomfort is not felt, one's body is relatively unobtrusive. It is often not until illness or pain is experienced that the body comes into conscious being; illness may then be conceptualized as the body taking over, as an external environment separate to the self.

Until recently, social and political theory and scholarship tended to ignore the human body, placing emphasis upon social structures and individual subjectivity with little discussion of where the corporality of the 'lived' body fitted in (Berthelot, 1986; Turner, 1991a, 1996). For much of the history and development of medical sociology the biological, human anatomy conception of the body has remained unchallenged: 'Sociologists support, criticize, collude with, and conspire against those health professionals whose claim to expertise is their sophisticated knowledge of the body – but rarely if ever question or criticize their biological vision of that body' (Armstrong, 1987a: 651). Likewise, social histories of medicine have neglected attention to the body (Gallagher and Laqueur, 1987: vii).

One reason for the reluctance to theorize or historically position the body was the desire of scholars in the humanities and social sciences to avoid the biological determinism of the 'hard' human sciences. As a result, for decades macro-sociologists have tended to focus on the 'social system', the structural, political and economic dimensions of social control, a theoretical space in which the body disappeared from view, while micro-sociologists were concerned with individual behaviour as socially constituted but neglected consideration of the embodiment of decision-making (Turner, 1996: Ch. 2). However, in the past two decades the body in late capitalist society has begun to attract the attention of social and cultural theorists. It is now the case that '[b]odies are in, in academia as well as popular culture' (Frank, 1990: 131).

This turn towards theorizing the body may be explained with reference to modern social movements such as feminism, the growth of consumer culture and the influence of poststructuralist and postmodernist theories (Turner, 1991a: 18). These movements, in concert with the release of the translated writings of Foucault, have focused new attention upon the body, its role in human subjectivity and its constitution by both elite and popular discourses. More specifically, the emergence of HIV/AIDS, public controversies over pornography and drug use in sport, and the burgeoning of the field of medical ethics have raised issues of interest to scholars engaged in the sociology of the body (Morgan and Scott, 1993: 4–5). So too, the increasing network of risk discourses surrounding the body, including the relationship between diet and health and the genetic dimensions of ill health and disease, have incited recent research.

In the wake of poststructuralism and postmodernism, in which a social constructionist position is adopted (Chapter 1), the human body can no longer be considered a given reality, but as the product of certain kinds of knowledge and discourses which are subject to change. As Haraway (1989: 10) remarks: '[B]odies, then, are not born: they are made.' From this perspective, scientific medicine is one important source of such discourses and knowledges, largely succeeding in excluding alternative portrayals of how the body functions and disease operates, such as those put forward in complementary or holistic medical therapies.

For the highly relativist social constructionist position drawing upon the postmodernist writings of Deleuze and Guattari, a philosophical model of a 'body-without-organs' has been identified. The body-without-organs is much more than the material or anatomical body (this is, the body-*with*-organs). It is the body-self, the 'self-inside-the-body', a phenomenon that is cognitive, subconscious and emotional as well as experienced through the flesh. It is intrinsically bound up with our sense of identity. Physical and social forces interact to produce the body-without-organs.

The body-without-organs is a site of cultural inscription – or in Deleuze and Guattari's words, 'territorialization' – which is constantly constructed and reconstructed as discourses and practices struggle to give meaning to it. Biomedical discourses and practices, for example, often territorialize the body, rendering it into a 'body-with-organs' by focusing largely on its anatomical aspects. At other times, other discourses and practices may prevail, 'reterritorializing' the body with different meanings. The body, therefore, is regarded as an always unfinished project, and the body-self is viewed as mediating notions of 'health' and 'illness' (Fox, 1993, 1998, 2002).

For contemporary poststructuralist and postmodernist theory, therefore, the body is viewed as 'an admixture of discourse and matter, one whose inseparability is a critical, though complex, attribute' (Rothfield, 1992: 102; see also Shilling, 1991: 664). It is conceived of as a collection of practices, or 'body techniques', which represent and regulate bodies in time and space (Frank, 1991: 48–9; Turner, 1992: 41). Bodies are regarded as not simply shaped by social relationships, but as entering into the construction of these relationships, both facilitated and limited by historical, cultural and political factors. The ways in which the state undertakes surveillance and control of bodies, and how in turn individuals come to self-regulate and discipline their bodily deportment, are of central interest for the poststructuralist project in medical sociology. Turner (1992: 12) has developed the notion of the somatic society, in which the body is a metaphor for social organization and social anxieties, the principal field of cultural and political activities. The regulation, surveillance and monitoring of bodies, of the spaces between bodies, are central to the somatic society.

While sociology and history have tended to ignore the symbolic interrelationship between bodies and the social order, anthropologists have traditionally taken an interest in the way in which body symbolism is used in small-scale societies to integrate communities and define social relations and spatial relationships. Mary Douglas (1980/1966: 128) argued that rituals concerning the body 'enact a form of social relations and in giving these relations visible expression they enable people to know their own society. The rituals work upon the body politic through the symbolic medium of the physical body.' For anthropologists Scheper-Hughes and Lock (1987: 8), there are three bodies at three separate but overlapping conceptual and analytical levels. The first is the individual body, understood as the lived experience of the body-self; how we each view our bodies, distinct from others' bodies. The second is the social body, or the symbolic, representational uses of the body in conceptualizing nature, society and culture, evident in discourses referring to a 'sick society', the 'foot of the mountain' or the 'head of state'. At the third level is the bio-politics of the body, in which the state controls, regulates and surveys the conduct of bodies on the individual and group level in order to maintain social stability.

For his part, Frank (1990: 134) suggests that there are four bodies: the medicalized body; the sexual body; the disciplined body; and the talking body. The boundaries between these typologies are necessarily fluid. Although the first typology of the body, the medicalized body, is most directly related in its title to the medical management of disease, it is the case that the other types of bodies are also bound up with the medical system. As is elaborated later in this chapter, the cultural influence of medicine is such that the sexual body has become drawn into medical discourse, and is in fact disciplined under the aegis of this discourse. The disciplined body is also evident in medical and public health discourses dealing with notions of control, asceticism and health, while the talking body is relevant to the medical encounter in which the patient is expected to verbalize his or her symptoms in the 'confession'.

Foucault, the body and the clinic

As previously noted, the writings of Foucault, as well as feminist critiques, have been extremely influential in establishing the current interest in the body in sociological, historical, philosophical and anthropological scholarship. Foucault was interested in establishing an historical 'genealogy' of the discourses surrounding and constituting contemporary medical practices. For Foucault and his followers, the body is the ultimate site of political and ideological control, surveillance and regulation. He argues that since the eighteenth century it has been the focal point for the exercise of disciplinary power. Through the body and its behaviours, state apparatuses such as medicine, the educational system, psychiatry and the law define the limits of behaviour and record activities, punishing those bodies which violate the established boundaries, and thus rendering bodies productive and politically and economically useful.

In his historico-philosophical accounts of the development of medical knowledge in France, Foucault identifies the establishment of the medical clinic and teaching hospital in the late eighteenth century as a pivotal point for ways of conceptualizing the body. He views medicine as a major institution of power in labelling bodies as deviant or normal, as hygienic or unhygienic, as controlled or needful of control (Foucault, 1979: 54). In *The Birth of the Clinic* (1975) Foucault refers to the 'anatomical atlas' that is the human body constituted by the medico-scientific gaze. He argues that in the late twentieth century, this notion of the body was accepted with little recognition that there are other ways of conceiving of the body and its illnesses. According to Foucault, as medical practices changed in the late eighteenth century, the introduction and routine adoption of the physical examination, the post-mortem, the stethoscope, the microscope, the development of the disciplines of anatomy, psychiatry, radiology and surgery, the institutionalization of the hospital and the doctor's surgery, all served to increasingly exert power upon the body. At the same time, bodies were subjected to increased regulation, constant monitoring, discipline and surveillance in other spheres, most notably the prison, the school, the asylum, the military and the workshop. The medical encounter began to demand that patients reveal the secrets of their bodies, both by allowing physical examination and by giving their medical history under questioning by the doctor: 'The patient had to speak, to confess, to reveal; illness was transformed from what is visible to what was heard' (Armstrong, 1983: 25).

For Foucault, the medical encounter is a supreme example of surveillance, whereby the doctor investigates, questions, touches the exposed flesh of the patient, while the patient acquiesces, and confesses, with little knowledge of why the procedures are carried out. In the doctor's surgery the body is rendered an object to be prodded, tested and examined. The owner is expected to give up his or her jurisdiction of the body over to the doctor. In severe cases of illness or physical disability the body is owned by the medical system, while in mental illness the body is the apparatus by which the brain is kept restrained, often against the owner's will.

The gendered body

The ways in which bodies are treated in medicine and how health and ill-health states are experienced are often shaped via sex or gender. Feminist critiques have been particularly influential in identifying the gendered aspects of embodiment over the past 30 years. The second-wave feminist movement has initiated many of the concerns surrounding the social construction of sexuality and gender, and 'the body' now holds centre-stage as the focus of feminist debate (Caddick, 1986: 60). Liberal feminists in the 1970s, drawing upon Marxist theory, began to stress the concept of gender, which sees femininity or masculinity as social roles, unrelated to the morphology of the female and male body. 'Sex', as a term related to physiological characteristics, thus became differentiated from 'gender', or cultural definitions of sexual roles. The notion of the essential human nature, common to men and women, the 'sameness of the sexes' was put forward as the ideal vision of subjectivity, serving to free women from the oppression of the feminine body. For gender theorists, the mind was viewed as 'a neutral passive entity, a blank slate, on which is inscribed various social "lessons"', while the body was regarded as 'the passive mediator of these inscriptions' (Gatens, 1983: 144). The relationships between femininity and the female body and masculinity and the male body were viewed as arbitrary, and therefore amenable to re-socialization to correct the oppression of women.

Certain, more recent, feminist representations of the body have attested to the necessity of the rational disembodiment of the person, rejecting the notion of the relation of sex (as given fact) to gender (as cultural artefact).

Such a view emphasizes the influence of cultural practices and discourses in constituting both dichotomously sexed and gendered bodies, rejecting the notion that nature and the body are outside culture: 'This approach allows us to shift the conceptual ground from the question "How is the body taken up in culture?" to the more profitable question "How does culture construct the body so that it is understood as a biological given?"' (Gatens, 1988: 62). For these feminists, the binary division between male and female is broken down to reform multiple sexed bodies, and the androgynous, or degendered, subject becomes the ideal (Caddick, 1986: 68; Gatens, 1988: 67). For example, the influential feminist and writer in the philosophy of science, Donna Haraway (1988), argues that the notion of the 'cyborg' performs this function, expressing an ideal of a 'humanoid hybrid', a combination of humanity and technology in which categories of sexuality, ethnicity, gender and indeed the distinction between humanity and technology are indeterminate and fluid. This is the supreme constructionist position, in which bodies are entirely texts, subject to rational, autonomous control in their constitution.

Not all contemporary feminist scholars adopt such a relativist viewpoint. There are currently a number of debates concerning the extent to which the feminine body is socially constructed or the product of biological factors, with feminisms ranging across the spectrum from biological essentialism to the most relativist of social constructionist perspectives, and combinations of theoretical positions (Jacobus et al., 1990: 3). Some feminists continue to argue that the denial of some degree of biological determinism of sexual difference ignores the lived experience of being born with either a female or a male body, and that the physical and the social bodies are inseparable (see, for example, Caddick, 1986; Lynch, 1987; Grosz, 1990; Rothfield, 1992).

It is contended by such writers that claims which deny the biological characteristics of lived bodies may prove to be self-defeating if it means that women who are pregnant, undergoing in vitro fertilization (IVF), childbirth, breast-feeding or abortion, taking hormonal contraception, subjected to female circumcision, experiencing premenstrual syndrome, menstruation or menopausal symptoms are denied acknowledgement of the sheer physicality and inevitable social consequences of these uniquely female physiological experiences, some of which, like menstruation, pregnancy and childbirth, are universal across cultures. As Pringle has commented: '[T]he most hardened social constructionists are likely to retreat rapidly into essentialism when faced with the unsettling questions raised by the practice of clitoridectomy [female circumcision]' (1992: 87). Calls have subsequently been made for feminists to pay greater attention to the relationship between bodily processes and social relations, including sexual pleasure, childbirth and infant feeding practices, as part of the struggle for resistance to patriarchal control (Reiger, 1987), for '[i]t is the *social inscription of sexed bodies*, not the imposition of an acculturized, sexually neutral gender that is significant for feminist purposes' (Grosz, 1990: 72–3, emphasis in the original). (Chapter 6 elaborates upon these issues with a more specific focus upon feminisms and medicine.)

While female bodies have received much attention in the critical social theory literature, until very recently little had been written about male bodies. In the 1990s this began to be redressed, as increasing numbers of articles and books began to examine the phenomenon of the male body. Part of this neglect was due to the 'taken-for-granted' nature of the male body, its representation as the idealized, 'normal' body against which women's bodies were compared and found wanting. So too, dominant assumptions about masculinity have tended to represent men as inherently stronger and less susceptible to ills than women. Hegemonic masculinities have emphasized the importance of men displaying little concern about the state of health or appearance of their bodies and exerting the power of rational thought over the weaknesses of the body. Indeed, illness is linked so strongly to femininity rather than masculinity that the notion of a man as a passive, weakened patient under the care of a doctor – relinquishing control of his body to another – challenges these dominant norms of masculinity (Davis, 2002; White, 2002).

With the advent of a literature devoted to male bodies has come a focus on the ways in which male bodies are represented and dealt with in medicine, and how men themselves experience embodiment. An American study of middle-class men and women (Saltonstall, 1993) identified important gendered differences in body conceptualizations; men tended to speak of themselves as 'having power' over their bodies, of 'owning' their bodies, while women referred to controlling a recalcitrant body, especially when it came to dietary practice. Men valued body maintenance work because it maximized their potential for action, while women were also concerned about their body's appearance in terms of acceptable standards of physical attractiveness. Saltonstall concluded from her research that 'gender played a key role in interpreting and constructing one's own and others' bodies as concretely and particularly healthy', with the existence of different bodily symbols of health for male and female bodies (1993: 12).

In recent years there has been growing attention paid in both medical and public health circles and the news media to men's health issues. Magazines focusing exclusively on men's health and well-being are now published, public health campaigns directed exclusively at men have been launched and a greater number of news stories devoted to men's health problems have appeared in the media. Such representations of men's bodies have drawn upon a number of dominant discourses. In magazines like *Men's Health*, which include articles and advertisements not only about health but also grooming, muscular development, weight control, cosmetic surgery and sexual technique, the healthy male body is conflated with the virile, conventionally slim and attractive male body. In news media accounts, men have variously been portrayed as vulnerable to illness, neglectful of their health and child-like, requiring the care and attention of their partners. In this way, gender stereotypes are perpetuated which represent men as oblivious to body-centred concerns such as health because of their preoccupation with work and their view of themselves as invulnerable to illness, while women are portrayed in caring roles, taking responsibility for their men's health (Lyons and Willott, 1999).

Men themselves tend to dismiss health needs as a means of constructing and performing dominant forms of masculinities. If to be ill and requiring of help and care are culturally represented as characteristically feminine, linked to vulnerability, weakness and loss of control over one's body, then avoiding the imputation of illness is a way for many men to establish masculinities by demonstrating difference from women. Some men may do this by not only ignoring signs of illness and failing to seek appropriate medical care but also deliberately taking risks such as drinking to excess, speeding or fighting, demonstrating fearlessness, lack of concern for one's health and control over one's body (Courtenay, 2000; Watson, 2000; White, 2002). These aspects of hegemonic masculinities have implications for the steps men may take to protect or otherwise neglect the health of their bodies and the ways in which they interact with health care providers.

The sexual body

Like the gendered body, the sexually active body is currently a primary site at which contesting discourses compete for meaning, particularly in the fields of medicine and public health. Debates about sexuality and gender have been carried out in a wider socio-cultural milieu in which sexuality is a sensitive topic. One reason for this sensitivity is that the sexual body is a constant reminder that humans are embodied, that rationality and reason may sometimes be overwhelmed by urges seemingly based in hormonal 'animalistic' imperatives, that 'nature' may predominate over 'civilization'.

The sexual body has occasioned much scope for debate in recent years around such issues as the manner in which sexual preference is developed and the appropriateness of certain expressions of sexual desire. These debates were fuelled by the second-wave feminist movement and the emergence of the gay movement in the 1970s, which called into question the biomedical orthodoxy which accepted that heterosexuality was genetically ordained. In the late twentieth century, the definition and deployment of sexuality was the centre of a number of political struggles and conflicts over such issues as pornography, child, adolescent and female sexuality, abortion, divorce, women's rights, homosexuality and sex education. A new area of knowledge developed in the wake of industrialization and gained prominence in the late twentieth century, bringing together the discourses of bodily control, commodity culture, self-expression and narcissism. Sexology, or the 'science of sexuality', developed to document, prescribe and provide advice upon the sexual government of the body.

Like the term 'sex', 'sexuality' itself is a word which has manifold and diverse meanings according to who is using it (Allen, 1992: 9); sexologists, criminologists, psychiatrists, gay activists, feminists and philosophers all have their own understandings of the term. It is around the sexuality debate that the most intense battles between proponents of naturalism and relativism have centred. Cultural theorists commonly draw upon social constructionism to argue for a view of the sexually active body as being a product of society/culture rather than biology. Sexuality thus becomes contingent upon cultural norms and historical trends rather than predestination as inscribed by the genes. At its most extreme, the liberal relativist position argues that 'prevailing representations of sexual norms in Western culture are little more than obnoxious and erroneous modernist and humanist fictions' (Allen, 1992: 14). The importance of language and visual representation, as in other poststructuralist projects, is emphasized in its role of bringing the sexual body into being: 'Desire is bound up with meaning, representation ... sexual relations are relations through language, not to a given other sex: the body is not a direct immediacy, it is tressed, marked out, intrinsically involved with meanings' (Heath, 1982: 154).

For Foucault and his followers, contemporary discourses around sexuality seek to categorize, document and explain the varieties of sexual expression available to humanity, rendering them ever more amenable to surveillance and disciplinary power. Rather than a plurality of sexualities being confined, Foucault suggests that modern discourses have constituted multiple 'perverse' practices by bringing them into the public forum: 'The extension of power over bodies, modes of conduct, sex, and pleasure produces not a repression but an incitement or proliferation of unorthodox sensualities' (Smart, 1985: 97). Foucault contends that the change to sexuality as medicalized, monitored, recorded and categorized, rather than resulting in lessening the sense of repression around sexuality, instead has resulted in sex becoming 'an object of great suspicion ... the fragment of darkness that we each carry within us' (Foucault, 1979: 69).

In line with his conceptualization of power and knowledge as they constitute the body, Foucault locates sex and sexuality in shifting relations of power and knowledge, seeking to identify the 'techniques of the self' through which individuals constitute themselves as sexual bodies. Foucault (1979: 155–6) contends that in contemporary western societies the individual's sexuality has reached such importance that it is deemed to constitute his or her subjectivity. He argues that the confession is the integral mechanism by which western societies have 'talked about sex' in the form of a religious ritual which centres on the production of 'truth'. According to him, the sexual confession became constituted in scientific rather than moral terms over the last 150 years. The inducement to speak about sexuality in the medical setting combined the confession with the physical examination. The act of confession was reformulated as a therapeutic exercise rather than penance, as was the case with the secular confession; the truths of the confession were categorized as normal or pathological. Sexuality was deemed to have an effect upon all aspects of behaviour, to intrude into all spheres of life. Sex was deemed elusive, needful of patient drawing out on the part of the doctor or therapist, the truth of which was hidden from the confessor until skilful questioning brought it to light; the expert became 'the master of truth' by deciphering the meaning of the confession (Foucault, 1979: 65–7). Thus, the sexual body became viewed as emblematic of the whole body, influencing all aspects of people's lives.

From the Foucauldian perspective, then, the obsession of researchers working within science, medicine and the social sciences in documenting the sexual body over the past century (for example, Krafft-Ebing, Freud, Havelock Ellis, Kinsey, Masters and Johnson and the 'AIDS industry' of sex research) serves to cast an ever-wider net of disciplinary control over citizens. Sexology is viewed as an ideology, a combination of discourses legitimized under the rubric of science which seek to control and confine certain forms of sexual expression (Weeks, 1987; Seidman, 1991; Clark, 1993).

Another issue of scholarly interest in which debates concerning the relative importance of biological destiny and enculturation have received attention is that of the determination of sexual preference. While biologists and psychologists have sought to locate the physiological basis for sexual preference in the structures of the brain, the hormones or the genetic code, arguing that homosexuality can be located as a 'deviance' from the norm, cultural theorists perceive heterosexuality and homosexuality as socially constructed, and therefore arbitrary and contingent, categories. They observe that homosexuality has been defined differently over various historical and cultural contexts, noting that it was not until the late nineteenth century that the category 'homosexual identity' emerged in western societies. Before that time, people may have engaged in homosexual *activities*, but not viewed themselves as homosexual (see Foucault, 1979; Plummer, 1981; Weeks, 1991, for expositions of this position). The word 'homosexuality' itself was not invented until 1869, and it was not until the 1880s or 1890s that the word was used in the English language (Weeks, 1991: 16).

Over the past century and a half, the homosexual body has been subjected to intense medical scrutiny. As part of the quest to categorize, label and define human bodily functions and behaviours, medico-scientific discourses have constructed 'the homosexual' as a distinct human type. The homosexual body was subjected to documentation, via photography, as scientists and sexologists sought to establish a 'norm' of sexuality by categorizing physical types. Homosexuality was believed to be expressed in individuals' body shapes and facial features (Marshall, 1990). Psychology researchers devoted themselves to explaining the cause of the homosexual 'condition' (Weeks, 1991: 17).

This production of the homosexual body was implicated in its repression; by identifying the homosexual, he or she could then be controlled. From the 1970s, sexual preference was constructed as a political category, intimately interbound with one's personal identity. People identified themselves as a 'homosexual' or a 'lesbian' or a 'gay' person, or less commonly (because it is taken as given) as a 'heterosexual'. To do so, argues Weeks (1987: 31) is to privilege sexual identity over identities such as class, ethnic or racial loyalties. However, as he points out, there is a paradox in this focus on identity in the light of modern acceptance of the precarious, transitory nature and cultural construction of sexual identity.

For gay men, the open labelling of their sexual identity, in conjunction with the free engagement in a diverse range of same-sex sexual practices, became a political act, a sign of their refusal to suppress their sexual preference in a society largely antipathetic to homosexuality. However, by the early 1980s, when HIV/AIDS appeared on the scene, male gay practices once again became subject to the clinical gaze as researchers sought to find the cause of this new disease in the body of the gay man (Watney, 1987; Marshall, 1990). Discourses celebrating the liberal position on sexual expression were problematized by the advent of HIV/AIDS. Sexuality and its dangers, for sexually active individuals of all preferences, became the subject of intense critical public scrutiny and private anxiety. A counter-discourse on sexual freedom emerged, in which it was argued that sexual 'promiscuity' was being punished by the fatal disease, and a return to the good old-fashioned values of monogamy and marital fidelity were espoused (Lupton, 1993a).

Over the past decade, the postmodern celebration of the diversification and fragmentation of sexual bodies has been subjected to criticism on the basis that it neglects embodiment and power relations, and legitimates sexual violence against the 'feminine' partner (whether that partner is a gay man adopting a feminine role, or a woman). Questions have been asked concerning who benefits from the freeing up of proscriptions concerning such bodily activities as incest and sado-masochism (Lonsdale, 1992). Although the feminist movement has traditionally been supportive of the provision of sexual choice, in the 1980s many feminists began to criticize the liberal ideology as supportive of men's power and sexual interests but neglectful of women's continuing oppression in sexual relations.

Moral panics in the late 1980s and early 1990s surrounding homosexuality, promiscuity and pornography centred around the view of a sexuality released from close intimate bonds as destructive, deviant and violent, calling for restrictions to be enforced upon sexual expression (Weeks, 1986; Watney, 1987; Showalter, 1990; Seidman, 1992). The result of these struggles is a diverse collection of discourses around the appropriate deployment of the sexual body. The discourses which claim that sexual attraction and love are one, and that sexual fulfilment is essential to personal happiness, continue to receive expression in the popular media, for example, the sexual advice offered by women's magazines such as

Cosmopolitan, which places an emphasis on 'finding yourself through sex', achieving satisfaction through communication by telling your partner what you want (Winship, 1987; McMahon, 1990). Steamy casual sexual encounters continue to provide titillation on prime-time television or in the cinema: for example, Madonna's book of soft-porn photographs featuring her own body was a best-seller in 1992. Yet the same popular media routinely report on the dangers of sexuality, providing the latest statistics on HIV/AIDS, publish features on the 'new' joys of monogamous marriage and techniques on making love with the same person for the rest of one's life, or depict people who engage in casual sex as being punished by unhappiness or even death for their actions (for example, the high-grossing films *Basic Instinct* and *Indecent Proposal*). Thus, at the beginning of the twenty-first century, the sexual body must struggle with a tension between the discourses privileging self-expression and satisfaction through sexual encounters and those emphasizing the fearful and potentially fatal consequences of the mingling of body fluids during sexual abandonment.

Public health and the disciplined body

In public health discourse the body is regarded as dangerous, problematic, ever threatening to run out of control, to attract disease, to pose imminent danger to the rest of society (Lupton, 1995; Petersen and Lupton, 1997). For centuries and up to the present day, concerns about the spread of infectious diseases such as cholera, smallpox, yellow fever and the plague have resulted in measures being taken by the state to confine bodies and control their movements. This control over bodies in the name of public health has often been coercive and discriminatory. For example, from the sixteenth to the early twentieth centuries, whole households of people were confined to their houses if public health officials designated one member as infectious, or people were removed to quarantine stations or lazarettos, sometimes by the police (Tesh, 1988: 12).

Those of foreign nationality, the poor and the working class have historically been singled out for attention by public health authorities as agents of disease, requiring forcible 'hygiene' programmes sometimes involving the destruction of their homes and isolation from the rest of society (Lupton, 1995). In the early twentieth century, for example, immigrants to Canada were especially targeted by quarantine regulations and subjected to medical examinations upon arrival, thus marking them as the dangerous, potentially contaminating Other (Sears, 1992: 70). Even in contemporary western societies, public health acts devised decades ago are used to constrain the movement of bodies in the name of health. One instance of this occurred in 1989 in Australia, when a section of the New South Wales Public Health Act of 1902 was instituted to detain for a time a sex worker who had publicly admitted to being HIV positive but not willing to enforce condom use among her clients.

Foucault (1984a) sees the modern state's preoccupation with controlling bodies *en masse* as developing in Europe in the eighteenth century in concert with the birth of the medical clinic, the growth of demand for individual medical care and a concern with the preservation and upkeep of the labour force. At that time, he argues, a new discourse emerged which problematized disease as an economic and political problem for societies, not just an individual concern, which therefore required some degree of collective control measures. By the turn of the eighteenth century, the charitable and religious institutions and foundations set up to deal with a range of bodily problems among the poor, including not only illness but old age, inability to find work and destitution, had begun to be supplanted by state apparatuses directed towards policing behaviours believed conducive to the spread of disease. Surveillance was directed in particular towards the family unit, including such behaviours as childcare, physical exercise, food preparation, inoculation and vaccination and the maintenance of hygiene (Foucault, 1984a).

The public health movement in the late nineteenth century developed a new rationale for the surveillance of bodies in the interests of gathering information to target better the health problems of populations. The emergence of the field of epidemiology, focused upon the documenting of patterns of disease across groups, intensified such practices, involving constant record-taking, measuring and reporting back to a system of government agencies. The medico-social survey became an important instrument in the disciplining of populations, 'an instrument of order and control, a technique for managing the distribution of bodies and preventing their potentially dangerous mixings' (Armstrong, 1983: 51). Disease became constituted in the social body rather than the individual body, and deviant types were identified as needful of control for the sake of the health of the whole population. As a result, by the early twentieth century everyone became a potential victim requiring careful monitoring: 'The new social diseases of the twentieth century, tuberculosis, venereal disease and problems of childhood, had been reconstrued to focus medical attention on "normal" people who were nevertheless "at risk"' (Armstrong, 1983: 37).

Such innovations as milk depots, which in the early twentieth century were opened in various towns in Britain to provide bottled cow's milk to mothers with young babies, provided the opportunity to record and scrutinize bodies individually. A separate file was opened for each baby, they were weighed each week, their heights were recorded by their mothers on a special card, and families were regularly visited by health visitors who reported their progress to the Medical Officer of Health (Armstrong, 1983: 14–15). This practice continues today. For example, health visitors in Scotland exercise surveillance over the bodies of children in underprivileged households by regularly visiting their homes to check the state of cleanliness and requiring their mothers to provide information about their diets (Bloor and McIntosh, 1990).

At the turn of the twenty-first century, the concerns of public health have remained firmly fixed on controlling bodies, but have moved from containing infectious disease to exhorting people to take responsibility for maintaining personal bodily health. Contemporary public health directed at 'health promotion' narrows its focus on the individual by associating the so-called lifestyle diseases with individual behaviours. Health promotion rhetoric maintains that the incidence of illness is diminished by persuading members of the public to exercise control over their bodily deportment. Health education is a form of pedagogy, which, like other forms, serves to legitimize ideologies and social practices by making statements about how individuals should conduct their bodies, including what type of food goes into bodies, the nature and frequency of physical activities engaged in by bodies, and the sexual expression of the body (Lupton, 1995; Petersen and Lupton, 1997).

Self-control and self-discipline over the body, both within and without the workplace, have become the new work ethic. State-sponsored health education campaigns in the mass media are conducted to warn the public about health risks, based on the assumption that knowledge and awareness of the danger of certain activities will result in avoidance of these activities. Such campaigns proliferated in the mid-to-late 1980s in Britain and Australia, warning of the dangers posed by HIV infection. Britons were warned 'Don't Die of Ignorance' and were asked 'AIDS: How Big Does It Have To Be Before You Take Notice?' in television and print advertisements featuring apocalyptic and forbidding images of coffins, tombstones, icebergs and volcanoes to signify looming large-scale disaster (Rhodes and Shaughnessy, 1990: 56). The notorious 'Grim Reaper' mass media campaign was run in Australia, using a horror-movie genre employing the image of the symbol of death laying waste to 'ordinary' Australians. These campaigns attempted to create awareness of the risks of HIV/AIDS by shock tactics and fear appeals, linking sexuality with guilt and death and positioning the public as ignorant and apathetic and the state as the guardian of morals in the name of preserving the public's health (Lupton, 1994a: Ch. 6).

The dialectic of public health is that of the freedom of individuals to behave as they wish pitted against the rights of society to control individuals' bodies in the name of health. For public health, the utilitarian imperative rules. Disciplinary power is maintained through the mass screening procedure, the health risk appraisal, the fitness test, the health education campaign invoking guilt and anxiety if the advocated behaviour is not taken up. The rhetoric of public health discourse is such that the individual is unaware that the discourse is disciplinary; health is deemed a universal right, a fundamental good, and therefore measures taken to protect one's health must necessarily be the concern and goal of each individual (Lupton, 1995; Petersen and Lupton, 1997). Initiatives to encourage individuals to change their behaviour, to know their risks are therefore seen as benevolent. Thus, in being aware of the public gaze, the individual unconsciously him- or herself exerts disciplinary power, both over others and over the self through self-regulation. In this process, power relations are rendered invisible, and are dispersed, being voluntarily perpetuated by subjects upon themselves as well as upon others: 'subjects thus produced are not simply the imposed results of alien, coercive forces; the body is internally lived, experienced and acted upon by the subject and the social collectivity' (Grosz, 1990: 65).

Cleanliness, dirt and body boundaries

Concepts of body imagery are central to an understanding of the ways in which individuals experience the lived body and its relationship to the environment. Policing the boundaries of the body by maintaining strict control over what enters and what leaves the body's orifices is an integral aspect of bio-politics. These actions often centre around symbolic conceptions of hygiene, cleanliness and dirt, and are inextricably intertwined with notions concerning societal order and control. As Douglas notes, the individual's ideas about what constitutes 'dirt' and the body's relationship to dirt are symbolic of the need to maintain control of the body politic:

> ... dirt is essentially disorder. There is no such thing as absolute dirt; it exists in the eye of the beholder. If we shun dirt, it is not because of craven fear, still less dread or holy terror. Nor do our ideas about disease account for the range of our behaviour in cleaning or avoiding dirt. Dirt offends against order. Eliminating it is not a negative movement, but a positive effort to organize the environment. (1980/1966: 2)

The cleanliness of the body is a central discourse in contemporary notions of disease and hygiene which focus upon the maintenance of body boundaries. Vigarello (1988), in his fascinating account of changing concepts of cleanliness in France from the Middle Ages, addresses notions to do with hygiene, dirt, privacy and the body. In the Middle Ages in Europe, he asserts, the use of water in cleaning the body was rare. To be clean meant to have no visible dirt on limited areas of skin. The code of cleanliness was thus dictated by social etiquette, limited to the visible surfaces of the body available to the view of others. The concept of cleanliness extended only to the external layers; how one's body felt to oneself was not considered important. The 'dry wash', or the rubbing of one's face and hands with a cloth, was considered the appropriate method of cleaning from the Middle Ages to the seventeenth century. Washing with water or regular bathing was uncommon. Water (especially hot water) was thought to be dangerous to the body, rendering it vulnerable and permeable to disease. Strengthening the body thus meant closing the pores by the application of skin coatings (used on newly born babies) or by wearing tightly woven clothing which did not allow the entry of unwholesome air to the body surface.

The prevalence of epidemics and plagues, and the miasma theory of disease common throughout the Middle Ages and up to the emergence of the scientific model of medicine, fed these notions of the body as permeable and highly susceptible to invasion and attack by disease. There are links between these notions and the still prevalent lay beliefs to do with vulnerability to infections such as colds and influenza in contemporary western societies. In one English study, for example, interviewees volunteered the beliefs that susceptibility to colds was increased by such behaviours as allowing one's head to get wet, going outside after washing one's hair, getting one's feet wet, going into a cold room after a hot bath and getting caught in the rain, all of which were viewed as allowing the illness to enter the body (Helman, 1978).

According to Vigarello (1988), notions about cleanliness changed from the eighteenth century. In the late eighteenth century the first ideas about bathing and its relationship to bodily hygiene became dominant. The idea of the body as a machine influenced notions about the properties of cold water as strengthening the body, to stimulate circulation and give firmness. Books on health advocated regular cold baths for invigoration, and as an ascetic practice of moral and physical toughening, ridding the body of 'softness' and feebleness. Cleanliness changed from values of appearance to notions of health, vigour, strength, austerity and morality. The body, rather than being perceived as passive and vulnerable to external forces as was the case in the Middle Ages, became endowed with endogenous power and vitality which could be released by such activities as cold bathing. Cleanliness induced by cold baths was viewed as the natural state of the body; the use of powder, perfumes and scented oils was decried as frivolous and artificial. The emphasis was now upon opening the pores rather than keeping them covered, to 'free the skin' by removing dirt, perspiration and oils which blocked the surface exits.

In the late eighteenth century, with the scientific discovery of microbes, external signs of cleanliness were no longer considered sufficient (Vigarello, 1988). These theories were legitimized by science; washing was seen to rid the body of microbes and release it from the danger of rotting matter. Microbes were viewed as 'invisible monsters capable of breaking down the body barriers' (Vigarello, 1988: 204), all the more dangerous because of their tininess. Appearances were viewed as deceptive, for cleanliness and dirtiness were now invisible states, on the imperceptible microscopic level: 'The clearest water might contain innumerable bacilli, the whitest skin might sustain every sort of bacteria' (Vigarello, 1988: 203). As a result, touching of parts of the body became prohibited, and frequent washing was advocated to protect against invasion. New areas of the body were named and appropriated by the discourse of cleanliness. To be clean now meant to be free of bacteria, protozoa and viruses.

This notion of cleanliness predominated in the twentieth century as medicine and science became ever more revered. One example is a Canadian women's magazine advertisement from the 1930s, which used the icons of a microscope and microscopic images to sell a household cleaning preparation. The heading of the advertisement proclaimed: 'Science shows why Old Dutch Cleanser costs less to use ... because it goes further, cleans quicker, doesn't scratch, cleans more things and brings Healthful Cleanliness.' The text later asserted that: 'It's your greatest aid in preserving the health of your family.' Another advertisement for Lysol disinfectant published in the American *McCalls* women's magazine, December 1933, was headlined 'The family's health is the family's wealth: let Lysol guard and protect it', and went on to claim, 'Lysol is the reliable general disinfectant which will protect the health of every member of the household, reduce infection from germs carelessly spread' (Leiss et al., 1986: 186).

Current television advertisements in anglophone countries for household cleaners and disinfectants continue to make such claims for 'protecting' the health of the household, especially that of young babies, who are considered particularly susceptible to the ravages of evil 'Dirt' and 'Germs'. There is a particular obsession with the cleanliness of lavatories, as demonstrated by the bewildering range of commercial cleaners which are marketed as having the sole purpose of disinfecting lavatory bowls, seats and S-bends, with cleanliness usually displayed by a bright blue chemical – being released every time the lavatory is flushed. Such fear and anxiety about germs and dirt is ironic, for in contemporary western societies members of the public are exposed to far less risk from deadly bacteria and viruses than in previous generations: 'Yet the fear of germs – codified during the Lysol and plastic-packaged 1950s – verges on a mass psychosis. Germs are bad guys: foreign, unnegotiable, dangerous' (Patton, 1986: 51).

The contemporary obsession with clean bodily fluids has been termed 'Body McCarthyism' and viewed by critics as an hysterical new temperance movement that targets the body's secretions and which expresses anxiety over the invasion of the body by viral agents. It has been argued that such anxiety concentrated upon eliminating 'Germs' and 'Dirt' reveals deeper concerns about the integrity of the body in an age in which potential contaminants are invisible, and where epidemics such as HIV/AIDS have served to heighten fears about the maintenance of body boundaries (Kroker and Kroker, 1988: 10ff). For the Krokers and colleagues, panic was the dominant adjective and theme of the late twentieth century, as in the terms panic sex, panic art, panic ideology, panic noise, panic theories, panic eating, panic fashion and panic bodies. They see burnout, discharge and waste as the characteristic qualities of the postmodern condition (Kroker and Cook, 1988: ii) and the body as portrayed in popular culture as both a torture chamber and a pleasure-palace (1988: 9–10). They describe the diseases receiving attention at the end of the twentieth century – anorexia, HIV/AIDS and herpes – as 'poststructuralist diseases, tracing the inscription of power on the text of the flesh and privileging the ruin of the surface of the body' (1988: 13).

Little empirical research has attempted to discover the ways in which people articulate their sense of body boundaries in this era of 'Body McCarthyism'. However, a range of notions concerning the boundaries and permeability of the body were identified in relation to contemporary French people's attitudes to the risk of infection from HIV (Douglas and Calvez, 1990). The first understood the body as 'a porous thing, completely open to every dangerous invasion' (1990: 454) of bacteria or viruses and therefore basically defenceless to the entry of HIV; the second notion of risk viewed the body as very strong, with a robust immune system to counter infection, and not requiring extra measures to counter the threat of HIV infection; the third conceptualized the body as having two protective layers, the physical skin, with exits and entry points, and the community, serving to control social boundaries but amenable to destruction by the wrong behaviour; and lastly, there was the view that the body is a machine with its own protective envelope, which, if pierced, admits vectors of infection that disrupt the body's functioning and therefore requires constant vigilance against HIV.

Such abstract concepts of the body and its defence against HIV infection cannot be simply reduced to a matter of ignorance, irrationality or lack of education about viral agents and disease. Rather, they are an integral dimension of the cosmology of humans, and the way that they place their bodies as parts of the natural and social worlds (Douglas and Calvez, 1990: 455–6). As I show in Chapter 3, in western societies there are several key metaphorical and discursive ways of conceptualizing the body in relation to health and illness, many of which are based on notions of the body/self and the Other from which this body/self's boundaries must be protected.

The commodified body

Recent theorizing of the body has discussed the manner in which the body in contemporary society may be regarded as a consumer commodity which must be groomed to achieve maximum market value. Some commentators have pointed to a strong element of narcissism in western societies' obsession with physical appearance, the purchase and consumption of commodities and the construction of self-identity. For example, Lasch argues that the increasing secularization of late-industrial societies has resulted in individuals seeking personal salvation and meaning in consumer goods: 'The contemporary climate is therapeutic, not religious. People today hunger not for personal salvation, let alone for the restoration of an earlier golden age, but for the feeling, the momentary illusion, of personal well-being, health, and psychic security' (1980: 7).

The consumption of commodities has become central to how people define themselves for 'consumer goods are the locus of cultural meaning'

(McCracken, 1988: 83). By the purchase and consumption of commodities, 'individuals create a personal "world of goods" which reflects their own experience and concepts of self and world' (1988: 86). In consumer culture the body itself has become a fetishized commodity, something to be attractively 'packaged' and offered for exchange. The discourse of commodification is a major contributor to the ideology of sexology; indeed, the development of sexology has been linked to western society's transition from a production-oriented to a consumer-oriented culture (Birken, 1988). The growth of commodity culture after World War I, which joined hedonistic and expressive values with the consumption of commodities, was a major impetus for the sexualization of wants, desires and pleasures (Seidman, 1991: 67). As part of the 'sexualization of the public realm', or the 'infusion into public spaces of sexual representations and discourses' (1991: 123), lucrative sex industries predicated upon the ideology of sexology emerged and prospered in the public domain. Sexual services, sex aids and pornography are now almost as openly marketed as are the commodities designed to enhance sexual attractiveness such as cosmetics, clothing and exercise products. In return, the sexual (usually female) body is used in advertising to sell such diverse commodities as cars, alcohol, sporting goods and industrial tools, in the attempt to imbue the product with erotic allure.

However, as previously discussed, for public health and medical discourses the body is also where discipline and control are physically expressed for both men and women; bodily 'maintenance' has become a central tenet. The discourse of body maintenance expropriates that of car maintenance in its emphasis upon regular servicing and care of the body for maximum efficiency (Featherstone, 1991: 182). In commodity culture, body maintenance in the interests of good health merges with the desire to appear sexually attractive, to be able successfully to market one's body, especially for women (Bordo, 1990). The emphasis placed on youth and beauty as the attributes of a desirable body has generated a huge industry devoted to bodily maintenance. The industries around cosmetics, fashion, fitness, sport, leisure, bodily cleanliness and diet rely upon the discourse which insists that youth and beauty equals normality and social acceptability. The primary message disseminated by this industry is that as long as the correct commodity is purchased and used, the body itself will be a tempting commodity in the market of sexual attraction. The ascetic lifestyle of constant body maintenance, involving strict dieting and exercising, is presented as being rewarded not by spiritual salvation or improved health, as it once was, but by enhanced appearance and a more marketable body with which one is then able to enjoy the pleasures of the flesh (Featherstone, 1991).

The appearance of the body has become central to notions of self-identity: '"Finding yourself" is today a common cultural quest and one's body is instrumental in solving this "puzzle" of self-knowledge. The "inner" world seems to have become transmuted into "external" flesh' (Lynch,

1987: 129). If the fleshly body represents oneself, then it is imperative to ensure that the appearance of the body is as attractive and conforming to accepted norms as possible.

Just as the 'primitive' rituals of body inscription by means of scarification and tattooing define the body as a socio-cultural and sexual body, so do such rituals and commodities as hairstyles, cosmetics and body-building construct the 'civilized' body in certain ways. Grosz and other poststructuralist theorists conceptualize the body as a text, 'a writing surface on which messages can be inscribed' (1990: 62). Featherstone notes that 'the tendency within consumer culture is for ascribed bodily qualities to become regarded as plastic – with effort and "body work" individuals are persuaded that they can achieve a certain desired appearance' (1991: 178). Slenderness and firmness of the body becomes strongly linked with moral control, self-discipline and 'caring about yourself'. As a result, for some individuals, particularly those from the middle class, the uncontrolled, non-exercised, overweight body, whether male or female, has become a grotesquerie, subject to public ridicule and private shame (Bordo, 1990; Morgan, 1993). 'The ideal here is of a body that is absolutely tight, contained, "bolted down", firm (in other words, a body that is protected against eruption from within, whose internal processes are under control)' (Bordo, 1990: 90).

This perspective demonstrates that the impetus to maximize fitness and avoid obesity is not necessarily strongly related to the desire for physical health but is associated more with the need for surface attractiveness. Thus the industries which support health and fitness activities such as aerobics feed off people's anxieties to conform to the desirable body shape and image. For some men and women, the activity of body-building represents an opportunity to reshape one's given body dramatically through hard work and discipline (Mansfield and McGinn, 1993).

Taken to its extreme, body work embraces cosmetic surgery, where the body is cut, reshaped and stitched together to conform to accepted notions of beauty. Women's magazines, as a genre of commodity culture directed towards providing role models for women, often glorify cosmetic surgery as a means of improving one's appearance and resisting the ravages of time. As noted above, in recent times men's health magazines have begun to similarly champion the bodily improvements offered by cosmetic surgery, including such newer techniques as Botox injections and penis, bicep and calf enlargement. Research into women's reasons for undertaking the risky and painful procedures of cosmetic surgery suggests that they do so to 'feel right' in their bodies, to 'feel normal'. Such women may not necessarily be seeking to achieve an ideal of physical perfection. Rather, they undertake cosmetic surgery as an intervention into identity, enabling them to reduce the distance between how they perceive themselves and how others see them (Davis, 1997).

The rise of commodity culture to prominence in western societies has resulted in the ageing body and the disabled body becoming sources of great anxiety. A body that does not function 'normally' or appear 'normal', that is confined to a wheel-chair or bed, is both visually and conceptually out of place, as evidenced by the lack of public facilities for people with disabilities or the elderly (Seymour, 1998). In the discourse of genetic screening and gene therapy, impairment in a foetus or newborn is typically represented as a tragedy, and one to be avoided if at all possible (Shakespeare, 1999). Genetic screening techniques such as amniocentesis and ultrasound (see Chapter 6) have attempted to identify disability in foetuses so that it may be 'dealt with' (often by termination of the pregnancy) before birth. Foetuses have been aborted following the discovery of such relatively minor defects as a cleft palate in people's quest for the 'perfect baby' (Robotham, 2002a).

Nor is it acceptable any longer to allow one's body to age gracefully, for age has become a negative cultural value. In popular culture, body maintenance is highly encouraged for those growing older, but not because of their cardiovascular health, but because the 'mask of ageing', the external signs of old age – sagging flesh, wrinkles, loss of muscle tone, overweight – are culturally stigmatized (Bordo, 1990; Featherstone, 1991; Featherstone and Hepworth, 1991; Bytheway and Johnson, 1998). The signs of ageing have become so abhorrent and pathological that they are conceptualized as distorting and hiding the 'real', essentially youthful self behind the 'mask', and as a disease needful of cure (Featherstone and Hepworth, 1991: 379). According to Featherstone (1987: 128), this belief is stronger among the middle class than the working class. Members of the latter class, he claims, tend to accept the deteriorating body as an unavoidable consequence of ageing, which in part explains why middle-class people engage more actively in exercise and weight-reducing activities than do the working class.

The obsession of some members of the middle class for the maintenance of the body to combat ageing is linked to a growing repulsion for bodily functions and frailty of the flesh, as well as the ideology that the body is a commodity. Likewise, participation in sporting activities is related to a constellation of cultural meanings of which the desire for a healthy body is only one. Sport is where the values of physical fitness, muscularity, youth and speed are given vivid expression (Hargreaves, 1986). Sports offer escape from everyday life in their combination of 'childlike exuberance with deliberately created complications' (Lasch, 1980: 100).

For women, sporting or exercise activities may represent a desire to engage with feminist ideals about the independence and strength of the female body rather than a concern to prevent against the ravages of ageing or extend longevity. Physical exercise for women as a socially acceptable endeavour represents 'a recent victory in women's struggle for equality with men' (Willis, 1991: 65). By allowing the female body to be physically active and strong, discourses on the value of exercise avoid the notion of the female body as weak, dependent, frail and sickly. These discourses are particularly evident among women who pursue such traditionally masculine activities as body-building (Mansfield and McGinn, 1993) and boxing (Hargreaves, 1997). However, exercise has only really been embraced by white, middle-class professional women; the response of working-class women is, according to Willis (1991: 65), '"Why exercise when you kill yourself working all day?"' The discourse of exercise urges women to achieve selfhood, empowerment and freedom from domination through toning and strengthening the body. Yet the potential for exercise to represent a political act challenging patriarchy is hampered by the other meanings around fitness; for example, while female body-builders enjoy adding muscle bulk to their bodies, they are denigrated if they go too far and become too 'masculine' looking (Mansfield and McGinn, 1993). The emphasis on individual rather than collective action, and beauty rather than health, commodifies exercise as something you buy and wear rather than simply something you do (Willis, 1991: 72), hence bolstering rather than undermining consumer culture's obsession with youth and physical beauty as characterizing the ideal female body.

Such discourses are evident in research studies of the ways in which people conceptualize the healthy body. Crawford's (1984) study of sixty people living in the Chicago area elicited responses about concepts of health that revolved around the notion of health as self-control, encompassing concepts of self-discipline, self-denial and will power. Health thus became a goal, to be achieved by intentional actions, involving restraint, perseverance and the commitment of time and energy. Crawford noted that judgement of others and self-blame were themes that recurred throughout the interviews, among both male and female respondents, reflecting a general moralization of health achievement similar to that of the work ethic. Body weight in particular symbolized self-restraint, with a thin body a testament to control and an overweight body signifying the lack of will power and self-indulgence. Crawford linked these accounts with the discourses on self-control and individual responsibility that predominate in health promotion rhetoric. He viewed 'health' as a moral discourse that incorporates the emphasis on individualism, hard work and material reward which predominates in contemporary American culture:

> Talking about health becomes a means by which we participate in a secular ritual. We affirm ourselves and each other, as well as allocate responsibility for failure or misfortune, through these shared images of well-being. The 'health' of the physical body – at the same time a social body – validates conventional understandings. (Crawford, 1984: 78)

For Crawford, the emphasis on restraint evident in people's accounts about health was related, amongst other social trends, to the economic downturn of the 1970s and 1980s, a cultural context in which self-denial must be fostered and which is reflected in the conduct of bodies. However, as he pointed out, there is also a competing discourse in American culture that privileges release, pleasure and consumption as the means to maintain health. Thus people's accounts of health incorporated both the need for self-control and the desirability of being able to 'let go' and relax, allowing them to rationalize the choices they made in the way they conducted their everyday lives.

Almost a decade after Crawford's study, Saltonstall (1993) interviewed American white, middle-class men and women about their notions of health, and in doing so elicited their conceptualizations of their bodies which revolved around the need for body maintenance to achieve 'health'. She found that health, for both men and women, was allied closely to physical standards that conformed to the ideals of being 'in shape'. Health was also something to be achieved by deliberate, intentional action involving the body, such as dieting, having enough sleep and physical exercise. The interviewees moved back and forth between describing themselves as having a body and being a body, and the maintenance of health was viewed as a matter of personal accomplishment.

In the early years of the twenty-first century, the link between the commodified body and health remains as strong as ever. Thinness remains an ideal for women, in particular, to aspire after. Female celebrities who dramatically reshape their bodies by losing weight, such as Geri Halliwell, are championed for their self-control, while those who allow themselves to gain some weight are pilloried in the popular media. While those celebrities (such as Kate Moss or Calista Flockhart) who are deemed to be 'too skinny' are frequently criticized for presenting unhealthy role models for young people, greater opprobrium and ridicule are reserved for those who have deemed to have 'let themselves go', apparently not able to muster the iron will required for body maintenance.

Food and the body

The act of incorporation of foodstuffs may be regarded as the apotheosis of the inscription of consumption choices upon the body, and one of the most permanent both externally and internally: skin tone, weight, strength of bones, condition of hair and nails, digestion are all commonly said to be directly affected by diet. These choices are not necessarily 'free'; they are constrained by the individual's social class position, in terms of both material wealth (which places boundaries upon the extent of choice) and the cultural expectations of different class fractions and stages in the life course (Featherstone, 1987): for Bourdieu 'the body is the most indisputable materialization of class taste' (1984: 190).

Bourdieu's (1984) notion of the *habitus*, or the pattern of unconscious preferences, classificatory schemes and taken-for-granted choices which differs between groups and classes and distinguishes them one from the other, is relevant to the understanding of the ways in which sub-cultures pass on eating practices and beliefs. This notion reincorporates the idea of class divisions in the practices of everyday life and the conduct of bodies, aspects of discussing bodily deportment which have often been neglected by Foucault and his followers. Bourdieu theorizes that if one belongs to a certain group and identifies with that group, then one will make choices in everyday consumption rituals which reflect the habitus of this group. Thus, for example, the working-class habitus produces a taste for cheap, filling and fatty foods, free consumption of alcohol and tobacco naturalized by the 'eat well and let yourself go' philosophy, while the middle-class habitus is characterized by valuing dietary restraint, bodily fitness and slimness. These tastes are thereby incorporated into body shape. Bourdieu argues that for members of the working class the body is a means to an end, for they have little leisure time to indulge the body and thus develop an instrumental orientation. However, for members of the ruling class, the body is an end in itself, a product of careful maintenance meant for aesthetic display rather than work (Shilling, 1991: 655).

The control of diet is a central feature of the government of the body, predominantly traditionally expressed in the discourses of religious asceticism and medical regimens (Turner, 1991b: 159), but in contemporary western societies now evident in secular discourses concerning sexual attractiveness and body shape: 'Today, it can be ventured, diet and body maintenance are increasingly regarded as vehicles to release the temptations of the flesh' (Featherstone, 1991: 171). Coward (1989), in her examination of the holistic, New Age health movement, made the observation that health has displaced sexuality as the new moralizing category for power to be exercised. This is especially the case with food, which Coward (1989: 126) argues has taken over the significance of sex as a major source of anxiety about the body.

Bodily obsessions currently appear to be centring around what foodstuffs are allowed to enter the body. In the age of controversies and complexities concerning such phenomena as 'mad cow disease' and genetically modified foods, and dire warnings about the growing 'epidemic' of obesity among the denizens of western countries, diet has become a focal point for anxieties about what is allowed to breach the boundaries of the body. Old certainties about 'good' and 'bad' food have been challenged and rendered more complex, as dieticians advise lay people, for example, about the difference between 'good' and 'bad' oils and 'good' and 'bad' carbohydrates. Achieving good health through diet has become a matter of acquiring expertise in the micro-constituents of foodstuffs.

The inducements of health, fitness, physical desirability and youth often merge in advertisements for food products. In western countries, the discourse of health and fitness has been incorporated in commercial practices whereby certain foods deemed 'healthy', such as low-fat milk, low-cholesterol margarines, lean meat and products with Omega 3 oils, are presented as aids to physical perfection and preservation of a youthful appearance. It is revealing that among the numerous advertisements for drugs in medical journals and medical magazines there are routinely glossy advertisements financed by corporations and companies market- ing food or beverages which advise doctors to 'prescribe' their products to their patients. The slippage between food as medicine and medicine as food in such advertisements is significant. Although such foods may not necessarily guarantee good health, the use of the labels 'low fat', 'low cho- lesterol' or 'high fibre' serve as reassuring (if often misleading) markers of goodness and virtue to the consumer.

Feminist scholarship has aroused extensive debate about the meanings and role of food for women living in affluent western cultures, where, as noted above, a thin body is considered desirable and therefore many women feel obliged to severely restrict their food intake, especially of foods deemed to be high in calories. Charles and Kerr (1986) found that many of the British women they interviewed experienced a constant struggle between depriving themselves and feeding their family. Few women had a positive body-image; indeed, most women felt that they should lose weight. Weight loss or gain was clearly linked to the women's self-esteem. However, the pressure on the women to maintain a sexually attractive figure for their husbands was at odds with their maternal role, which dictated that women should feed their families nutritionally and socially satisfying meals. Charles and Kerr assert that food is a tempting enemy for many women, against which they feel obliged to practise self- denial. The patterns of the women's lifestyles often make it difficult for them to exert control over their diet because of external constraints. For many women the role of food as comfort in times of depression, boredom or stress also results in food having ambiguous meanings of both a relief and a cause of anxiety and unhappiness.

Some feminists have gone further in their analyses of women's rela- tionships with food, and linked food intake with women's lack of power in society. They argue that body image is not necessarily the primary motivation for some women who suffer from eating disorders (Chernin, 1985; Caskey, 1986; Brumberg, 1988; Orbach, 1988; Banks, 1992). Rather, these theorists suggest that women's bodies are the only sphere over which they can effectively exert control. Sometimes the need to reduce body weight becomes an obsession, and some women develop eating dis- orders such as anorexia nervosa, compulsive eating and bulimia. It has been suggested that anorexia nervosa, the deliberate starving of oneself, is a form of control and a demand for freedom. The ability to control hunger, for the anorexic, signifies control over her body and her life: 'Refusing to eat is supremely defiant and supremely obedient at the same time' (Caskey, 1986: 181). In anorexia nervosa, the restriction of food intake is an obsession, overtaking everyday lives and thoughts. Many anorexics are sophisticated in their knowledge about nutrition, and per- ceive food in highly abstract and symbolic terms. Once ingested, the meaning of food changes:

It is no longer a matter of numbers or chemical composition; suddenly food is metamorphosed into a dark dragging force that threatens to take over the anorexic, to sink her under suffocating waves of unwanted flesh. To anorexics, food seems to linger ominously in the body; it has a living presence inside them which overpowers them and which they resent, whence their frequent use of laxatives and their manic exercise habits. (Caskey, 1986: 183)

The control over food can take on a spiritual dimension in the quest to renounce the demands and bonds of the corporeal body. Some women (and men) are motivated by religious or quasi-religious beliefs concerning the purity of the body and the control over appetite and hunger (Brumberg, 1988; Bordo, 1990; Banks, 1992; Turner, 1996; Garrett, 1998). The renunciation of food becomes a symbol of asceticism, 'lightness' and holiness, not a quest for the perfect figure. The dimensions of control, discipline, virtue and strength of character, however, are comparable between food denial as symbolizing religious purity and food denial as symbolizing beauty. Like the fasting of women in the name of religion in previous centuries, fasting today may represent a statement of secular piety, of moral purity, of metaphysical discipline over the flesh and its desires.

The dead body

The changing meaning of death over the centuries provides an example of the way in which a physical event is constructed through cultural custom. While death would seem to be the ultimate biological essentialism, there is a wide boundary around which death is negotiated, culturally, historically and politically: 'Death is not a thing or event existing independently of human consciousness; it is simply the word given to a certain threshold, interface, space or point of separation' (Armstrong, 1987a: 655). The dead body has changed form and substance in western society over the past few centuries, in concert with notions of what death is and how it should be achieved. Before the advent of medicine, the most potent symbol of death was the grim reaper, a skeletal figure dressed in black and carrying a scythe. In the late twentieth century, death is represented by a biological lesion or a test result; for example, a positive result for the presence of cancer in a Pap smear or biopsy.

Historical writings on the body have demonstrated the ways in which western societies' notions about corporeality have changed over the centuries. In the sixteenth century and the first half of the seventeenth century in Europe, death was a largely non-medical ceremony. Both the Protestant and Catholic religions insisted that a member of the clergy should be in charge at the deathbed, rather than a medical practitioner, who left when it became clear that nothing more could be done. Friends and family were present to give encouragement to the dying person to resist the temptations of the devil. It was important that the dying person give outward signs that he or she was dying well, displaying serenity, calmness, fortitude, faith and welcoming death as the entrée into heaven (Wear, 1992: 124–5). Enlightenment ideals of rationality, with their emphasis on the present rather than the future life, lessened the religious meaning of death by the end of the seventeenth century, at least among the elite classes, and by the end of the eighteenth century, the medicalized death was beginning to take shape, reflecting the growing secularization of society (1992: 125).

Ariès (1981) traced the history of the social rituals of dying, noting a major change in death customs in the middle of the nineteenth century when death became under the control of the doctor, removed to the hospital rather than taking place in the home. He argues that, at this time, death became hidden away, mystified and 'driven into secrecy' (1981: 562). Armstrong (1987a), however, challenges Ariès' conclusions, asserting that since the mid-nineteenth century rather than there being a silence on death and dying, there has been an explosion of discourse around these subjects with the moving of death from the private to the public domain. He points to the death certificate, in particular, as a symbol of the increased attention paid to the documentation of death and its causes. While death may have been a public affair before the mid-nineteenth century, involving shows of mourning and bedside vigils, this was only so for the immediate family and community within which the dying person lived. Armstrong argues that after the introduction of the death certificate and the commonplace removal of the dying to hospitals, death became a more publicly controlled event: 'In the old regime knowledge of death was restricted to within earshot of the church bell: beyond there was silence; in the new regime no death was to be unknown' (1987a: 652). Following death, dead bodies became the object of analysis to confirm and document the cause, sometimes resulting in the opening up of the corpse for pathologists and coroners to peer inside to discover the 'truth' of death. The means of disposal of the dead body became an issue of great importance, around which a constellation of rules was developed (Armstrong, 1987a).

Before the emergence of scientific medicine and epidemiology, death was connected with luck and chance, as random, unpredictable and untamed, as an event that could strike anyone at any time. By the end of the eighteenth century, a new image of death became current, where death was not located in the individual, but in the entire population (Prior and Bloor, 1993; Prior, 2000). The development of the life table, used to calculate the length of life spans based on sex and age employing mathematical laws, symbolized this change, for it was an attempt to rationalize death, to subject it to a formalized pattern which could be predicated using statistical methods: 'The life table, then, is one of the most significant representations of life and death that our own culture has produced. It not only expresses a vision of life as a rationally calculable object, but also provides a set of background expectancies of normal, natural lifespans' (Prior and Bloor, 1993: 356). This cultural artefact is currently relied upon by doctors in their judging of what is and what is not a normal, natural death, and is vital in the construction of reasons for death as reported on the death certificate.

The use of the corpse for medical training and research has been a focal point of concepts of death. In medicine today, the corpse is regarded as a necessary teaching tool, but prior to the nineteenth century, dissection was surrounded with moral prohibitions. Dissection of the corpse violated a number of beliefs about the sanctity and mystery of death and the dead body. By the sixteenth century, dissection was recognized in law as a punishment, a fate worse than death, even while it was serving the purposes of medical knowledge (Richardson, 1988: 32–4). While anatomical dissection was undertaken for teaching and research purposes in medieval France from the fourteenth century onwards, general society did not consider it permissible to open up the secrets of the body for such purposes. Dissection was seen as punishment for criminal behaviour, as a prolongation of the suffering inflicted by the executioner, and its disordering of the body's organs was regarded as symbolic of societal chaos (Pouchelle, 1990). The cutting open of bodies, even in the quest for medical knowledge, was subjected to deeply rooted taboos at that time. Such exposure of the internal workings of the human body was deemed an unacceptable invasion of the microcosm which harboured the soul, laying bare the intimate parts of the person: 'The human body was seen not only as a "little world" (microcosm), but also as the reflection and model of human society … If the members and organs of the microcosm were dispersed, disturbing the order of the world, would not the "body politic" fall apart as well?' (1990: 83).

Blood, in particular, was regarded as sacred and poisonous, and to be avoided by surgeons if possible. Surgeons had to follow rituals before an operation which were designed to purify them, preserve their bodily integrity and keep their strength and power intact; for example, when treating a fracture of the skull, one document of the day noted that the surgeon must, the night before, avoid contact with women and speaking with menstruating women, must not eat any garlic, onion or hot sauces on the day, and must clean his hands thoroughly before the operation (Pouchelle, 1990: 87). It was not until the end of the fifteenth century that official dissections were carried out at the Faculty of Medicine in Paris, accompanied by pomp and ceremony, including a banquet, to highlight the unusual nature and symbolic danger of the event (1990: 84).

Despite the strong moral prohibitions surrounding the cutting open of dead bodies, by the eighteenth century the medical gaze had extended into the previously hidden world of the corpse. Because of the prohibitions surrounding dissection, however, the obtaining of corpses for surgeons and anatomists was difficult, and by the seventeenth century corpses had become a commodity (Richardson, 1988). Condemned prisoners were encouraged to barter their bodies for money, and grave-robbing became rife. 'By 1800, in medical circles, market terminology was being applied to human corpses apparently without embarrassment' (1988: 55) and human bodies were 'dismembered and sold in pieces, or measured and sold by the inch' (1988: 72), yet public opinion did not approve. At the time of the British 1832 Anatomy Act which provided for the requisition of the corpses of the poor for anatomical uses, the corpse was viewed with a mixture of solicitude and fear, with ambiguity concerning both the definition of death and the spiritual status of the dead body expressing a mixture of pagan and Christian beliefs (Richardson, 1988).

Funereal practices in the seventeenth and early eighteenth centuries foregrounded the corpse, and demonstrated beliefs that there was a period between death and burial in which the human being was regarded as 'neither alive nor fully dead', including the custom of placing food and wine beside the corpse in case it woke, and watching over it (Richardson, 1988: 15). In the interim before the onset of rigor mortis and putrefaction, death could only be unreliably defined by listening for a heartbeat or testing for breath on a mirror or glass, and thus could not be decreed with certainty. There was also uncertainty about the time of separation of the soul from the body, whether it left the body at death, or slept in the grave with the body (1988: 15–16). While death in the eighteenth century was considered in medical discourse as an absolute fact, the end of life and the end of disease, it was also relative, because examination of the corpse could not reveal the distinction between the cause and the effect of death, especially once decomposition had set in (Foucault, 1975: 140–1). Following the spread of the dissection of corpses, death became not a single moment in time, but a series of 'partial deaths', of small changes in parts of the body at different times (1975: 142).

The above discussion suggests that there is historical evidence of a schism between the conceptualization of the dead body in medicine and that of the lay person; the former viewing the body as a commodity and teaching tool, the latter continuing to invest the corpse with respect and fear. Thus, dissection 'represented a gross assault upon the integrity and identity of the body *and* upon the repose of the soul, each of which – in other circumstances – would have been carefully fostered' (Richardson, 1988: 76, emphasis in the original). When the stealing of corpses from graveyards in Britain became widespread, customs of protecting graves came into being to foil the bodysnatchers, and public opprobrium was high. As a result, British medical schools could not gain access to enough corpses, and the Anatomy Act was drawn up and passed, allowing anatomists to obtain the 'unclaimed' bodies of people who had died in workhouses, hospitals and other charitable institutions as well as prisons, the reasoning being that such people, who had been kept alive by the public purse, had no relatives to protest against their deployment for dissection. The Act thus discriminated between the bodies of the poor, deemed suitable for dissection, and the wealthy, protected from the ravages of the grave-robbers (Richardson, 1988).

It is worthy of note that in contemporary western societies it is generally considered entirely appropriate for individuals to pledge their dead bodies for transplantation purposes. In some western countries this choice is enshrined on drivers' licences, while in others organs are deemed automatically available for donation at death unless individuals or their relatives specifically request they not be. Allowing medical dissection for the purposes of helping another is generally valorized in the popular media rather than being represented as fraught with moral prohibitions; they routinely depict organ donation as saving lives and the 'ultimate sacrifice', as in the headline 'Organ recipients plead for gift of life for others' printed in a national Australian newspaper in January 1993. The possible discourse highlighting the commodification of bodily parts used in transplant surgery is replaced by that of altruism, or the invoking of the ideal of prolonging one's material existence by living after death in another's body. Ironically, at the same time as the western media champion the altruistic ideal of giving one's organs for transplant surgery, an international trade in human organs exists in which impoverished people from developing countries such as India and the Philippines undertake to have their own organs surgically removed while they are still alive, including kidneys, eyes and pieces of skin, and sold to western nations. It seems that among some medical quarters at least, there is no compunction in removing organs from living bodies and treating them as commodities, just as grave-robbers in the nineteenth century sold pieces of human flesh by the inch.

Since the introduction of medical technology that allows the prolonging of the life of people who previously would have been pronounced dead, the issue of defining death has become even more problematic. When can death be said to have occurred if a body is on a life-support machine, the brain shows no sign of functioning, and breathing could not take place if the machine were to be switched off? Muller and Koenig (1988) emphasized the social nature of defining death exploring the processes by which doctors interpret selected information about patients to reach conclusions about whether the patient is 'dying' or 'still has a chance' (and is thus deserving of further medical intervention designed at forestalling death). What is the status of a person's organs which have been taken from a body pronounced to be dead and transplanted into a living person's body? Are these organs 'dead'? The difficulties of defining death in such situations is evidenced by the three categories of death that currently exist in medical discourse relating to the viability of human body organs and tissue for transplantation or other medical use: tissue may be described as 'dead', 'double dead' or 'triple dead' (Clarke, 1993). Due to such conundrums, death has now moved from the province of the clinician to that of the medical ethicist (Armstrong, 1987a: 656).

Here again is evidence of a schism between the ideals of medical science in its quest for progress and the beliefs of lay people. Twenty people living in England, of both middle-class and working-class origins, were asked what they thought about a range of medical procedures including medicine and drugs, elective surgery, reproductive technology and life-saving technology (Calnan and Williams, 1992). Findings revealed that certain forms of western medicine, such as IVF or heart transplantation surgery, transgress 'natural'–'unnatural' boundaries in the view of the lay population, and thus are less readily accepted. For example, one woman said, 'Well I don't think that anybody should give transplants to other people because their heart is different from what the other's have been, it's unnatural isn't it?' (1992: 245). Such comments attest to a lingering suspicion about the desirability of using parts of other people's bodies to prolong life. However, it should be noted that the interviewees in this study gave different views based on whether they found procedures acceptable for themselves and their family members, or for the population as a whole, demonstrating the tension that exists between fear of illness and death on the personal level and global, generalized beliefs about right and wrong.

Where once death was considered under the auspices of fate or God's will, contemporary understandings tend to suggest that early death is preventable and therefore, in many cases, subject to the individual's control. Public health discourses claim that taking the appropriate measures will protect against premature death: driving safely, eating well (as in 'the anti-cancer' diet), reducing alcohol consumption, taking regular exercise, avoiding smoking, engaging in safer sex practices and so on (Lupton, 1995; Prior, 2000). Ever greater hopes are pinned on biomedical advances in the effort to vanquish early death and prolong lifespans. In the context of an intensified focus on control over death, to succumb to a fatal disease or accident before old age becomes viewed as a loss of control over one's body. Such deaths can no longer be regarded as simply misfortune: instead, someone must be held accountable.

Part of this need for control over death is the sequestration of dying, death and corpses from everyday life, in such places as hospitals, hospices and cemeteries (Prior, 2000). Although images of the dead body are routinely portrayed in the popular media (violent television or cinematic dramas, for example), the material corpse is hidden from view, so that people may go through their lives never viewing a dead body in the flesh. Even news media portrayals of the dead body tend to be highly censored in deference to public sensibilities. For example, although the 11 September 2000 terrorist acts in the US received blanket media coverage for many days, great pains were taken by the media to edit out direct images of the corpses and body parts resulting from the attacks.

Conclusion

The intensified interest in the body on the part of scholars and researchers in the humanities and social sciences over the past two decades has provided a wealth of theoretical insights relevant to understanding the human body as defined by medical discourses and practices. Scholarship using the social constructionist perspective in particular has demonstrated the dynamic and mutable nature of concepts, knowledges and lived experiences of the body in the context of illness and medical care, and highlighted the relations and techniques of power evident in the regulation and deployment of bodies under medicine and public health. By far the most important insight is that which views the body and its ills not as universal biological realities but as a combination of discursive processes, practices and physical matter which have a symbiotic and symbolic relationship with the discourses and ideologies governing societal regulation. This conception of the body has challenged the ways in which sociologists, anthropologists and historians have undertaken studies of medicine as culture.

3
Representations of Medicine, Illness and Disease in Elite and Popular Culture

Along with the increasingly intense interest in language and discourse in scholarship in the humanities and social sciences there is a growing focus on narrative accounts of disease and illness (Frankenberg, 1990: 351), including those evident in popular cultural texts and works of elite literature. Writers who have suffered serious illnesses often incorporate their experiences into their work, using dramatic imagery in their attempts to convey the meaning of the illness as they experienced it. Such accounts of the effects of illness and disease upon the body, both fictional and autobiographical, provide insights into the ways in which illness is experienced which other, more prosaic, forms of expression sometimes fail adequately to achieve. Indeed, it has been suggested that medical students and practising physicians should be encouraged to read literary accounts of illness, pain and death so that they learn to treat their patients with empathy and compassion and become more sensitive to the human dimension of the illness experience and the complex moral implications of medical practice (Pellegrino, 1980).

Cultural theorists are beginning to focus their attention on these expressions of discourse to identify recurring narrative structures and tropes in the portrayal of the illness experience. Two important and pervasive ways of conceptualizing illness and disease are the use of metaphor and visual imagery. Following a general discussion of the ways in which disease and death have been portrayed in elite and popular culture, this chapter examines these features of the representation of medicine, illness and disease in western societies, including an historical dimension to demonstrate how linguistic and iconographic representations have changed together with wider socio-cultural and political shifts in understanding the world and maintaining social order.

Disease and death in elite culture

The terrors of physical decay, pain, suffering and death are the very stuff of drama. As a result, descriptions of ageing, illness and disease have received the attention of western novelists, poets and playwrights for centuries, especially leprosy, the plague, tuberculosis, cancer, syphilis and mental disorders (Horst and Daemmrich, 1987: 90). Indeed, several renowned literary figures either were doctors themselves (for example, Rabelais, Chekhov, Maugham, Keats, William Carlos Williams) or were the sons of doctors (including Proust, Flaubert and Hemingway) (Peschel, 1980). Even in the nineteenth century, as epidemic disease was in regression in Europe, paradoxically the sick body was expressed more and more frequently in literary works (Herzlich and Pierret, 1987: 78). Disease used as a recurring motif or as a theme in literature has focused attention 'on the intractable, capricious, and mysterious forces beyond human control or comprehension' (Horst and Daemmrich, 1987: 90).

Disease and death have traditionally been used as devices in novels to reveal the psychological development of characters and to structure events (Meyers, 1985: 12). The functions of disease in literary texts have included illness as a sign of divine power or providence (common in biblical writings and the *Iliad*); illness or epidemics as the test of the moral fibre of the afflicted individual and society, exposing their true nature (for example, Camus' *The Plague*, 1947); disease as a recurrent metaphor for moral or social decay (Ibsen's *Ghosts*, 1881); as a vision of collective social disaster; as a sign of the individual's inability to escape from a destined fate; a catalyst for artistic or intellectual genius and a sign of emotional, intellectual or moral curiosity or superiority (Beecher Stowe's *Uncle Tom's Cabin*, 1852 and O'Neill's *Long Day's Journey into Night*, 1956); as a means of redemption for the fallen or the outcast (Dumas' *Lady of the Camellias*, 1848); as a way of heightening the awareness of death, calling up questions of mortality and life's complexity (Joyce's *The Dead*, 1914); and as an alien, incomprehensible force penetrating human life and destroying it (Solzhenitsyn's *Cancer Ward*, 1968) (Horst and Daemmrich, 1987: 90–1).

In novels, '[d]isease has always been a great mystery: a visitation, a curse, a judgement' (Meyers, 1985: 2). In Oscar Wilde's short novel *The Picture of Dorian Gray*, for example, first published in 1891, the decadence of the protagonist is reflected in his painted visage, which, as the years go by, becomes more and more frightful in its external signs of old age, decay and corruption while the man himself remains youthful and handsome. The Gothic novel emerging in the Romantic era (spanning the late eighteenth century to the 1830s) portrayed the fearsomeness of nature wrought upon humanity, depicting diseases and the bodily symptoms of illness or physical decay as evil demons and monsters to evoke horror and to symbolize the internal sufferings or evil of characters. The Victorian period of literature following was obsessed with death and the supernatural. One example is the writings of Edgar Allan Poe, which centred around characters' horror of tortures and the physical wages of sin, including his short story 'Masque of the Red Death' (1840) in which the protagonists fall prey to a plague-like illness after daring to trivialize and mock Death. Mary Shelley's *Frankenstein* (1818) dealt with the moral issue of humans usurping God as creator of the human body, while Bram Stoker's *Dracula* (1897) focused on themes to do with the sexual body, gender, death and immortality with a particular emphasis on the symbolic nature of blood. It is telling that both these latter literary works remain central in contemporary popular culture as horror stories, demonstrating the resonance of their themes for audiences even today.

Representations of illness and disease in literature have closely followed changes in medical discourses on the body. During the Romantic period the creativity of the writer or artist was believed to emerge from suffering due to travails such as serious illness. Above all illnesses, tuberculosis, a common cause of death in the nineteenth century, was believed to stimulate the creative impulse, fuelled by the early deaths from that disease of literary figures such as Chatterton, Keats, Percy Shelley and Byron and the success of the romantic and tragic operas *La Traviata* and *La Bohème* (Meyers, 1985: 4). With the advent of scientific medicine, naturalist writers in Europe began to incorporate clinical descriptions of illnesses and neuroses into their novels (Herzlich and Pierret, 1987: 29). By the twentieth century, novels were beginning to include clinical discussions of illness and disease to represent not only dissolution, decay and physical corruption but metaphysical despair, loneliness, alienation and self-doubt (Meyers, 1985: 13). In such writing, the medical treatment foisted upon the patient becomes torture to be endured by sheer strength of will, while the existence of illness forces characters to confront their mortality, the threat of nothingness (1985: 13–14). Mann's *The Magic Mountain* (dealing with tuberculosis), *The Black Swan* (uterine cancer) and *Death in Venice* (a cholera epidemic) and Solzhenitsyn's *Cancer Ward* are examples of such works.

Medicine, illness and death in popular culture

Representations of medicine, illness and death are not limited to elite cultural texts such as literature and opera, but also routinely feature in the popular mass media. Fictitious portrayals of doctors and other health professionals and patients have been common in popular fiction and film and particularly television dramas and soap operas since the 1950s. Successful and often long-running television dramas since that time have included the high-rating American *Marcus Welby MD*, *Dr Kildare*, *St Elsewhere*, *Doogie Howser MD*, *Chicago Hope* and *ER*, and the British *Dr Finlay's Casebook*, *Casualty*, *Cardiac Arrest* and *Peak Practice*. In soap operas, sickness, injury and death have provided vital themes for plots, especially accidents and violent events, suicides, homicides, psychiatric disorders, pregnancy-related conditions, heart disease and infectious disease (Cassata et al., 1979). Medical breakthroughs and the personalized stories of people suffering from disease regularly make newspaper headlines and provide the basis of television and radio news and documentaries.

In most fictional television programmes, sickness is treated, usually competently and successfully, by doctors in hospitals using the latest technology and fast-acting drugs (Turow and Coe, 1985). The status of the doctor is usually indicated by his or her white coat, signifying authority, the objectivity and power of laboratory science and hygienic purity, and the stethoscope, ultimate symbol of medical technology and the ability of the doctor to gain access to the patient's body to hear or see bodily functions denied patients themselves, while retaining a certain distance between doctor and patient (Krantzler, 1986: 936–7). For many years, until quite recently, members of the medical profession were most often represented as omnipotent figures who had the power to save lives against all the odds, while nurses were depicted either as maternal, nurturing figures, dispensing kindly care and assisting doctors, validating their superiority, or as promiscuous sex objects (Karpf, 1988; Turow, 1989; Lupton and Chapman, 1991). For example, analyses of the depiction of doctors on American television dramas have found that they were generally portrayed as successful, benevolent, knowledgeable and authoritative, with almost mystical power to dominate and control the lives of others (McLaughlin, 1975; Turow, 1989).

Doctors as characters in television dramas have tended to dominate over other professional occupations, and to be shown as more successful, peaceable and fair-minded than most other characters (Gerbner et al., 1981: 902). They have routinely been depicted as 'saving patients from themselves', by forcing patients to confront truths or show courage in the face of pain or death (Turow, 1989: 146). So too in the news media, doctors are routinely presented as superhuman figures, the secular equivalent of clergy, and medicine is portrayed as the avenue by which miracles may be wrought (Lupton and Chapman, 1991; Lupton and McLean, 1998).

Documentary representations have similarly been very positive in their portrayals of members of the medical profession and of scientific medicine generally. *RPA*, a 'reality' docudrama made in Australia and focusing on the experiences of real patients and staff in Royal Prince Alfred Hospital, Sydney, especially underlines the power and benevolence of the medical practitioners working at that hospital. In scenario after scenario, grateful and passive patients are cured of their illness and are shown thanking their doctors profusely before leaving the hospital. While the medical staff often appear realistically awkward in their face-to-face dealings with their patients, this very popular series rarely shows them making mistakes or a procedure going wrong. The fantasy that doctors will do the right thing all the time and that they can cure any malady is strongly perpetuated in this series.

In popular media representations, medical technology, in particular, is singled out as the apotheosis of medical magic. The trappings of technology: the complex machinery, the flashing lights, the 'blips' of the monitors, the graph measuring the strength and regularity of the pulse dwarf the figure of the patient, shown in medical dramas and news and documentary features as lying passively on the bed, connected to the machinery by various tubes and wires, rendered part-human, part-machine.

Despite the long-term dominance of positive portrayals of medical practitioners and medicine itself in popular culture, in the later decades of the twentieth century and into the twenty-first century there have been a growing number of portrayals of doctors and scientific medicine as fallible. News coverage of doctors commonly reports cases of professional negligence, sexual harassment and assault of patients by doctors, fraudulent behaviour and other scandals (Bradbury et al., 1995; Lupton and McLean, 1998). Television dramas such as *Casualty* and *ER* have represented doctors as flawed and all-too-human characters, capable of making mistakes or lapses of judgement under pressure and coping with complicated private lives which sometimes affected their work. For example, some physician characters in *ER*, such as the surgeon Dr Robert Romano, are portrayed as thoroughly unpleasant and unlikeable, although technically very competent. *Chicago Hope* commonly dramatized the ethical and legal issues around the practice of medicine in a large hospital, and a new Australian medico-legal drama, *MDA*, focuses entirely upon the stories involved in cases brought against doctors by their patients.

Nevertheless, in both news and fictional portrayals of doctors and scientific medicine, positive representations continue to outweigh those that are negative. Doctors remain the voice of authority in news stories on medical issues, receiving privileged access to frame debates in the news media. Medical negligence, malpractice and other misdoings on the part of doctors have proved newsworthy, but so too have the skills, expertise and dedication of members of the medical profession and the advances of medicine (Lupton and McLean, 1998; Hodgetts and Chamberlain, 1999). While the doctor characters in *ER* and several other medical dramas are presented as beset with human failings, most programmes tend to continue to represent them as competent in most cases and above all as highly dedicated to their profession and concerned about their patients' welfare and well-being.

Illness and metaphor

Literary and popular culture accounts of the illness experience have provided fertile ground for scholars of rhetoric, especially those interested in the use of metaphor. Individuals who have experienced illness or disease have often reverted to metaphorical discourse to conceptualize and articulate to themselves and to others their experiences. In the context of illness, metaphors enable people to render indefinite physical sensations such as pain more concrete (van der Geest and Whyte, 1989: 354). This reliance is partly due to the lack of linguistic expressions for effectively conveying bodily feelings. As Virginia Woolf, in her essay 'On Being Ill' (first published in 1930), commented:

English, which can express the thoughts of Hamlet and the tragedy of Lear, has no words for the shiver and headache. The merest schoolgirl, when she falls in love, has Shakespeare or Keats to speak her mind for her; but let a sufferer try to describe a pain in his [*sic*] head to a doctor and language at once runs dry. There is nothing ready made for him. He is forced to coin words himself, and, taking his pain in one hand, and a lump of pure sound in the other (as perhaps the people of Babel did in the beginning), so as to crush them together that a brand new word in the end drops out. (Reprinted in Enright, 1989: 19.)

The frequent use of metaphor in the medical context is not surprising, for metaphor is used in all areas of verbal communication as an epistemological device, serving to conceptualize the world, define notions of reality and construct subjectivity (Lakoff and Johnson, 1981; Clatts and Mutchler, 1989). Metaphor works by association, by comparing two non-associated entities with each other centring on the ways in which they resemble each other. In doing so, the metaphor shapes perception, identity and experience, going beyond the original association by evoking a host of multiple meanings (1989: 106–7). As Geertz has argued: 'In metaphor one has ... a stratification of meaning, in which an incongruity of sense on one level produces an influx of significance on another' (1973: 210). The establishment of metaphorical associations both relies upon pre-established knowledge and belief systems to establish meaning and extends these meaning systems in other directions.

There is a reflexive relationship between metaphorical discourse applied to illness and disease: just as other concepts or things are used to describe disease, so is disease used as a metaphor. But metaphorical representations are not politically neutral; in fact, metaphors are commonly used in ideological struggles around a contested site of meaning, a linguistic strategy used to persuade the acceptance of one meaning over another (Kress, 1985: 71). Metaphor works to 'naturalize' the social, turning that which is problematic into the obvious (1985: 72–3). For example, disease metaphors are most commonly used to describe disorder, chaos or corruption, as when describing communism as 'a cancer on society', or describing a psychopathic murderer as 'sick'. The word 'invalid' is also suggestive of loss of integrity:

In English, we use the same word to describe an expired passport, an indefensible argument, an illegitimate legal document, and a person disabled by disease. We call each of them *invalid*. To be an invalid, then, is to be an invalidated person, a human being stamped *not valid* by the invisible but invincible hand of public opinion. (Szasz, reprinted in Enright, 1989: 1454, emphasis in the original.)

Metaphors describing the body, illness and disease are strongly associated with the commonplace objects of everyday life. Pouchelle examined the treatise on surgery written between 1306 and 1320 by Henri de Mondeville, surgeon to the French King, Philip the Fair, and the 'unacknowledged father of French surgery' (Pouchelle, 1990: 2). She traced the dominant metaphorical systems evident in de Mondeville's medical writings. Architectural metaphors were often used to describe the body; the body as house, as fortress, as edifice, cell, cage, box, coffer, with the womb as 'ultimate dwelling place, intended to shelter the foetus' (1990: 134). The eyes were represented as sentinels, with a porter (the duodenum) guarding the lower door of the stomach against the arrows of flatulence and needles of pain caused by bile, while the stomach itself was the kitchen of the household (1990: 108–9). The orifices and openings of the body were variously described as doors, passageways and bridges, with cracks and holes in the body's fortress serving to expose its occupant to the outside world. While the escape of bodily secretions was considered normal and necessary, an accidental or surgical wound provided a dangerous outlet for vital warmth and spirits and allowed contact with the outside pestilential air; the body was viewed as being in constant threat from outside.

Other conceptions of the body in de Mondeville's treatise described diseases as 'Nature' invading the body with her mineral, vegetable and animal forms, or represented the body as a tool, or a workshop full of tools (Pouchelle, 1990: 106). The choice of metaphorical systems in this medieval medical text suggests the terror felt against the 'animality' of the flesh at that time. The view of the body as a potential for 'wilderness' against which all good Christians should guard is evinced by the metaphors of disease as the invasion of Nature, and of the body as fragile, imperfectly protected by a skin riddled with holes that allow easy penetration. They imply a subsequent need to conceptualize the body as an ordered, reasoned, 'civilized' system that is not of Nature. As Pouchelle comments: 'Through architectural metaphors the body becomes a building, ordered and controlled by man; to see the mouth as a door is to feel reassured that this gap in the body's defences is under control' (1990: 147). Hence, the medieval doctor-surgeon was charged with the responsibility for controlling the traffic between the inside and outside of the body, protecting culture, as represented by the body as dwelling or fortress, against the incursions of untamed Nature.

In seventeenth-century England, religion and health and illness were closely intertwined and religious metaphors were common in depicting the body. Writers represented the body as God's workmanship, a temple to be kept pure, clean and in good order. As one commentator of the time stated:

> Whereas our bodies are God's workmanship, we must glorify him in our bodies, and all the actions of body and soul, our eating and drinking, our living and dying, must be referred to his glory: yea we must not hurt or abuse our body, but present them as holy and living sacrifices unto God. (From William Perkins, *A Golden Chaine*, published in 1612, quoted by Wear, 1985: 63.)

Medical metaphors were also employed to describe the religious experience: the sinner was described as a sick man, while sin was said to be 'cured' or 'healed' by Christ the 'healer' of the soul. The words 'health' and 'salvation' were exchangeable (Wear, 1985: 67–8). Illness was commonly spiritualized by the Puritans as a corrective or punishment of God the Father, and often seen in providential terms, in which guilt and a sense of sin were prominent: 'Health, a good night's sleep or recovery from illness were noted as a sign of God's favour, but the onset of illness stirred up anxiety, self-doubt and guilt' (1985: 71). However, even devout Puritans often used medical or physically-based explanations of illness as well as those relying on religious belief, although medical remedies were often couched as 'God's gifts' (1985: 78–9).

The use of language when referring to disease and those at risk of contracting it has a direct effect upon the way in which ill people deal with their condition and the ways in which others treat them. In relation to HIV/AIDS, for example:

> ... to say someone has AIDS is to say much more than that person is experiencing the progressive exposure of fragile vital organs to the ravages of common infections. It is to say that he or she is a certain type of person, socially and morally defined ... the metaphoric predication of AIDS opens a door to the dark musty cellar of cultural associations of the profane, the defiled, the denied, the unshown, the forbidden, the feared. (Clatts and Mutchler, 1989: 108)

Susan Sontag has published two influential essays which consider contemporary metaphors of illness and disease and their use to make moral judgements about the ill. In her introduction to the first essay, *Illness as Metaphor*, first published in 1978, she commented that, 'it is hardly possible to take up one's residence in the kingdom of the ill unprejudiced by the lurid metaphors with which it has been landscaped' (Sontag, 1989: 3–4). Although Sontag's work has been the subject of criticism for her belief that metaphorical associations can and should be stripped from diseases (notice her own use of metaphor when writing about the illness experience in the sentence quoted above), she was one of the first modern critics to cogently argue that disease is rendered meaningful through the use of metaphor. In *Illness as Metaphor* Sontag focused upon two diseases, cancer and tuberculosis. She examined the ways in which these diseases, and later HIV/AIDS, achieved an extraordinary cultural resonance in western society over the past two centuries. Sontag drew upon the understanding of metaphor not only as a rhetorical device, which compares unlike objects and concepts to emphasize their relatedness, but as a vital epistemological device, by which we understand the world.

Writing from the perspective of one who had been diagnosed and treated for cancer, Sontag commented upon the stigmatizing and discriminatory effect of metaphorical discourse: 'As long as a particular disease is treated as an evil, invincible predator, not just a disease, most people with cancer will indeed be demoralized by learning what disease they have' (1989: 7). In comparing tuberculosis and cancer, Sontag described the former as being mythologized as a disease of romance and passion, a sign of 'inward burning' or ardour, conceptualized as disintegration, transparency, hyper-activity alternating with elegant languidness, leading to a noble and often lyrical death. By contrast, cancer is a disease of uncontrolled, abnormal growth that invades the body, 'a demonic pregnancy' (1989: 14), a disease of industrial society and also the wages of repression of feeling. Cancer is thus a shameful disease, a metaphor for evil. Sontag argued that the stigmatizing nature of the metaphors that surround diseases such as cancer has a direct effect on practices, for people feel inhibited and frightened to seek diagnosis and early treatment.

In her essay on the metaphors of HIV/AIDS (1989), Sontag saw HIV/AIDS as attracting the same metaphors of invasion, but also those of pollution, implying invasion from outside rather than from within. The virus that causes the immunodeficiency characterized by HIV/AIDS is represented as an invader of the body, removing its defences and allowing the opportunistic infections associated with the onset of HIV/AIDS to colonize and overwhelm the body: 'Cancer makes cells proliferate; in AIDS, cells die' (Sontag, 1989: 107). Thus both cancer and HIV/AIDS are represented as punishments for living unhealthy lives, for taking health risks, for excesses of diet and lifestyle, weaknesses of will, self-indulgence and addiction (1989: 113).

The comparing of HIV/AIDS to plague inspires centuries-old fears of incipient illness, spread mysteriously and striking down large numbers of people almost without warning. As Sontag (1989: 142) noted, plagues are 'invariably regarded as judgements on society', and the use of the plague metaphor in describing another illness imputes such moralism. Other metaphors commonly used to describe HIV/AIDS have invoked the detective story, the wrath of God, apocalyptic visions, Gothic horror, silent assassins, tombstones and the grim reaper to 'make sense' of the new disease and its impact on society (Watney, 1987; Clatts and Mutchler, 1989; Sontag, 1989; Williamson, 1989; Rhodes and Shaughnessy, 1990; Lupton, 1993a). These choices of metaphor to give meaning to HIV/AIDS throw light upon the stigmatized nature of the disease and the discriminatory attitudes towards people living with HIV/AIDS and those who are believed to be at high risk of HIV infection.

The machinery of the body

Since the industrial revolution, the mechanical metaphor has been frequently used in discourses on the body. As described above, even pre-industrial revolution metaphors adopted the imagery of the body as a workshop full of instruments and tools, including the lungs as blacksmith's bellows. Such conceptualizations have proved long-lasting in the ways that the body is represented in both medical and lay forums. Even when the mysteries of the human body were finally revealed by medical dissection, ages-old metaphorical understandings of the body's interior were not unduly disturbed, because such pre-established beliefs served to shape the perceptions of the newly exposed interior: 'Thus dissection, far from dealing the death-blow to metaphor, used it as a jumping-off point, and afterwards, for anatomical knowledge progressed via a complex and almost incomprehensible dialectic of visual perception and mental images deeply rooted in language' (Pouchelle, 1990: 196).

The French philosopher Rousseau wrote of his body the following: 'After having read a little physiology, I began the study of anatomy, and took a survey of the number and working of the individual parts which composed my bodily machine. Twenty times a day I was prepared to feel the whole out of gear' (quoted by Herzlich and Pierret, 1987: 91). Today we speak about 'recharging our batteries', 'blowing a fuse', of feeling 'run down'. Clockwork metaphors – 'I'm all wound up', 'What makes him tick?' – and hydraulic metaphors – 'bottled-up emotions', 'overflow of feelings' – are also commonly used when talking about bodily processes or human behaviours (Seddon, 1993: 183). These expressions adopt the language of technology in conceiving of the internal workings of the body as a combustion engine, a battery-driven machine or a plumbing system. Indeed, the concept of the heart as a 'pump', which can 'break' and which contributes to low or high blood 'pressure', has been so naturalized as to be rendered a dead metaphor, or an expression which we no longer recognize as a metaphor (1993: 183). However, the heart is itself a powerful metaphor of emotion, especially romantic love, and heart problems are also often said to be linked to emotional rather than physical causes using older concepts of heart function; one is 'heartsick', 'heartsore', 'heavy' or 'light' of heart and may die of a 'broken heart' caused by emotional distress (Helman, 1985: 321; Seddon, 1993: 184).

The mechanical metaphor includes the idea that individual parts of the body, like parts of a car or plumbing system, may 'fail' or stop working, and can sometimes be replaced. The metaphor has the effect of separating mind and body, of valorizing medical techniques which focus upon locating a specific problem in a part of the body and treating only that part, and devaluing healing relationships which rely upon spirituality, personal contact, intimacy and trust (Helman, 1985; Martin, 1987; Scheper-Hughes and Lock, 1987; Stein, 1990; Turner, 1996). Hence the importance of the technological imperative in biomedicine: the dependence upon the use of machinery to fix machinery. Thus the routine employment of organ transplants and artificial organs or parts such as pacemakers, plastic joints and hearing aids in high-technology medicine both is supported by and reinforces this image (Stein, 1990: 81).

It was a logical conceptual leap in the late twentieth century to imagine the body as a computerized system. There developed a symbiotic metaphorical relationship between computers and humans, in which computers were anthropomorphized (for example, they are said to have a 'memory'), while humans have increasingly been portrayed as 'organic computers' (Berman, 1989: 7). Indeed, the notion of 'biofeedback' originated in computer terminology (Stein, 1990: 81). As a result of the computer metaphor, argues Haraway (1989: 15), bodies have become cyborgs and disease has become viewed as 'a subspecies of information malfunction or communications pathology'. Such a metaphor serves to restore order, rationality and predictability into our visions of the body (Montgomery, 1991: 353).

One example of the machine/computer metaphor as applied to the human brain is an article published in the British popular science magazine *New Scientist* (Young and Concar, 1992) as part of the series entitled 'The secret life of the brain'. In the article were references to 'how the brain stores information', 'memory's hardware', 'the internal filing system', 'the machinery that enables us to retain a sequence of digits, letters or words', 'electrical impulses', 'the brain's cellular architecture', 'fine-tuning connections between neurons' and 'memory networks'. The article then discussed attempts to perfect silicon chips that mimic the behaviour of the human brain. By this imagery there occurs 'the transformation of the human subject into an object, a repository, or else a collision site, for various types of detectable and usable information' (Montgomery, 1991: 383).

The bio-information metaphor may be linked to the discovery of the genetic material DNA in cell nuclei in 1953 and the later introduction of the term 'genetic code'. The DNA molecule was described by Watson and Crick (the scientists who discovered DNA) as a 'template', a 'mechanism for self-duplication' and a 'copying process' for important information (Montgomery, 1991: 368). With the discovery of DNA and RNA, the human body began to be represented in medical and scientific texts as a complex 'chemical factory' manufacturing 'chemical building blocks' using 'blueprints' (Nelkin and Tancredi, 1989: 16). The current enthusiasm towards identifying or 'mapping' the structure and sequence of the genetic material in the human genome presents an image of the body and mind 'as machine-like "systems" that can be visualized on a computer screen and understood simply by deciphering a code' (1989: 15). The use of the word 'map', and the visual depiction of the alternating dark and light bands of chromosomes in identified genes like an aerial photograph of the earth's continents, invoke a related cartographic metaphor (Lippman, 1992: 1469) in which the human genome is portrayed as undiscovered and uncharted territory awaiting exploration and documentation of its secrets.

These metaphorical systems reduce individuals to their DNA codes. They are reworkings of the mechanical metaphor in representing the body as being comprised of a multitude of tiny interchangeable parts, rendering the body amenable to objectification and technological tinkering in the interests of developing the 'perfect' human. Sickness becomes viewed as the product of biological destiny, located within the individual and therefore requiring the intervention of technology to 'correct' the faulty code, hence drawing attention away from the examination of the social context of illness such as poverty, racism and sexism (Lippman, 1992; Conrad, 1999).

The military metaphor

The language of warfare is extremely common in modern medical and public health discourses that deal with cancer, infectious diseases and other illnesses such as HIV/AIDS. The immune system, for example, is commonly described as mounting a 'defence' or 'siege' against the 'invasion' of 'alien' bodies or tumours which are 'fought', 'attacked' or 'killed' by white blood cells, drugs or surgical procedures. Such metaphors are common not only in literature dealing with medicine and individual treatment, but in public health campaigns directed at large populations.

Sontag traces the use of the military metaphor in public health education to campaigns mounted in World War I to educate people about syphilis, followed after the war by educational programmes against tuberculosis. She cites one example of a campaign conducted in Italy in the 1920s, using a poster called *'Guerra alle Mosche'* ('War against Flies') which depicted the flies as 'enemy aircraft dropping bombs of death on an innocent population' (Sontag, 1989: 98). On the bombs were inscribed the words *'microbi'* (microbes), *'germi della tisi'* (the germs of tuberculosis) and *'malattia'* (illness). Sontag (1989: 99) asserts that the military metaphor has such resonance in western society's discourses on illness and disease because it appeals to the need to mobilize against an emergency, to make sacrifices, to do everything possible to counter a threat to life. Montgomery (1991: 343) goes even further into history for the origin of the military metaphor, commenting that images portraying disease in the form of an 'attacker' armed with spear or quiver go back centuries to the Middle Ages. He argues that contemporary images of violence and warfare tend to 'connect disease in its connotative charge with the greatest evils and atrocities of the twentieth century: fascism, Stalinism, even the Holocaust' (1991: 349).

In the modern era, a dominant image around which notions of the internal workings of the body have been organized is that of the germ theory of disease. Illness is no longer predominantly conceived as an evocation of evil incurred by the wrath of God, but as a microscopic invader, intent on entering the body and causing trouble. 'Germs' are commonly believed to have motivation and evil intentions: 'There are no "good" Germs or "normal" Germs; all Germs are bad' (Helman, 1978: 119). Among lay people, bacteria and viruses are conceived of as:

> ... living, invisible, malevolent entities [which] have no free existence in nature, but exist only in or among people. They are thought of as occurring in a cloud of tiny particles, or as a tiny, invisible, single 'insect'. They traverse the spaces between people by travelling in the air, or in the breath. Germs causing gastro-intestinal

symptoms are seen as more 'insect-like' ('Bugs'), and are larger in size than those Germs causing other symptoms. Germs have personalities; these are expressed in, and can be recognized by, the various symptoms they cause. (Helman, 1978: 118)

By Edwardian times, the germ theory of disease had become central to medical and lay discourses on illness, centring around anxieties over pollution, purity and boundary maintenance. An example is the constant use of such words and phrases in the media and political forums as 'social purity', 'mothers of the race', 'the imperial race', 'British stock', 'degeneration' and 'purification of the race'. This usage may be interpreted as emerging from concerns about maintaining the boundaries between inside and out and protecting against internal pollution, decay and degeneration (Wright, 1988: 322). The terminology of germ pathogeny 'fell into easy harmony with such imagery, strengthening it and vicariously endowing it with some of the added weight of science. Germ pathogeny came to serve as a trope for society and social affairs – a model for making sense of disease' (1988: 322). This was evident from the phraseology of a hygiene reader, E. Hood's *Fighting Dirt: the World's Greatest Warfare* (1916), in which it was asserted that:

While the boy and girl yearn to handle a sword and go to the wars, deadly enemies surround them, lurk in their clothes, cling to their flesh, penetrate into their mouths, and only wait a favourable moment to attack their bodies in force, as soldiers have attempted the capture of some great fortress, such as Gibraltar. (Quoted by Wright, 1988.)

Military metaphors continually emerge in contemporary popular media accounts of medical science and immunology. For example, an article in the American *Time* magazine (31 August 1992) entitled 'Attack of the superbugs' described the increasing resistance of bacteria to drugs such as penicillin, using the following rhetoric:

In the battle against old scourges, magic bullets are losing their power, and invisible legions of drug-resistant microbes are again on the march ... medicine is no longer confident of winning the battle ... Using marvellous powers of mutation, some strains of bacteria are transforming themselves into new breeds of superbugs that are invulnerable to some or all antibiotics ... scientists are worried about the future. 'We forgot that microbes are restless and that they would counterattack,' says Richard Krause, a senior scientific adviser to the National Institute of Health ... Researchers who once thought they had won the war with microbes now know better. 'Disease,' observes chemist Irwin Kuntz of the University of California at San Francisco, 'is an ongoing battle between one species and another.' (Nash, 1992: 46–7)

In such texts, bacteria are anthropomorphized into wily aggressors, deliberately changing themselves to elude detection and attack from their human foes. Even the scientists interviewed for the article used colourful metaphors of war to describe their efforts; language that perhaps gives their endeavours legitimacy and a sense of great importance, positioning them as the 'generals' in the battle against disease. The military metaphor has been particularly dominant in representations of HIV/AIDS. For example, in an article on HIV/AIDS recently published in *New Scientist* (Brown, 1992), such phrases as 'HIV can reproduce only by hijacking its host's genetic material ... the virus is winning ... a moving target ... why is the war against the virus proving so difficult? ... the virus attacks the very cells that should defend the body against it ... know your enemy' prevail. Yet the use of such metaphorical systems is not confined to scientific, medical or media representations of HIV and AIDS. Autobiographical accounts of HIV/AIDS draw upon similar imagery to describe personal experiences of illness, suggesting the difficulty of resisting dominant military metaphors even for those who are ill. As Dreuihle vividly described in his account of his experience as a person who is HIV positive:

> My personal war began two years ago when I was mobilized by AIDS. All the pleasures of peacetime and my carefree life were suddenly banished, as if an orchestra had stopped playing to let the theatre manager announce that war had just been declared, that Pearl Harbour had been bombed. Since then I have devoted myself exclusively to the war effort, because the futility of civilian life (my thirty-six years of good health) is absurd when survival itself has become the main imperative. (1988: 6–7)

Medical practitioners themselves may draw upon a complex series of metaphor systems to describe their work and patients. Stein (1990), as a medical anthropologist working in an American hospital, engaged in participant-observation of physicians treating their patients. From this position he identified a series of common metaphors within western medicine, including those of military/war; sports; technology/engineering/mechanical; family; life cycle; religion; economics/business; freedom; masculinity/femininity; and time. These metaphor systems were evident in the informal and formal discussions between doctors, talk between doctors and patients, at medical seminars and conferences, in drug advertisements and articles in medical journals and in representations of medicine and disease in the popular media. Doctors working in the hospital repeatedly described themselves as being 'on the front line', in need of 'getting aggressive' with patients and using 'shotgun therapy' or 'magic bullets'. They commonly described working in the emergency room as being 'in the trenches'.

The doctors in Stein's study saw themselves as battling not only against disease, but also against the masculine world of the medical system and other physicians, attempting to master their work as 'winners', never allowing themselves to lose control or to fail in the clinical setting. In this context, the patient became the feminized, passive object, to be poked, prodded and 'attacked' as the focus of the battle for medical male supremacy (regardless of the gender of the patient or physician) (Stein, 1990: 67–73). Hence such statements made by doctors as 'He tackled the real difficult patient. He handled it aggressively. But he got shot down', and 'In the clinic I hit her with everything (antibiotics), but she still came in the hospital door', which combine military and sporting metaphors (1990: 72).

The body against itself: metaphors of the immune system

The discourses of science as an heroic quest, nuclear exterminism, space adventure, extra-terrestrialism, exotic invaders and military high-technology are dominant in popular accounts of the immune system (Haraway, 1989: 5). The anthropology of immunology was the subject of an inquiry by Martin (1990a), who drew upon major mass media articles and popular monographs on the immune system published in the United States in the 1980s for her source of data. Martin concluded 'that the dominant imagery used was that of 'the body as nation state at war over its external borders, containing internal surveillance systems to monitor foreign intruders' (1990a: 410). She later found that the dominant metaphorical systems she had identified as recurring in popular medical and media texts on the immune system were emerging in lay people's descriptions of their bodies (Martin, 2000). They commonly used violent imagery such as 'the policing system', 'the defence system', 'like an army' to articulate their understandings of the processes of their immune system, and often compared the strength or effectiveness of their immune response to that of others, evincing beliefs that one can 'train' or 'build up' one's immune system.

Such phrases demonstrate the pervasiveness of value judgements made about relative superiority in which some groups or individuals are said to have 'better', 'stronger' or 'tougher' immune responses than others. Martin (1990a, 2000) views this discourse as being part of a metaphorical 'currency' of health which is a response to an increasing focus of media and medical literature over the past decade on the immune system and its link with such diseases and disorders as HIV/AIDS, allergies, cancer, heart disease, arthritis, diabetes and chronic fatigue system. She sees this change in popular body imagery as shifting from the centuries-old notion of the body as defended from disease at its external borders, like a fortress, to a body defended by a complex internal system.

Under the ideology of the 'currency' of health, the discursive way in which the 'deficient' immune systems of those people who have an auto-immune system or immunodeficiency disease (such as systemic lupus erythmatosus [lupus] or HIV/AIDS) are described becomes emblematic of their imputed moral deficiencies. People whose immune systems are 'inferior' become members of a new stigmatized and victimized underclass, subject to 'Body McCarthyism' where 'political discourse is reduced to the purity of your bodily fluids' (Kroker, 1992: 325). One example of the use of discriminatory language is an article entitled 'Self Destruction' published in a weekly Sydney community newspaper (*Western Suburbs Courier*, 15 January 1992) as part of a series of regular medical columns by Professor John Dwyer, an immunologist known largely for his work in HIV/AIDS. In his article, Dwyer outlined the symptoms, causes, risk factors and treatment of lupus, using revealing terminology in his attempts to describe the immunological intricacies of the disease to a lay audience. The title of the article itself implies blaming the victim and punishment: the illness is 'self' destruction, not externally imposed destruction; it is the body turning against itself. Dwyer gives a detailed explanation of the immune system and the reasons for auto-immunity: 'that unfortunate set of circumstances which sees our normally impeccable immune system, designed to attack "foreignness", make a mistake and instead attack "self" – a biological form of self-destruction. How can such a terrible thing happen?'

These sentences are revealing of the discourses of military strategy, xenophobia, purity and blame which recur in medical and media representations of the immune system. In this account, the onset of auto-immunity is described as an 'unfortunate set of circumstances' and a 'terrible thing'. The purity, normality and balance of the body have been overturned, the 'impeccable' status lost. Instead, the body has made a 'mistake' and turned against itself rather than against 'foreignness'. Later in the article, when Dwyer is describing the treatment for auto-immune diseases such as lupus, he uses the phrase 'The punishment must fit the crime', in which there is a curious slippage between the criminal (the disease) and the patient's body. The 'punishment' is the treatment, and therefore is administered not only to the condition, but to the patient's body.

The metaphors used to describe the immune system thus construct and maintain the boundaries and binary oppositions between inside and outside, the normal and the pathological. Haraway (1989), in her essay on the bio-politics of postmodern bodies, contends that popular medical and scientific discourses surrounding the immune system seek to mark out difference. She notes that: 'Just as computer design is a map of and for ways of living, the immune system is in some sense a diagram of relationships and a guide for action in the face of questions about the boundaries of the self and about mortality' (Haraway, 1989: 18). Like other uses of military metaphors to describe disease causation and control, both scientifically and in lay discourses, they reflect wider divisions, anxieties and concerns in society. While military imagery may overtly connote decisive action and the refusal to 'give in' to the disease, at a deeper level of meaning this discourse serves to draw boundaries between Self and Other by representing the body as a nation state which is vulnerable to attacks by foreign invaders, invoking and resolving anxieties to do with xenophobia, invasion, control and contamination. The ideological work performed by such imagery is to make violent destruction seem ordinary, prosaic and domesticated, and xenophobia acceptable (Haraway, 1989; Martin, 1990a).

In the arena of public health, military imagery also serves to justify the intervention of the state in the everyday habits of its citizens, granting power to external agencies to control individuals' bodies in the interests of the health of the body politic.

Cancer metaphors

Like HIV/AIDS, cancer is a disease that has occasioned a constellation of metaphorical systems, largely due to its severity, mystery and evasion of medical solutions. Indeed, Herzlich and Pierret assert that for the populations of western societies, 'cancer is THE illness of our time' (1987: 55). As they note, the name of the disease is itself a metaphor, derived from the Latin word for crab, and denoting a swollen protuberance like the legs of a crab. In medieval times, cancer was commonly represented as a hungry animal, 'gnawing' at the body (Pouchelle, 1990: 169). Even today, 'cancer is also fraught with phantasms of rot invading the body, animals that gnaw and destroy it' (Herzlich and Pierret, 1987: 56). This metaphor was vividly evident in the view of one Frenchman, who commented that, 'I have the feeling that I am in a pre-cancerous state, in the condition that favours its hatching' (1987: 65).

In modern times, notions of moral culpability have surrounded people suffering with cancer. This disease in modern western societies is often viewed as brought upon oneself through irresponsibility, either by indulging in injudicious diets or tobacco consumption, or by suppressing negative or angry thoughts (Sontag, 1989). Pinell (1987) analysed letters sent by cancer patients in France in response to a call by the French minister of health to instigate public debate on cancer. She examined the way in which cancer patients deal with the dominant discourses on their disease which are often contradictory; on the one hand, the victorious and hopeful 'winning the battle against cancer' discourse, often expressed in advertisements for cancer agencies and benefits; on the other, the 'cancer equals death' discourse that is also common. Pinell found that a homology between social disorder and biological disorder appeared in many letters that referred to poor working conditions or low socio-economic status as a cause of their cancer: for example, one woman noted that, 'I am convinced that there will be no cancer in a better world' (quoted by Pinell, 1987: 32). Such interpretations pointed to a cause of cancer which was located external to themselves, and thus for which they could not personally be blamed. Letter-writers wrote of the stigmatization they had experienced: 'Friends avoid you, not knowing what to say, and it's a mistake, one should speak about it; it is less frightening' (1987: 36). Cancer was often referred to as evil, sometimes with a capital E, or as 'the thing', 'the scourge', 'an invisible enemy, whose weapons we know nothing about', or 'that contemporary plague, which has taken other forms in the history of the world' (1987: 37–8).

Like other medical writing aimed at lay audiences, popular media accounts of cancer often incorporate metaphors in the attempt to 'simplify' explanations. For example, in a self-help book entitled *Your Cancer, Your Life*, Dr Trish Reynolds describes cancer cells as disorderly and out-of-control: 'Cancer growths are made up of cells which belong to our body but which have stopped behaving in a co-operative and orderly fashion' (1987: 26). Later in the book she observes that the multiplication of cancer cells 'has no purpose – it is not in order to replace or repair. The cells do not differentiate into useful cells. They keep growing to the detriment of the body and regardless of normal control mechanisms. Unlike normal body cells we can think of cancer cells as unco-operative, disobedient, and independent' (1987: 27) and further comments that '[n]ormal cells exist peacefully side by side with their neighbours. Cancer cells damage and destroy them' (1987: 33). The over-riding metaphor used here is that of the cellular dimension of the human body as a society, peopled by 'good' and 'useful' cells that serve a function, but with social order threatened by deviant cells that refuse to obey societal laws. Cancer is portrayed as a challenge to rationality; 'It seems as if cancer – an outcome of social disorder – inscribes analogical disorder into the sick person's body, bringing about death' (Pinell, 1987: 27).

Military discourse is often linked to other discourses in representations of cancer. Thus, for example, mass media accounts of people's experiences of illnesses such as cancer may incorporate military language, bringing together 'battle' and 'warrior' with such words as 'God', 'Jesus', 'faith' and 'miracle' to represent cancer as a 'challenge to the spirit' (Hoffman-Goetz, 1999). A study of American press accounts of men with testicular cancer found that articles frequently drew upon both sporting and military discourses (Clarke and Robinson, 1999). Indeed, sporting metaphors are common in media representations of various types of cancers for both men and women, depicting their 'heroic struggle' against the disease (Seale, 2001).

As mentioned above, a dominant discourse surrounding cancer in modern western societies is that of hope. This discourse is related to military and sporting metaphors and discourses, for it postulates that 'winning' the battle against cancer is intimately linked to having a positive attitude to getting better. To despair, to lose hope, are frowned upon as strategies of dealing with diseases such as cancer. People with cancer are lauded if they appear to be brave, never allowing themselves to 'give in' to the disease. There is an emphasis on 'will' which argues that 'if one has enough hope, one may will a change in the course of the disease in the body', an emphasis which is related to notions of individualism, fighting spirit and the power of thought to shape one's life course which are particularly evident in American society (Good et al., 1990: 61). This discourse supports the current practice of informing a patient of his or her diagnosis in the United States, a practice which is not followed in Japan or Italy where it is believed best to withhold or mask the diagnosis of cancer in order better to protect the patient (1990: 62).

The discourse of hope can be problematic when, despite the patient's and the doctor's best efforts to remain optimistic, the illness worsens, for the patient can then be held culpable for not being positive enough. When this metaphor dominates, cancer victims are expected to fight the sickness, providing them with the 'glories of a war hero' even if they do not actually get better (Erwin, 1987: 202). In interviews with cancer patients and oncologists, Erwin (1987: 207) found that both patients and their doctors constantly referred to the disease as an enemy and an aggressor, and perceived themselves as allies against cancer. As these data suggest, in western anglophone societies, cowardice, giving in, fear and 'denial' are not considered socially acceptable ways of dealing with the disease. Rather, optimism, a coping attitude, cheerfulness and strength are required. Dying bravely becomes a victory. Likewise, the physician must respond with military-like leadership, authority, precision, confidence, lack of emotion and an aura of control: 'For the medical doctor, the long range goal is to determine which treatment protocols produce the best statistical curves – that, in his [sic] opinion, is the way to win the war. The war is his career. Fighting a single battle is the concern of the individual patient/soldier' (1987: 216).

The discourse of hope is often evident in popular representations of people with cancer, especially if they are well-known. Women's magazines are particularly fond of personalizing stories about famous women's experiences of breast cancer in terms of their triumph over the scourge. An example is an account of ex-First Lady Nancy Reagan's experience with breast cancer. The article noted that after her recovery from mastectomy, Reagan 'raised her arms in the air like a boxer giving a victory salute' (*New Idea* magazine, 5 December 1987). Another example is an article printed in the *Australian Women's Weekly* (Olivar, 1993) in which singer/actress Olivia Newton-John was interviewed about her recent diagnosis and treatment for breast cancer. The article featured a number of recent photographs of Newton-John with her husband and child, smiling brightly and looking attractive and healthy. Titled 'My Fight for Life', the article comments that 'positive thinking is proving to be Olivia's greatest weapon in fighting her cancer, and, if attitude can cure, she has every reason to be optimistic … As she chats, you would never guess she was suffering from a life-threatening illness.' When describing her feelings after being told her diagnosis, Newton-John is quoted as saying, 'I don't consider myself ill. I had cancer and I'm having treatment for it, but papers write that you're this, you're that, you're depressed, you're really sick. That makes me cross. I need people telling me that I'm doing well and giving me support, not the other way round.' Such cases are held up as a public example of how personal courage and the constant maintenance of a positive hopeful attitude, in conjunction with medical knowledge and skill, can save people with cancer from death.

Metaphor, gender and medicine

In her book, which examines the discourses around medicine, science and gender between the eighteenth and twentieth centuries, Jordanova (1989) suggests that the biomedical sciences in eighteenth- and nineteenth-century France and Britain were characterized by a discourse which linked nature with women and culture with men. The Enlightenment privileged an epistemology that was rooted in empirical information derived from the senses. The methods of science and medicine were considered to avoid superstition and dogma, and were addressed to investigating phenomena surrounding sexuality. In so doing, she argues, the discourses of science and medicine employed sexual metaphors to describe their endeavours: 'for example by designating nature as a woman to be unveiled, unclothed and penetrated by masculine science' (1989: 24).

For Jordanova, the wax anatomical models of women used in the medical context, complete with eyelashes, eyebrows and pubic hair as well as detachable organs, are representative of and contribute to a constellation of practices which constituted central discourses on gender, medicine and science in the Enlightenment: 'The late eighteenth-century wax models occupy the same space as political theory, advice books, medical theory and practice, art and literature, and accordingly, we can see this space as having political, social, cultural, ideological and aesthetic dimensions' (1989: 54). She views these wax models as ultimately erotic, in that they allowed penetration beneath the surface of the skin by the successive removal or 'unveiling' of layers. The metaphor of 'unveiling' signifies the feminine mystique rendered open to the masculine gaze, allowing possession and mastery.

Jordanova uses other texts – medical textbooks and illustrations of the eighteenth century, the writings of the nineteenth-century French historian Jules Michelet, a statue of a woman made in 1899 entitled 'Nature Unveiling Herself before Science', paintings of dissections of female corpses, the Fritz Lang film released in 1927, *Metropolis*, and contemporary medical advertisements – to inquire into the historical linkages between science, medicine and the constitution of gender and sexuality. The woman/nature metaphor was characterized by ambivalence: women were represented as softer, more sensitive and more vulnerable than men, but also tougher and more tenacious of life. The breast was of particular interest to practitioners concerned with moral philosophy and ethics: 'It symbolized women's role in the family through its association with the suckling of babies; it defined the occupational status of females within the privacy of the family, as opposed to public life. It was the visible sign of femininity that men recognized' (Jordanova, 1989: 29). The women-as-nature and men-as-culture dichotomies became key terms in struggles around child-care and midwifery in the period. Women as mothers and as midwives were represented as irrational and irresponsible, their knowledge based on tradition rather than experience, needing the guidance of men who possessed scientific knowledge.

Martin's (1990a) analysis of the metaphorical systems evident in medical and popular portrayals of the immune system noted that even at the cellular level, gender differences were reproduced in descriptions of 'masculine' and 'feminine' cells: 'there are obvious female associations with the engulfing and surrounding of phagocytes and obvious male associations with the penetrating or injecting of T cells ... "Male" activity is valued as heroic and life-giving, and "female" activity is devalued as ordinary and mortal' (1990a: 416–17). Martin's (1987) earlier study of contemporary writings on childbirth and women's reproductive organs in medical textbooks uncovered the dominant metaphors organizing medical praxis. A common metaphor was that of industrial production. Women were depicted as the sites of production, alienated from their work by medical praxis, the baby the end product, the uterus the labourer and the doctor the supervisor.

A later study published by Martin (1991, 1992) examined visual and print media's representations of scientific explanations of human reproduction. She observed that while both male and female reproductive organs were metaphorically represented as 'systems for the production of valuable things', menstruation was described as the death of tissue, implying wastefulness, chaos and 'production gone awry' (1992: 411). The processes of male reproduction, by contrast, were portrayed as awe-inspiring, productive in the capitalist sense, successful. This representation was evident in a medical textbook in which the following sentence appears: 'Whereas the female *sheds* only a single gamete each month, the seminiferous tubules *produce* hundreds of millions of sperm each day' (1991: 486, emphasis in the original). Ova were anthropomorphized in a feminine manner, depicted as passive, holy, lying hidden in wait: 'a dormant bride awaiting her mate's magic kiss, which instils the spirit that brings her to life' (1991: 490); while sperm were described using active masculine words connoting strength and aggression: they 'deliver' their genes to the egg and 'burrow through the egg coat' and 'penetrate' it (1991: 489).

Such metaphors appear to pervade popular descriptions of human fertilization in the western mass media. For example, in a segment of the Australian popular science television programme *Quantum* (7 April 1993), the ovum was described as coyly preparing itself for its romantic interlude: 'patiently waiting' for 'that ultimate encounter – with the sperm'. Sperm production was described as 'a *very* flamboyant affair ... one of the processes where you get these spectacular volumes of cells produced ... The sinuous passageways of the testes are a vast production line, an impressive three metres long when uncoiled.' It is notable that the 'journey' undertaken by the sperm through the vagina up to the fallopian tubes was portrayed as dangerous, the sperm struggling to survive in a 'treacherous' environment, competing amongst themselves to win the battle against the vagina dentata: 'they must escape the acid secretions of the vagina and then negotiate the mucous-covered folds and recesses of the uterus … By the time [the sperm] actually reach the egg, only a couple of hardy survivors remain.' The union of the sperm with the ovum was described as a violent, almost rape-like attack: the sperm were said to wear 'a protective cap, a kind of chemical crash helmet' which helped them to 'hurl themselves against the cell wall [of the ovum] to batter a tunnel right through'. Yet the ovum enjoyed the encounter: 'at the moment of contact between egg and sperm, the sparks fly. A wave of electric excitation sweeps across the egg membrane … as if to celebrate the happy union, the cell almost immediately begins to split in two.' The subtextual ideologies of these descriptions are transparently drawing upon stereotypical concepts of masculine and feminine sexuality in describing the behaviour of cells.

It seems that such stereotyping is difficult to avoid. Even when it became recognized amongst biophysicists that the ovum plays an active role in fertilization, Martin (1991: 498) notes that metaphors of entrapment and aggression, the representation of the ovum as 'femme fatale' replaced the passive metaphors in medical texts. Like her observations of gender stereotypes in representations of the immune system, Martin suggests that these portrayals are revealing of the dichotomies constructed in medical and scientific discourses between masculine and feminine. The imagery also has implications for debates over human reproduction. By ascribing personhood to gametes, this discourse can play an important role in legitimizing medical scrutiny of reproductive processes, and has implications for legal and other initiatives concerning abortion, foetal surgery, genetic screening, artificial reproductive technologies and contraception.

The iconography of illness, disease and death

Over the centuries, the visual dimensions of disease, death and the body have provided much inspiration for artistic works. Herzlich and Pierret (1987: 75) quote vivid descriptions drawn from historical accounts of illness such as syphilis and the plague, which represented the ill body as a monstrous sight, an 'exteriorized horror' of rotting flesh, in which the presence of disease was immediately visible to onlookers and sufferers themselves. Given the hideous visual nature of illness and disease, it is not surprising that attempts to portray death and the fear of death recur frequently in medieval and Renaissance art, particularly the image of the 'Dance of Death' during the years of the Great Plague that devastated Europe in the late sixteenth century. In the fifteenth and sixteenth centuries, Death was commonly portrayed as a skeleton, hovering about and ready to pounce, riding on horseback, or gleefully celebrating his victories over humanity in a dance. Depictions sought to convey the ubiquity and arbitrary nature of death: 'in Hans Holbein's woodcuts of the dance of death (1538) we see death snatch at one moment a healthy child from the hearth, and at another a robust woman from a nunnery' (Prior and Bloor, 1993: 353). To illustrate the idea that death was caused by chance, a stroke of fate, dice and playing cards were often depicted in paintings and engravings of death, and time pieces were used to denote the inevitability of mortality (Prior and Bloor, 1993: 352).

By the Renaissance, the need to understand death and disease was expressed in illustrations and paintings which sought to portray the inside of the body, often placing the anatomically detailed form in a naturalistic setting so as to imply morality. Anatomical engravings of the sixteenth century often had a hint of sadism as well as a feeling of compassion for the exposed bodies, their skin flayed to reveal the muscular and venous systems below. By the seventeenth century, the machine metaphor had received expression in portrayals of the human body in fanciful illustrations which represented heads and bodies as comprised of wheels, cogs, bellows, pistons, metal plates and other industrial objects (Lucie-Smith, 1975).

Over the history of western medicine, visual representations of illness have played an important political role in the categorizing of the Other, those deemed abnormal or dangerous to a society. For example, portraits of patients were commissioned by doctors in the early nineteenth century in the attempt to construct a 'pathological identity' by documenting physiognomies of deviant types institutionalized for insanity or 'crimes against nature' (Marshall, 1990: 22). By the late nineteenth century, with the development of photographic techniques, many doctors began to document the manifestation of illness in their patients using photography. Patients were routinely depicted facing the camera, displaying the marks of their illness. The disempowered – male homosexuals and other sexual 'deviants', prostitutes, criminals, drunkards, women hysterics, sufferers of sexually transmitted diseases (especially syphilis), the poor and the mentally ill – were subjected to such recording of their bodies in the interests of the clinical gaze, effectively extending the surveillance techniques of the medical profession (Fox and Karp, 1988: 183; Marshall, 1990: 24–5).

This enterprise of detection, labelling and categorization conducted by nineteenth-century medics, psychologists and sexologists can be compared to voyages of botanical discovery in the seventeenth and eighteenth centuries when a new world of exotic flora and fauna was discovered by the early colonialists exploring the 'dark continent' – the 'other' of western civilization (Marshall, 1990: 26).

The practice of documenting pathology by photographing the diseased body remains central to medical literature, especially medical journals, textbooks and magazines. While patients' faces are perhaps not shown as freely now as they were in the late nineteenth century, parts of their bodies are routinely depicted, often in full colour and gory detail, for the interest of medical practitioners and researchers, including close-up shots of diseased or deformed genitalia. The news media also routinely publish or broadcast images of the disempowered diseased body: the starving, emaciated child in Africa, the equally thin gay man dying with HIV/AIDS and marked by the lesions of Kaposi's sarcoma, the brutally exposed, pulsing internal organs of a person undergoing surgery.

The iconography of medical advertising is a revealing insight into the ideologies and mythologies surrounding the doctor–patient relationship in the context of the biomedical system of healing. I undertook a study examining the representation of patients in Australian medical advertising in magazines directed towards the medical profession readership (Lupton, 1993b). I found that common to several medical advertisements was the pictorial dismemberment of the human body, featuring 'sawn-off' bits of bodies. Bodily parts were sometimes transformed and distorted through graphic design techniques. The mechanical model of the body received overt expression in a number of striking visuals which departed from any naturalistic representation of body parts by using symbolism which rendered organs, limbs or biological processes as parts of machinery. Indeed, some advertisements avoided *any* direct reference to the shape or appearance of bodily organs, using highly symbolic imagery to connote body processes. For example, an advertisement for a stomach ulcer treatment used a photograph of a large brass switch mounted on a metallic surface, as if part of industrial machinery. Next to the switch was shown a begrimed gauge with clock-like face. The switch was labelled with the word 'ACID' in big brass letters, followed by the engraved words 'ON' and 'OFF'. The switch lever was set at 'OFF', implying the effect of taking the drug upon the patient's stomach is like a mechanical switch which is able simply to 'shut off' acid production by cells in the gastro-intestinal tract. Few of the advertisements examined showed a doctor actually touching a patient, evidence of the diminishing importance of human contact in the medical encounter. The effect of such fragmented representations is to dehumanize the doctor–patient relationship by rendering patients' bodies as distinct from their individuality. When only part of the patient's body is depicted without a face, the result is dehumanizing and promotes anonymity.

In his collection of essays (1988), Gilman undertook a wide-ranging enquiry into how disease and illness have been represented in visual media over the centuries. The sources he used to trace representations included the illustrations used by the ancient Greeks and the nineteenth-century Chinese in their medical literature, drawings of sexual intercourse by Leonardo da Vinci, medieval paintings and engravings of madness, photographs of mental patients from the nineteenth century, a German opera libretto dramatizing homosexuality, the paintings of Blake, Goya, Delacroix, Vincent van Gogh and others depicting asylums, and recent mass media images of people with HIV/AIDS. Gilman's thesis is that the iconography of illness is an indication of the ways in which society deals with and conceptualizes disease: 'The portrait of the sufferer, the portrait

of the patient, is therefore the image of the disease anthropomorphized'
(1988: 2). Gilman argues, like Sontag, that the construction of stereotypes
of an illness and the patient suffering from the illness through images and
language influences the way in which the illness and the patient are
treated by others, and is internalized by patients, shaping their experience
of the illness. His tracing of common images over centuries of western
development demonstrates the resonance of certain images even today.

Gilman asserts that these images result from society's need to organize
a chaotic, frightening world, to draw (literally) the boundaries between
ourselves and the diseased Other so as to provide control over the randomness of disease. By portraying the diseased Other in art, it is labelled
and stereotyped for ease of identification, providing 'a basic reference
against which all images of disease, whether literary or visual, are measured' (Gilman, 1988: 3). Images of disease remain relatively stable over
centuries, influenced only slightly by shifting popular or medical views.

There are two levels in which the visual imagery of disease is coded:
first, on the level of the social construction of categories of disease; and
second, on the level of the internalization of such images in individuals or
groups who are labelled as at risk (Gilman, 1988: 4). Thus Gilman examines myths of madness in Renaissance paintings as well as the art produced by those who have been labelled insane. The most recent icons of
disease examined are American newspaper and magazine photographs
and drawings of people living with HIV/AIDS. Gilman draws a direct historical parallel between such representations and the centuries-old
iconography of syphilis, demonstrating how the stigma of sexually transmitted disease was similarly appropriated by visual imagery. By doing so,
he places representations of HIV/AIDS in their historical context and casts
light upon society's response to people living with HIV/AIDS.

While the female body has been subjected to 'an excess of visibility' in
medical and popular media representations, the male homosexual body
has been virtually invisible. It was not until the advent of HIV/AIDS that
gay men began to be represented visually, albeit in a manner that tended
to objectify and stigmatize them, linking death and homosexuality as
almost inseparable (Marshall, 1990: 20–1). Crimp (1992) recently discussed an exhibition of photographs which included images of people
with HIV/AIDS which was shown by the Museum of Modern Art in New
York. He argued that such visual images serve not only to invade the privacy of those pictured, and to give the impression that HIV/AIDS is an
inevitable death sentence, but personalize the disease in such a way as to
obscure the social conditions of the epidemic. Crimp (1992: 118) observes
how the photographs overwhelmingly portrayed people with HIV/AIDS
as 'ravaged, disfigured, and debilitated by the syndrome; they are generally alone, desperate, but resigned to their "inevitable" deaths'. He suggests that '[p]eople with AIDS are kept safely within the bounds of their
private tragedies' by such representations (1992: 120). His argument here
is similar to that of Gilman's: visual imagery of disease serves to safely

define the Other, to create a stereotype, and in doing so dehumanizes the sufferer.

Iconographic representations of health, illness and disease have become more important as western societies have moved towards mass communication via the visual media. As I noted above, medical 'breakthroughs', surgical techniques and the use of medical technology often receive the attention of high-rating television infotainment programmes, and often feature on the front page of newspapers, news magazines, women's magazines and popular science magazines. Computer graphics and electro-microscopes have realized in three dimensions and full colour the T cell and HIV, and intimate colour photographs of the foetus in the womb and the moment of human fertilization have become the stuff of coffee table art books and prime-time television documentaries. Such images, allowing access into the very interior of the body using the technology of the endoscope (a tiny television camera), are seductive, extending the clinical gaze into the colourful landscape of the body's interior: 'the endoscope triumphs over [the] tradition of the morbid anatomist by dispatching the curtain of light' (Vasseleu, 1991: 56). Like the 1966 science-fiction film *Fantastic Voyage* (1991: 55), which portrayed the adventures of a group of miniaturized scientists injected into the bloodstream of a living person and journeying around the highways and byways of his body, 'the publications of Lennart Nilsson's photographs, in the coffee table art book *The Body Victorious* and in the *National Geographic*, allow the "land, ho!" effect unmediated scope. The blasted scenes, sumptuous textures, evocative colours, and ET monsters of the immune landscape are simply *there*, inside *us*' (Haraway, 1992: 320, emphasis in the original). These images vividly render the internal body as a form of 'inner space', colonized and busy with the violent activities of foreign bodies engaged in warlike activities, destabilizing the sense of perspective people have about their bodies as a self-contained, knowable part of Self: 'We seem invaded not just by threatening "non-selves" that the immune system guards against, but more fundamentally by our own strange parts' (1992: 320).

There seems little doubt that the scientific technologies which produce images of reproductive processes contribute to the constitution of individuals' perception of their bodies: 'For a woman patient in an IVF clinic, the ovum being visualized in the screen ... has all the reality of a metonymic assimilation. It is becoming part of the text which is her body' (Vasseleu, 1991: 64). Of concern is the way in which iconographic images of the interior of the body have been used to serve political purposes, especially in the area of struggles over abortion, assisted conception technologies and prenatal screening. Anti-abortion groups have often used the power of the visual image of the foetus to sway opinion to their argument by depicting the foetus as an independent being, unconnected to the mother except by the umbilical cord, floating in undefined space like an astronaut, and deserving of human rights as an autonomous human. Likewise, the ultrasound image allows obstetricians to take charge of the pregnancy by commandeering the first images of the foetus, applying surveillance techniques out of control of the pregnant woman, and constructing a 'patient' out of the foetal images: 'Obstetrical technologies of visualization and electronic/surgical intervention thus disrupt the very definition, as traditionally understood, of "inside" and "outside" a woman's body, of pregnancy as an "interior" experience' (Petchesky, 1987: 65). While anti-abortion ideology and medical writings contend that knowledge of the foetus, including the visual representations offered by ultrasound, contributes to mother–infant bonding, some critics argue that the focus of such screening on the foetus conversely tends to separate the woman from the foetus by portraying it as an individual identity, with its own rights and autonomy (Ginsburg, 1990: 67; Rapp, 1990: 35; Rowland, 1992: 1354).

Countering the oppressive image: cultural activism

With the advent of the HIV/AIDS epidemic there has been an increased interest on the part of cultural commentators in deconstructing representations of illness and sexual 'deviance'. A number of scholars who have criticized the discursive and iconographic formations around HIV/AIDS and people living with HIV/AIDS have gone beyond criticism to shaping resistance. In an attempt to challenge oppressive stereotypes, people with HIV/AIDS have worked to resist the dominant media iconography of HIV/AIDS. The AIDS Coalition to Unleash Power (ACT UP) groups in several western countries, including the United States, Britain and Australia, have staged protests and 'media events' using clever performance art and graphics. Groups such as the London-based 'AIDS and Photography Group' have produced cultural artefacts and staged exhibitions which challenge the way HIV/AIDS has been represented in the media. Crimp has termed this work 'cultural activism' and claims that 'art does have the power to save lives, and it is this very power that must be recognized, fostered and supported in every way possible' (1989: 3).

People with disabilities and their advocates have also been active in attempting to overcome the negative discourses and meanings surrounding disability. Drawing attention to language use has been a central part of their activism, including contesting the words used in relation to disability. Some activists, for example, argue that 'impairment' is a better and more empowering term than 'disability', a term which itself had replaced the more stigmatizing 'handicap' (although there is by no means agreement on this issue within the disability politics movement). Many disability activists also assert that the individual who has been labelled as 'disabled' should not be described and viewed as 'disabled' or 'dependent', but rather that the social conditions and meanings surrounding them create their disability and dependence. Such people therefore experience a form of social oppression that serves to isolate them, render them deviant and impair their functioning (Shakespeare, 1994; Williams and Busby, 2000). Thus, for example, a person who cannot use her legs and is reliant upon a wheelchair is rendered 'disabled' by the lack of facilities – such as ramps and lifts – available to her to move around freely. Activists have focused attention on these issues to highlight the ways in which language and discourse are inextricably intertwined with practice and experience.

The late British photographer Jo Spence used the creative process to challenge the mythologies of illness. Drawing upon her experience as a breast cancer patient, Spence and her colleague Rosy Martin invented a technique called phototherapy, a synthesis of photography and aspects of psychoanalytic theory. The technique, as employed by Spence, used photography to document the diseased body and her experiences of bio-medical treatment. It was concerned with the politics of representation, struggle over discourse and the creation of identity (Martin, 1997). Spence's work engages with discourses surrounding health, disease, the body, pornography, religion, fashion, ageing, death and motherhood, reflecting upon the loss of dignity and power accompanying illness and medical intervention. Her own body formed the subject of her photography where she deliberately exposed images of age, ugliness and pain. Spence used her work to empower people with disease, to resist medical dominance of the body and to render problematic the functioning of the health care system (Spence, 1986).

In collaboration with Rosy Martin, Spence re-enacted her emotions as she underwent hospitalization for cancer: her feelings of powerlessness, the reversion to infantilism in the face of medical authority, the need to reassert control over her own body. In a television documentary on her work (*Arena*, 1988), Spence noted that:

> Eventually I began to see the body as a battle-field. In fact, the medical establishment sanctions only three methods for the treatment of cancer: that's surgery, radiation and chemotherapy, which is a form of chemical warfare. And this is analogous to the three major weapons used by the police and the military against social eruptions and revolt, and I think what we need to do is to ask ourselves why our bodies are in revolt, and not just have lumps hacked off and be given tranquillizers to keep us quiet.

Spence's photographs were displayed in two exhibitions: 'The Picture of Health?' (1986), which positioned health and ill-health as major political issues and critiqued the loss of dignity and power that accompanies disease and the way a cancer patient is silenced and professionally 'managed'; and 'Narratives of Dis-ease: Ritualized Procedures' (1990), which dealt with Spence's repressed anger about her health and her ageing and surgically-scarred body. In a later BBC documentary, filmed in 1991, Spence had recently been informed that she had developed leukaemia. The documentary portrays the regime of holistic medicine she adopted to treat her illness, as well as examining Spence's relationship with her brother and her parents. Towards the end of the documentary, Spence, with her brother, visits the hospital where her leukaemia was diagnosed, and comments:

> We came out of this building absolutely aghast at the glibness of this high tech-nology that can tell me to a millionth of something-or-other what's going on in my blood, but actually can't see me as a human being. And I want to be seen as a human being: I am a human being, and I'm taking control of my own body again.

Other artists have drawn attention to the ways in which damaged women's bodies are marginalized and represented as deviant in wider society. The photographer Matuschka, for example, documented her own body in a series of self-portraits after she had undergone a mastectomy. She uses the term 'invasive' to describe both the breast cancer she experi-enced and the ways in which she has sought to create an awareness of the politics of breast cancer through her artistic and activist efforts. A self-portrait that appeared on the front page of the *New York Times Magazine* in 1993 inspired controversy because of its open depiction of her chest following surgical removal of one of her breasts. Matuschka's intention was to represent her body as heroic, beautiful, strong and dignified, countering negative representations and resisting pity (Malchiodi, 1997: 56–9).

The French multi-media performing artist Orlan addresses notions of how women may assert power over their bodies using medical tech-niques – specifically, cosmetic surgery. In her long-term performance piece entitled 'The Re-Incarnation of Saint Orlan', Orlan underwent a series of cosmetic surgery procedures and video-taped each one. She instructed the surgeons to give her facial characteristics from classical paintings, including Mona Lisa's forehead, the chin of Venus in Botticelli's *Birth of Venus*, the nose of Gerard's *Psyche* and the lips of Moreau's *Europa*. These operations were later shown in a video installation, with a glass vessel containing the pieces of flesh cut from her face and Orlan herself present as a 'living work of art'. Orlan claims that she is not attempting to achieve an ideal of beauty through her operations (she chose the charac-teristics above because of their cultural meaning, not their beauty). Rather, she uses the idea of the plasticity of appearance as it may be achieved via medical procedures as a way of demonstrating the malleability of identity as it is experienced through embodiment. Surgical alteration has allowed her to transform her physical appearance in ways that she has dictated, to create a 'self-portrait' using new technologies. In doing so, she explores the pressures that are placed upon women to conform to the conventional norms of beauty (Davis, 1997).

Engaging in artistic and creative pursuits has the potential of serving several purposes for people who are ill and their supporters. Expressing their feelings and experiences creatively allows a cathartic release of the fears, confusion and anxieties surrounding serious illness, and thus fulfils a personal need. But when the work is received into the public domain, when it is exhibited, published, transmitted or screened, the personal experience of disease fulfils a collective goal of drawing attention to the ways in which linguistic and visual representations of disease constitute practices. It is rarely that the oppressed voice is heard, that the disabled or ill person has a say in the public domain. By exposing the underlying ideological bases of metaphorical and iconographic images of illness, and the linguistic practices around illness and disease, the politics of representation are uncovered and a space emerges for passiveness to give way to active agency and the opportunity to express one's views. The potential to resist oppressive and stigmatizing discourses and practices is liberated, and artistic or cultural criticism endeavours become activism.

Conclusion

The linguistic and visual representations of medicine, illness, disease and the body in elite and popular culture and medico-scientific texts are influential in the construction of both lay and medical knowledges and experiences of these phenomena. The metaphorical systems describing illness, disease and the body are important linguistic choices which are revealing of deeper societal anxieties about the control and health of the body politic as well as that of the body corporeal. Likewise, iconographic representations of the ill body are inherently political, seeking to categorize and control deviancy, valorize normality and promote medicine as wondrous and ever-progressive. As shown, common ways of conceptualizing illness or the threat of illness often incorporate imagery associated with war, fear, violence, heroism, religion, xenophobia, contamination, gender roles, vilification and control. Awareness of these latent meanings as expressed in elite, scientific and popular texts is vital for scholars and students in the humanities and social sciences who are interested in medicine as culture, and provide the basis of efforts on the part of cultural activists to resist or subvert stigmatizing or disempowering representations of the ill.

4

The Lay Perspective on Illness and Disease

The onset of illness, especially if severe, constitutes a threat to the integrity of the body and self-identity, and requires a status change from well person to patient. Regardless of the type of culture in which an individual lives, the dysfunction of the body represented in illness disturbs the harmony between the physical, social and moral being (Comaroff, 1982: 51). Even relatively minor symptoms occasion people suffering illness to question aspects of their lives, seeking to find a satisfactory explanation for their sickness (Frank, 1998). Being ill is therefore intimately related to notions of one's sense of self. Giving meaning to the illness experience involves drawing on a range of dominant discourses and cultural resources, including those from folk knowledges about the body and illness, as well as expert discourses originating from biomedicine and alternative medicine and those circulating in the mass media. People draw selectively on these sources in making sense of illness. They often choose narrative as a means of organizing their experiences, giving them meaning and representing them to others.

Phenomenology is a good starting point for understanding the meaning of the illness experience. Some anthropologists and sociologists working within the phenomenological tradition have centred their interpretations upon detailed studies of lay knowledges and experiences of health and illness states. The phenomenological approach to understanding the social world places importance upon the everyday activities in which people engage and the meanings invested in these activities. It rejects the assumptions of positivist research that human behaviour can be observed in the same manner as the natural sciences. Phenomenology employs the techniques of ethnomethodology – participant observation, depth interviewing and the construction of case studies – to understand the human lived experience. Hermeneutics, or the interpretation of the meaning of the human experience, is part of the research method of phenomenology.

This chapter discusses medicine, health and illness from the patient's perspective, a facet of biomedicine which hitherto has been frequently neglected, particularly by historians of medicine. Changes in the patient's experience of illness over time are discussed, as are contemporary accounts of illness ranging from autobiographical narratives to participant-observation and ethnographic research by anthropologists and sociologists, and doctors' own experiences of being a patient. The moral meanings of illness and lay beliefs and understandings of illness and disease causation and treatment are also reviewed.

Historical perspectives on the illness experience

To refer to patients in the historical context is somewhat misleading, for the term has connotations of passivity, of 'placing oneself under the doctor', and medical advice was not routinely sought in pre-industrial society (Porter, 1985: 3). The sick in past time constitute important objects of historical study, for they illuminate contemporary aspects of the illness experience. Yet until recently, the experience of people affected by illness or disease rarely received the attention of medical historians. The history of medicine tended towards documenting the discoveries of the 'great men' of biomedical science in the inexorable progression towards modernity. The ways in which people dealt with illness or disease, how they felt about their body and its ills, their relationship with the medical profession and other health care givers, their experience of treatment were aspects of the medical encounter which were little explored. One reason for this neglect was the difficulty of obtaining accounts of illness by lay people to use as historical data (Porter, 1985).

With the development of the sub-disciplines of medical sociology and medical anthropology during this century, greater attention has been paid to the illness accounts of the patient elicited by means of the depth interview and case study. The social history of medicine has since incorporated these means into its own method. Historians have turned away from public documents to private artefacts written by lay people to trace their responses and experiences of illness in past times. The subject matter – one's body and its state of health – has provided a source of concern and inspiration for writers over the centuries to document in such personal artefacts as diaries, journals and letters. Medieval Europe was a 'universe of disease' and subsequently, '[m]uch of medieval writing – private letters as well as religious and literary texts – reveals an obsession with illness' (Park, 1992: 60–1). Death rates were high and life expectancy was low compared with contemporary times, although life expectancy was lower for women than for men, for city dwellers compared with country dwellers, and for the poor compared with the rich. It has been estimated that between 15 and 30 per cent of infants died before achieving the age of one year. Periodic famine and chronic malnutrition were common, and disease was easily spread through a low level of collective and personal hygiene, particularly in the cities (1992: 61–2). While detailed study of medieval diseases has yet to be accomplished, fragmentary evidence suggests that in these conditions, diseases flourished, including those which were non-lethal but rendered life highly uncomfortable and miserable, such as skin diseases (rashes, boils, ulcers and sores) and diseases of the eyes and teeth (1992: 62–3).

During the Middle Ages the monasteries played an important role in preserving medical knowledge formed as part of the general literary culture of the Greek and Roman world. There was a disjunction between the literary tradition in medicine, as maintained in the monasteries, and medical practice as carried out by physicians, apothecaries and surgeons. Religious and secular healing systems co-existed. For the chronically ill, recourse was to the 'heavenly' medicine of Christ, mediated through shrines and the saints. Healing was thought to require direct contact with a saint's relics, and hence, a pilgrimage (Park, 1992: 72–3). By the Enlightenment, religious explanations of illness, while decreasing in their potency, continued to coincide with medical models in the lay population's ideas about the causes of illness and disease. In England between 1660 and 1800, both doctors and lay people regarded good health as an outcome of the proper workings of the individual constitution, while sickness boded malfunctioning of the body (Porter, 1992). Good health was seen to be secured and maintained by a regime of proper diet, exercise, regular evacuations, adequate sleep, a healthy environment and the regulation of passions. It was believed that the individual should take care not to allow the body to become too hot or cold, wet or dry. It was also widely believed among members of the lay population that 'disease might be the result of *maleficium*, or spells cast by witches, or of satanic or demonic possession' (1992: 95), and that the sins of humankind were visited by disease as a divine punishment: 'God used affliction for a multitude of higher purposes' (1992: 96).

Until the mid-eighteenth century, the causes of illness were related to both the corruption of the air and the corruption of morals, over which hovered the will of God, viewed as the ultimate cause of illness (Herzlich and Pierret, 1987: 103). Notions of the miasmic, or air-borne, theory of contagion were prevalent in early seventeenth-century England, according to Wear (1992). The moist air of marshy and low-lying places was considered detrimental to health, as was the foul-smelling air of cities and towns, while the countryside, and in particular high and dry areas, was considered the healthiest, having free, pure, open air.

If air smelt bad, it was believed to be disease-carrying, and hence in times of the plague or other epidemics, people took to carrying bunches of sweet-smelling flowers or herbs to ward off foul vapours (Wear, 1992: 137–8). The Garden of Eden was a powerful symbol of the beneficent powers of nature in providing a healthful environment, free of the impurity and foul air of the cities and towns. It was believed that the healthiest foods were those originating from the countryside, while the purest water came from rain water or springs running swiftly rather than stagnant pools (1992: 139–43). There was a 'perceived dichotomy between town and country, short life and long life, the unhealthy and the healthy, the stultifying and the fresh, the stagnant and the moving, dark and light, crowded and uncrowded, the tame and the wild' (1992: 145). Such ideas remain dominant today, in the form of condemnation of the 'artificiality' of crowded cities and industry and the idealizing of 'nature', the country-side, light and cleanliness, particularly in the New Age and environmental movements (1992: 146–7).

The examining of life documents such as diaries kept over a number of years has provided medical historians with rich material detailing personal illness experiences. Beier (1985) examined the diaries of the Reverend Ralph Josselin, who was born in 1616 and died in 1683, for his discussions of health and illness in his family over a 40-year period. She notes that Ralph Josselin and his family were unwell, or at least uncomfortable, most of the time, due to continual colds and occasional bouts of ague, eye and skin disorders, and in the case of Josselin's wife Jane, 15 pregnancies and at least 5 miscarriages. Of the 10 live births to the Josselins, 5 children predeceased their father. Worms, rickets, boils, measles and smallpox were suffered by the children, while Ralph Josselin himself suffered pain, swelling and ulceration in his left leg for the 11 years before his death, and inflammation of the navel for almost 4 years.

In the era in which the Josselins lived, death was a familiar and expected outcome of illness, believed to come at any time: 'Thus it was natural to think of death for oneself or one's loved ones in almost any situation' (Beier, 1985: 127). While there were expectations that people sick enough to be confined to bed should stay in bed, be waited on and take medicine if required, it was expected that people well enough to be out of bed should bear their discomfort and carry on with their normal duties. The family relied upon herbal remedies, some of them made at home, rather than the compound medicines sold by apothecaries and physicians. They almost never consulted physicians and surgeons, but relied on their own knowledge or that of others such as friends, nurses and part-time healers for treatment of ailments and attendance at childbirth. This was the case because the Josselins believed that God's will was of the ultimate importance in determining the outcome of an illness: 'Josselin truly felt that the best remedy was prayer and the best preventive medicine was a sinless life' (1985: 122). While explanations involving the humours may be used to understand why an illness eventuated, it was divine intervention which determined the outcome. Josselin was terrified of epidemic illnesses, especially smallpox and plague, for he was convinced that epidemics were God's punishment for collective sin, and thus could not use his usual weapons against disease: righteous behaviour and prayer (1985: 126).

In the sixteenth and seventeenth centuries, even the privileged members of royalty were not immune to the ravages of daily or recurring illness in adulthood. Excerpts from the writings of an English physician of the time, Sir Theodore Turque de Mayerne, concerning the current

King, James I (then aged 57 years), describe his sovereign's problems with poor sleep, biliousness causing vomiting, colic and flatus (wind), regular bouts of diarrhoea, arthritis (which from the age of 50 caused the King constant acute pain), and kidney disorders so severe that '[f]or many years past, after hunting, he often had turbid urine and red like Alicante wine'. Yet, for all these problems, de Mayerne observes that the King 'laughs at medicine, and holds it so cheap that he declares physicians are of very little use and hardly necessary. He asserts the art of medicine to be supported by mere conjectures, and useless because uncertain' (reprinted in Enright, 1989: 155–7).

The emergence of scientific medicine

The time of the Enlightenment, spanning roughly one hundred years between the late seventeenth century and the late eighteenth century, is believed to be the period in which many of the ideologies, discourses and practices surrounding contemporary biomedicine developed and became dominant. Among the ideals of the Enlightenment were faith in the progress of society assisted by developments in science and technology, and belief in the power of reason in shaping human understanding. These were accompanied by a rejection of the 'superstitions' of religion and the privileging of utilitarianism as a dominant ethic for the functioning of society. Medicine based on scientific principles was seen as providing the solution for the ills of humankind (Risse, 1992).

By the late eighteenth century, medical advice books provided the lay public with details on how to prevent against illness which focused on maintaining temperance, or avoidance of unnatural excess, in the individual's daily habits, including diet, exercise, sleep and regular exposure to fresh air and cold bathing. These were based on the principles of the 'non-natural' elements, which comprised air, diet, drink, motion and rest, sleeping patterns, evacuation and the human passions. Health was seen to depend upon the individual's control and proper regulation of these non-naturals, while sickness was an avoidable evil, regarded as endangering both the individual and the community, and thus blamed on the individual should it occur. The role of medicine was to re-establish lost health by dealing with diseases, their symptoms and causes by restoring bodily fluid balances. In concert with the ideals of rationality, it was believed that medical knowledge would eventually improve understanding of the human body through systematic observations and classification, and hence provide solutions for sickness (Smith, 1985; Porter, 1992; Risse, 1992).

While healing powers are valued in most societies, the rise to power of the medical profession in western societies is historically recent. As the comments of the physician to King James I quoted above suggest, physicians and surgeons before the Enlightenment were deemed as little more than tradespeople. Because surgeons had contact with blood, that dangerous substance believed to be a poisonous residue of the humours, and were engaged in the blasphemous dissection of bodies, they were deemed impure and polluted (Pouchelle, 1990). Even as little as a century ago, the medical profession had much less prestige, influence, income and power than it currently enjoys. As late as the eighteenth century most people medicated themselves, or changed their lifestyle when ill, and tended not to seek the help of medical practitioners, for they were not considered appropriate to deal with divine intervention or witchcraft (Porter, 1992: 103). Hence, the massive extension of orthodox and conventional medicine developing in the eighteenth century augmented rather than appropriated lay medical culture and self-medication, stimulating the proliferation of a repertoire of new discourses and practices about sickness (1992: 114).

When people did seek practitioners' help, the role of the medical investigator was to interpret the signs of illness, based on the sick person's account of his or her unique pattern of bodily events and subjectively defined sensations and feelings. Treatment and cure thus depended upon the sick person's self-report, and emphasized all aspects of emotional and spiritual life as well as physical disposition (Jewson, 1976: 228–30). The system of patronage upon which medical practitioners depended meant that the ill selected their practitioners using their own personal assessment of the moral integrity and professional skill of the practitioner, and thus the consultative relationship 'was joined on the basis of personal empathy between the parties' (1976: 233). The valorization of rationality in the Enlightenment was accompanied by an increasing importance being placed on scientific principles, the establishment of university training in medicine and greater control over licensing of medical practitioners. These developments, accompanied by recent changes this century in medical practice which led to greatly improved recovery rates of patients, resulted in a rise in the status of the profession of medicine (Herzlich and Pierret, 1987: 51–2).

An important feature of this rise in status was the growing acceptance in the nineteenth century that diseases were caused by specific entities occurring within the tissues, of which the ill person was unaware (Jewson, 1976: 235). This new area of knowledge was assisted by the invention of the microscope, which was able to identify disease agents such as bacteria and protozoa which were previously invisible to the human eye. From the late 1800s onwards, the dramatic discovery and isolation in the laboratory of the causes of the dread diseases cholera, tuberculosis, typhoid and diphtheria provided occasion for front-page news glorifying the progress of scientific medicine. Professional excellence in medicine came to be associated with scientific prowess and laboratory research rather than library-based knowledge and empathetic bedside skills (Rosenberg, 1988: 20–1). Today, because medicine is seen to be informed by objective and rigorous modern scientific knowledge, which is out of the reach of understanding of most lay people, and because medical practice is directed towards therapeutic ends, it has a privileged status by comparison with other authoritative institutions such as law and the clergy (Starr, 1982: 4–5).

It was not until the development of the biomedical model of illness and disease, founded as it was upon scientific techniques of objective observation, that the importance of the patient's interpretation of his or her illness began to diminish. The bedside medicine model of the late eighteenth century, with its emphasis on patients' explanations and interpretations of their symptoms, was superseded by the hospital and laboratory models. There was a shift away from a person-centred cosmology of illness to an object-centred cosmology (Jewson, 1976: 232). It was no longer the responsibility of the sick person to select the practitioner based on perceptions of individual worth, for there was now instituted a system of formal qualifications, and those who possessed such qualifications were deemed worthy of respect on the basis of the authority inherent in their occupational role. The institution of the hospital and dispensaries and clinics in the late 1700s allowed physicians and surgeons considerable authority over patients, and gave them the opportunity for continuous observation, as well as placing the practitioners in a situation where their own activities were more closely monitored and scrutinized by their peers and the public. Journals and ledgers documented successes and failures of prescribed treatments, and the description of clinical case studies in medical journals served to help share observations based on experience (Jewson, 1976: 235; Risse, 1992: 184–5).

The sick person became the 'patient', 'designated a passive and uncritical role in the consultative relationship, his [sic] main function being to endure and wait' (Jewson, 1976: 235) and subject to the rules and regulations of the hospital, as the following passage illustrates:

> All Patients admitted into this Hospital must, before they be received into the Ward, be clean from Vermin and furnished with a Change of Body-Linen, Stockings, Neck-cloth, Stock, or Handkerchief, and to pay to the Sister Two Shillings and Ninepence ... If any Patient curse or swear, or use any prophane [sic] or Lewd Talking, and it be proved on them by two Witnesses, such Patient shall, for the first Offence, lose their next Day's Diet. (Benjamin Harrison Jr, Treasurer of Guy's Hospital, London, 1797, reprinted in Enright, 1989: 123.)

With the rise of the modern European states in the seventeenth and eighteenth centuries, medicine's sphere of influence began to extend from the sick bed to the community. The welfare of the population and maintenance of its growth in changing conditions caused by industrialization, urbanism and the free market economy became a paramount concern, and with the greater emphasis on environmental health, epidemiology, infant and maternal welfare and the new prominence of the institutions of the clinic and the hospital, society became more medicalized. Programmes of public health and hygiene, and systems of accreditation for the medical profession, were instituted to police the activities of medical practitioners in order to provide a coherent health care policy for the general population (Foucault, 1975; Jewson, 1976; Armstrong, 1983; Fee and Porter, 1992; Risse, 1992).

According to Foucault (1975: 35), up until the end of the eighteenth century medical practice was related more to 'health' than 'normality'; that is, it referred to elements of the patient's lifestyle and general functioning, comparing the patient against him- or herself rather than against a norm. By the nineteenth century the concept of the 'standard' had developed, and medicine became concerned with determining to what extent patients deviated from that norm and how they could be restored to normality. Patients were not privy to the standard of the 'generalized state of health' against which they were judged, while the earlier form of medicine relied upon the patient's judgement to determine what was amiss. The establishment of the clinic and the hospital allowed the surveillance of many patients, the classification of their ills, the maintenance of detailed records on populations. The clinical method became reliant upon the observance and classification of disease based on symptoms and signs: 'The symptoms allow the invariable form of the disease – set back somewhat, visible and invisible – to *show through*. The sign announces: the prognostic sign, what will happen; the anamnestic sign, what has happened; the diagnostic sign, what is now taking place' (1975: 90, emphasis in the original). These techniques of normality were positioned as neutral and impartial, creating categories of the deviant subject which medical and psychiatric technologies of discipline were designed to eliminate.

By the turn of the twentieth century, the views of the patient had lost their relevance and power in the medical encounter, and the responsibility for discovering and labelling illness had become the preserve of the medical practitioner. The disease had become more important than the person who harboured it (Doyal, 1983: 31). However, Armstrong (1984: 739) notes that by the 1950s, the medical gaze was in a state of transition. At this time, he asserts, the passivity of the patient under the medical gaze was beginning to be challenged. While disease was still seen to exist within the human body, discovered through interrogation of the patient, there was a second strand to medical perception that viewed illness as existing in the social spaces *between* bodies. Clinical method now required techniques to map and monitor this space, demanding that the patient's view be heard. Armstrong contends that the exhortations upon doctors to devote more attention to the social context of illness merely extended medical surveillance into all areas of patients' lives:

> The patient's view was no longer a vicarious gaze to the silent pathology within the body but the precise technique by which the new space of disease could be established: illness was being transformed from what was visible to what was heard. The patient's view was not, in this sense, a discovery or the product of

some humanistic enlightenment. It was a technique demanded by medicine to illuminate the dark spaces of the mind and social relationships. (1984: 739)

The patient's compliance to medical orders came under question, and it was accepted that obedience to medical advice could no longer be assumed. Patients were ascribed personalities and were not simply viewed as objects. The central problem was perceived as being one of communication, and by the 1960s and 1970s 'effective communication' between health care professional and patient was championed in the medical and social science literature to 'improve' patient compliance, and a concern with patient satisfaction manifested itself in the literature (Armstrong, 1984).

Contemporary perspectives: rationality, morality and control

Drawing on the traditions of the Enlightenment, contemporary western culture is based upon the tenets of naturalism, autonomy and individualism, and the philosophist assumption that the mind is separate from the body: 'the image of the modern self, capable of nearly absolute freedom from social determinacy, able to disengage in order to reach a higher level of truth, is a western ideal of what it means to be human' (Gordon, 1988a: 40). These tenets pervade biomedicine, and underlie many of its practices as well as constituting the illness experience. They are central to the treatment of diseases as independent entities which may be located within the patient's body and treated separately, and the scientific biomedical model of illness as cause and effect (Comaroff, 1982: 59; Gordon, 1988a: 26).

Medical care is becoming more, rather than less, scientific, with increasing emphasis upon making clinical judgement and medical decision-making 'more rational, explicit, quantitative, and formal' (Gordon, 1988b: 258) in which 'intuition' is replaced by calculation. This trend supports the ideology of rationality underlying much of western culture, with 'science' being privileged as a way of overcoming uncertainty, both physical and metaphysical. This change has been related to concern about the uncertainty of medical science, in which the outcome is never able to be predicted perfectly, and to increasing demands for medical accountability and cost containment on the part of patients, lawyers, the medical profession itself and outside agencies (1988b: 261–2).

Within the mind/body dualism predicated by scientific medicine is a series of essentialist binary oppositions: mind is contrasted with body, spirit with soul, active with passive, form with matter, rational with irrational, reason with emotion, free with determined, objective with subjective, voluntary with involuntary, master with slave, adult with child, male with female, immortal with mortal, right with left, culture with nature, purity with coarseness (Gordon, 1988a; Kirmayer, 1988). The healthy body parallels the mind, but when sickness strikes, the essential nature of the body is exposed. Sickness is a threat to rationality, for it threatens social life and erodes self-control. Hence the ability of the rational bio-medicine to deal with sickness is privileged (Kirmayer, 1988).

Western medicine is thus directed towards controlling the body, keeping it from subsiding into the chaos and disorder threatened by illness and disease. As a series of advertisements for MBF, an Australian private health insurance firm, stated: 'Being in MBF is about being in control.' The advertisements depicted scenarios in which worried mothers consult male doctors about the health of their children. The doctor suggests that an operation is the only solution to the problem (in one case, a squint, in another, a hernia). The mother is told that her child must wait several weeks or months for the operation, and responds with alarm and anxiety. But when she informs the doctor that her family is covered by MBF, she is assured that all is well – the operation will go ahead within a matter of days. These advertisements position 'the operation' as the ultimate cure and suggest urgency, even though the conditions discussed are non-acute. Health insurance is portrayed as facilitating control over the irrationality of disease by allowing swift medical treatment: it is suggested that if you *really* care for your family, you must protect their health by subscribing to private health insurance. In Australia, where all residents are covered by the publicly-funded health care scheme Medicare which subsidizes medical treatment, there is little need for most people to subscribe to private health insurance, although it is the case that patients must wait a little longer for elective surgery if they are treated in the public system rather than the private system. Hence advertisements for health insurance sell their product by emphasizing the anxiety caused by one's child falling ill and wanting to have medical intervention as soon as possible, in order to supposedly regain 'control' over the potentially disruptive force of illness.

Today's sick person is predicated upon the understanding that illness is not necessarily followed by death. People who are ill now survive their illnesses, and may become chronically ill for a long period of time before death, 'so that it can be a form of life as well as of death' (Herzlich and Pierret, 1987: 23). Illness is reduced to a unifying general view; that of clinical medicine. As a result, 'the diversity of bodily ills will give birth to a common condition and a shared identity: that of the sick person' (1987: 23). The ill in modern western societies are expected to place themselves in the hands of the 'science' of medicine: being sick and being treated have become synonymous (1987: 52).

It has been argued by some sociologists that the state of *illness* is fundamentally different from that of *disease* (Kleinman, 1988; Posner, 1991; Turner, 1996). Illness refers to the social, lived experience of symptoms and suffering which is innately human. It includes recognizing that bodily processes are malfunctioning and taking steps to rectify the situation, such as seeking treatment. Disease, on the other hand, is not limited to humans: animals or plants can be diseased. Indeed, to describe someone as 'diseased' implies a lack of humanity (Turner, 1996). In contrast to illness, the term 'disease' is defined as denoting a technical malfunction or deviation from the biological norm which is 'scientifically' diagnosed.

This definition, of course, does not necessarily imply that disease is an objective state, for as scholars from the social constructionist perspective argue, the categorizing of disease is influenced by the social, historical and political context as is the definition of illness. The biomedical model of disease is not a rational scientific reality which is internally consistent; rather, it is open to differing interpretations even among health care professionals. Diseases, far from being homogeneous, are definitions that vary according to the speciality of the medical practitioner, the context, the audience, the type of condition, as well as the personal characteristics of the doctor, and his or her position in a professional hierarchy (Helman, 1985: 293–4). For example, doctors may use one type of explanatory model when explaining to a patient, while using another to a medical audience.

Each of the three types of clinical information used by doctors – the medical history, the examination and the pathology test – is open to a considerable degree of interpretation, despite being viewed as 'objective' evidence. For example, Helman quotes a case study in which a male patient's chest pain was diagnosed as muscular aches by a general practitioner, as a heart attack by a junior resident doctor, as angina by a senior registrar and as pseudo-angina by a cardiologist and chest physician, caused by, respectively, external stressors, coronary artery thrombosis, narrowing of the coronary arteries and hyperventilation. The explanatory model held by the patient himself was a combination of elements from both biomedical and lay models of heart function, as well as being influenced by his subjective physical experience of symptoms. Helman (1985: 322–3) calls such an explanatory model 'folk angina', developed from such diverse sources as the electronic mass media, 'home doctor' books, novels, medical advice columns in newspapers and magazines, health education material, personal experience of symptoms and physical changes, discussion with others experiencing similar symptoms and contact with physicians.

The illness experience

As in other times and other cultures, in modern western societies the ill still experience alienation and a search for meaning, which in most cases is dealt with by seeking medical advice and treatment. The illness experience, if related to acute or life-threatening conditions, can be disabling not only of the body but also of an individual's peace of mind and sense of security. Receiving bad news about one's health and entering into 'deep illness' can lead to a profound state of shock, disorientation and the feeling that one's control over one's life has suddenly been called into question.

The illness comes to affect virtually all life choices and shape the individual's identity. Illness or disability, if incapacitating, removes people from their social roles and activities, including work, relationship and family obligations. The seriously ill or incapacitated person becomes a permanent patient, involving a major change of status. In such a situation, the definition of self can be severely challenged. The ill can become socially excluded and isolated (Frank, 1998; Little et al., 1998). People with cancer, for example, are often treated like lepers. Others avoid mentioning or discussing their illness with such people, or even avoid social contact with them, sometimes seeming to fear them. As a result, people with cancer find themselves placed in a position of having to conceal from others their own distress and anxiety, as well as the physical signs of their illness, such as surgical scars (Broom, 2001).

Serious illness can redefine close relationships and become an occasion for questioning the direction of one's life, including confronting one's own mortality, perhaps for the first time. As the American journalist Joyce Wadler wrote about her experience of breast cancer:

> Nothing is real until you are close to it, and for a few weeks I was given something few people have: a dress rehearsal of my own mortality … my experience with serious illness has changed me. Death, I now see, may not come when I am 85 and weary, or after I have solved all my problems or met all my deadlines. It will come whenever it damn well pleases; all I can control is the time between. (1992: 134)

Such narratives enable ill people to give voice to their suffering in a way that transcends narrow biomedical accounts of illness. Often the question 'Why me?' is answered through the construction of illness narratives. It is a means by which people seek to give meaning to their experiences, to make sense of them and to begin to formulate a revised identity and new context for living after the disruption of illness (Hyden, 1997; Frank, 1998). Indeed, both patients and doctors tend to recount illness events in the form of 'stories'. Doctors ask patients questions to elicit the 'story' of their illness, and the subsequent case histories and case presentations developed by doctors to communicate to each other are likewise presented as 'stories' (Good and Good, 2000).

Very ill people – the 'deeply ill' – tend to draw upon certain narratives when making sense of their predicament. Three basic narrative types of illness stories have been identified by Frank (1998): the restitution story, the chaos story and the quest story. The restitution story is culturally preferred in western cultures such as North America, Britain and Australia, for it is optimistic and emphasizes regaining control, focusing on becoming well and 'doing something' about the illness. Disease is an enemy and biomedicine is represented as the weapon of choice against this enemy. Those whose stories of illness cannot include recovery may be marginalized by the cultural dominance of the restitution story. The chaos story is diametrically opposed to the restitution story in its emphasis on physical decline, lack of success of treatment and resultant social, financial and other problems. Loss of control reigns in the chaos story, and it is therefore a difficult narrative to recount and listen to. The quest story involves representing the illness experience as lived as a quest, a condition from which something can be learned. This story is more optimistic than the chaos story, although it may not involve recovery from the illness as it focuses on the positive ways in which the illness experience has changed the ill and their lives: for example, realizing and valuing the important things in life.

In one study of people with cancer of the colon (Little et al., 1998), it was found that such individuals typically entered a liminal phase following diagnosis of their disease, in which they felt uncertainty and an acute sense of loss in general and loss of control. They experienced the world contracting to embrace their 'cancer patientness', including the immediate impact of their diagnosis and persistent identification as a cancer patient, and felt as if they could not adequately communicate to others the horror of their experience. These people became aware of limits to space, available time and empowerment once they entered the 'cancer patient' role, began treatment and were 'taken over by the system'.

A study of interactions between doctors and patients focusing upon the ways in which diseases and the body parts are referred to in common speech usage (Cassell, 1976) found that diseases and symptoms were frequently described using the impersonal terms 'it' or 'the' disease, rather than referring to 'my' or 'I'. This usage signifies that patients do not view their disease as part of themselves, but as entities which exist apart. This was especially true if the organs affected were internal. For example, one patient with cancer of the oesophagus, when asked how he felt, spoke of 'the bomb inside', while another, speaking of a kidney disorder, said that 'They said it was all infected, one of the kidneys' (1976: 143–4). Diseases thus are conceptualized as invading, alien objects, which must be removed before bodily integrity can be restored. The literature suggests that this conceptualization of disease is expressed in practices used to treat illness: people in many cultures use such measures as emetics, purgatives and sweat baths to remove sickness from the body (van der Geest and Whyte, 1989: 356), and in biomedicine, surgery is directed towards cutting the diseased part of the body out.

It is now medical treatment, rather than illness or disease itself, that causes alterations in the body which can mark and mutilate. For example, respondents interviewed by Herzlich and Pierret (1987: 88–90) found that the iatrogenic side-effects of surgical and radiation treatment rendered their own body 'foreign': people said that they 'no longer recognized themselves' because of mutilation and overwhelming pain. Radical surgery which permanently alters and disfigures the body has a profound effect upon people's body images and relationships with others. Kelly (1992) interviewed people who were left permanently faecally incontinent after radical surgery (ileostomy) to treat ulcerative colitis (inflammation of the large bowel) and who had to wear a bag hidden beneath clothing to collect waste matter. He notes that such surgery, which disrupts the body's conventional way of disposing of waste matter, is bound up with cultural meanings associated with dirt, pollution, loss of control and the transgression of body margins. For the person who has undergone such surgery, knowledge of the new and changed private self conflicts with a public persona for which the surgical effects are hidden. As most of the patients are in early adulthood, their sexual relationships can be severely disturbed by the need to wear the waste bag at all times. Kelly (1992: 405) suggests that 'for the person with an ileostomy, the body is experienced as attached to an alien object', for the physical functioning of the body requires constant attention, including the need to hide the waste bag from others and prevent leaking in public.

The decaying and dying body in which the boundaries of the body have been severely challenged may be subject to extreme stigmatiza-tion and even disgust on the part of the person her- or himself, family members and those caring for such patients. There is very little tolerance in western societies for such 'grotesque' bodies. Because the disintegrat-ing body is no longer controlled by the will and emits foul substances and smells, those suffering from such events are typically removed from the presence of others. Patients themselves may request isolation, seda-tion or euthanasia because of the challenge to their sense of self and social relationships incurred by the unboundedness of their bodies (Lawton, 1998).

People who are permanently and severely disabled as a result of an accident or sudden illness, such as paraplegics and quadriplegics, must also come to terms with disruptive transformation in the way they per-ceive their bodies and engage in everyday activities. Body maintenance activities that were once routine and private, such as cleaning one's teeth, washing or eliminating waste matter, become major hurdles to accom-plish on a regular basis and involve the help of others, who must observe or touch parts of the body normally shown only to sexual intimates. The identity and self-image of people who become quadriplegic and para-plegic is disturbed and must be reconceptualized, incorporating loss of physical sensation as well as dependence upon others. Yet once they leave intensive care and begin rehabilitation, such people are not 'ill' and cer-tainly do not have a disease. Rather, they are in a liminal state in which they are subject to bodily dysfunction, often constant medication and medical or para-medical attention and are viewed by others as abnormal and possibly 'unhealthy' but do not necessarily feel unwell. Like people who have had an ileostomy, the sexuality and gender identity of people with paralysis is challenged by their condition, including their lack of sen-sation and reflexes and their inability to conform to some aspects of stereotypical 'masculine' and 'feminine' roles (Seymour, 1989, 1998; Taleporos and McCabe, 2002).

The moral dimension of the illness experience

Moral meanings are frequently ascribed to illness experiences. The advent of a serious illness may cause individuals to question whether there is a connection between the illness and their moral values, or how they live their lives, forcing them to evaluate their lives in moral terms. People may ask themselves whether they 'deserved' the illness (Hyden, 1997).

As discussed in Chapter 1, the functionalist perspective on the illness experience views illness as potential 'deviance' which is alleviated by interaction with members of the medical profession. According to the 'sick role' model, once patients have sought help from a physician, their withdrawal from societal expectations is legitimized and they are no longer regarded as 'deviant'. However, there are instances for which the sick role concept is unable to adequately account. The sick role changes according to the cultural meanings ascribed to the illness. Some illnesses or diseases are not considered the 'fault' of the sick person – for example, most non-sexually transmitted infectious illnesses such as influenza or measles – while others are laden with opprobrium which emphasizes the guilt of the victim for bringing the illness or disease upon themselves. Parsons' sick role model cannot be applied to these diseases, because one of his conditions, that the patient is not blamed for his or her illness, is not applicable. Such individuals, even though under medical care, are still regarded as 'deviant' because they have allowed themselves to fall ill; they have ignored the moral proscriptions of society and are paying the consequences. Illness may thus be designated as originating from either accidental or wilful 'deviance', the sick person categorized as either 'inno- cent' or 'deserving' of his or her fate. In the latter case, 'deviance' is not abrogated by entering the sick role.

So, too, the curability of the illness influences the state of 'deviance', and questions the utility of the sick role concept. While the sick role con- cept fits acute, curable illnesses, it is not easily adapted to the features of chronic illnesses or permanent disability. If a person becomes ill with a chronic or life-threatening condition, which does not seem to respond to medical intervention, he or she may be seen to flout the third and fourth conditions of the sick role outlined by Parsons by failing adequately to escape the 'deviant' state of illness, and also by failing to benefit from the socially sanctioned solution to illness. In these cases, chronically ill or dis- abled patients must adapt to their role, 'manage' their illness and accept impaired functioning as a normal state rather than a 'deviant' state. Unlike acute illnesses, in which patients are generally passive and abro- gate responsibility for their bodies, placing themselves in the hands of the practitioner and not required to contribute anything to overcoming the problem, chronic or disabled patients, in the face of the failure of medical treatment, are expected to make changes in their lives to adapt to their continuing illness or pain (Turner, 1995).

Illness as symbol therefore serves to make moral distinctions in the attempt to control the social disorder it threatens. The 'rationality' and 'objectivity' of medicine are assumed to rise above value judgements. Yet the implicit moral evaluation which pervades the biomedical model of disease agents is reflected in everyday rhetoric, such as the basic terms 'poorly', 'bad' and 'better' when speaking about health states; 'as our popular usage suggests, the term "sick" has itself become a powerful metaphor of moral condemnation' (Comaroff, 1982: 62). Epidemic disease is particularly potent in inspiring drama, panic, irrationality, stigmatization and attempts to locate the blame. This is particularly the case if the epidemic is new or strikes in a new way, generating much more extreme reaction for its unexpectedness. For example, Europe in the Middle Ages became quite accustomed to regular outbreaks of bubonic plague, and thus plague became institutionalized. However, when an epidemic is new, it provokes a number of different explanations, interpretations and suggestions for strategies to counter it, including many which are inherently moral (Strong, 1990: 252). The emergence of a new outbreak of disease becomes an occasion to question the tenets and moral values of everyday life. This is the case because:

> ... most of the time, in the dull grind of our daily lives, our dominant perception is of order. But every now and then chaos erupts in a wholly unexpected and spectacular fashion: epidemics and revolutions erupt, empires suddenly rise or fall, stock markets crash. The world appears brittle, flimsy and open, at least for a moment. (1990: 256)

That is when the symbolic nature of illness is asserted, in attempts to provide explanation, to 'make sense' of threatening events.

Morality encroaches when rationality seems not to be espoused; if patients are chronically ill, if they have appeared to have brought the illness upon themselves, or if they fail to comply with doctors' directions: 'Sickness makes the patient's stewardship of the body suspect' (Kirmayer, 1988: 62). Even before the rise in importance of the germ theory of disease, ill individuals were considered responsible for their disease, particularly if the disease was thought to be contagious. For example, in the cholera epidemic in the United States in the 1830s, the victims (most of whom were from the poorer classes) were blamed for deliberately weakening their bodies by engaging in unseemly behaviours and vices, including Sabbath-breaking, intemperance and debauchery, and thus were viewed as being punished for their sins (Risse, 1988: 46).

In modern western societies, the emphasis upon lifestyle choices and individuals' responsibility for preserving their health and avoiding 'risk' has come to dominate explanations of illness. Self-indulgence and lack of self-discipline are viewed as the reasons why people become ill with such diseases as coronary heart disease, diabetes, lung cancer or cirrhosis of the liver, which have been strongly linked to diet, weight, tobacco and alcohol consumption (Nelkin and Gilman, 1988; Sontag, 1989; Lupton, 1993c, 1995). As Coward has commented of the current emphasis on diet: 'It is here that attitudes towards food enter firmly into the realm of morality. According to this way of thinking, what we eat is about making choices, choices between illness and health, the perfect body as opposed to the obese, unhealthy or diseased body' (1989: 147). If the behaviour is viewed as socially deviant, such as excess alcohol consumption, cigarette smoking or homosexual activities, then the ill person is held up as courting illness. For example, in the 1990s surgeons in Britain had begun to refuse heart by-pass operations to people who smoke, arguing that such patients are less likely to benefit from surgery. There is a strong implication here that people who smoke are also less *deserving* of medical care.

The common modern tendency to view illnesses such as cancer as the result of internalized stress and anger constitutes 'a powerful means of placing the blame on the ill. Patients who are instructed that they have, unwittingly, caused their disease are also made to feel that they have deserved it' (Sontag, 1989: 57). Clarke (1992) compared the discussion of cancer, heart disease and HIV/AIDS in articles published in popular magazines in North America between 1961 and 1965 and 1980 and 1985. She noted that there were differences in the moral meanings ascribed to the diseases and those who suffered from them. For example, cancer was described as an evil, immoral predator, an enemy, a mysterious disease which engulfed the whole self and which was associated with hopelessness, fear and death. In contrast, heart disease was portrayed as a strong, morally neutral, active and painful localized attack, which was represented as a breakdown of the machinery of the cardiovascular system and was therefore preventable and manageable through lifestyle modification and technological intervention. The person with HIV infection or AIDS was described in moral terms, suffering the punishment of an immoral lifestyle, while AIDS was represented as the scourge of society, a nemesis for promiscuity. Clarke believes that such portrayals have implications for the self-worth of people suffering these diseases: for example, 'a person with cancer could be vulnerable to feelings of shame because his or her previous moral self is forfeited by the invasion of an evil predator that is so fearsome that it is not even to be named, but fought as a powerful alien intruder that spreads secretly through the body' (1992: 115).

The imputing of blame for illness based on the assumption that ill people have indulged in 'risky' activities means that the ill are forced to protest that they have done all they can to avoid its onset. For example, in the magazine article about Olivia Newton-John's breast cancer discussed in Chapter 3, she was quoted as saying, 'Initially, I was puzzled that this had happened to me, because I eat sensibly, exercise regularly, don't smoke and hardly ever drink. My stress level was really high, though, so perhaps that's why this occurred' (Olivar, 1993). Such a claim is telling that in an age in which a lifestyle choice rather than an act of God is viewed as the cause of disease, the ill are placed in a position in which they must justify themselves. Another contemporary example is media reports of people with HIV or AIDS, where the source of their infection is invariably mentioned so that we know whether they were 'guilty' of homosexual activities or injecting drug use, or 'innocent' victims who have been infected through no 'fault' of their own, such as recipients of blood transfusions, children born to women with HIV infection or hetero-sexual women who simply 'fell for the wrong man without knowing that they were injecting drug users or bisexuals' (Lupton, 1993a).

The increasing focus on medical research on the genetic basis of illness and disease – or what has been termed 'the new genetics' – has also influ-enced ways of viewing risk. The emergence of the Human Genome Project, a massive research undertaking involving mapping the whole human genome, has been a dominant instigator of the new genetics. Increasing numbers of behaviours – from alcoholism to obesity – have become linked to specific genes and gene clusters. Scientists involved with the Human Genome Project have claimed that identifying the genes on the genome will allow much greater understanding of genetically-determined disease and assist the development of new forms of therapy for such disease, as well as screening programmes directed at identifying genetic risk (Cunningham-Burley and Bolton, 2000).

When the cause of disease is genetic, emphasis to some extent shifts away from personal responsibility, at least in relation to the control of lifestyle factors. But greater focus then turns towards such strategies as testing for incipient disease and engaging in prophylactic behaviours designed to prevent disease before it can manifest itself. Examples are the termination of foetuses that have been found to have a genetic abnormal-ity such as Down's syndrome or cystic fibrosis, deciding not to have children because of a high risk of inherited illness, or, for women who have a high risk of developing breast cancer due to inherited risk, pro-phylactic mastectomies. In these cases, moral meanings may be imputed to the refusal by individuals to engage in such preventive behaviours. This is particularly the case for women, who are portrayed in discourses on genetic risks as bearing the responsibility for passing on their own and their partner's genes via reproduction, and for ensuring their own well-being so as to protect the well-being of their partners and children (Hallowell, 1999).

Hospitalization

The hospital is a place fraught with competing meanings of anxiety, threat, despair, hope, fear and punishment. Most people, ill or well, feel uneasy in a hospital, yet the hospital promises salvation and remediation for those who are ill: 'The hospital calls up some of our deepest anxieties – about pain, decay, and death – in the promissory rhetoric of the remedial'

(Singer, 1993: 101). Because it is the place where one goes, or is sent, when something is wrong (except when women go there to give birth), the hospital as an institution signals visible social deviance (1993: 100–1). When patients enter the hospital or clinic, they enter the medical world, in which they must conform to a set of rigid rules and routines with which they are unfamiliar. The hospital is almost a total institution like a prison, in which patients have little or no control at all over when they eat or sleep, the clothes they wear, the level of noise or light to which they are exposed, and the manner in which they defecate or urinate. Many bodily processes are tied to nurses' shift changes, which involve 'a departure from "normal" patterns of crossings of body apertures and translating of body fluids from outside to inside as well as extra-body substances in the other direction. Fluids leave at the wrong time, the wrong place, and in the presence of the wrong significant others' (Frankenberg, 1988: 29).

Everyday notions of temporality are changed and disrupted in the hospital setting for both patients and medical staff. For patients, the disruption of normal temporality results in diminished status, as they become the inmate of the institution, their bodies subject to total control, and the boundaries of public and private space are dissolved. The disruption of time experienced by specialists when they are summonsed at any time by the omnipresent 'beeper', however, is 'a symbol of almost sacred power' (Frankenberg, 1988: 15), for they are seen to cross the boundaries of night and day, life and death, public and private. Unlike the nursing staff and patients, members of the medical staff have the choice of 'foregoing the privilege of private time' (1988: 15). Patients and their relatives are made to wait, perpetuating uncertainty and dependence on doctors (Frankenberg, 1988; Singer, 1993). Indeed:

> To be in a hospital is to lose time; the time of productivity and activity in a waiting game where one is cast as receptacle and consumer of whatever is dished out. In the hospital one's time, like one's sentence, is determined by the institution and its power to extend an eternal present in a way that obscures any agency with respect to the future. (Singer, 1993: 103)

People who have been in hospital frequently mention the alienation and vulnerability experienced during treatment. One case study discussed by Kleinman (1988) is that of a young man with severe eczema on large parts of his body. The young man's account tells of the shame involved with a disfiguring skin disease, which he must expose for the sake of medical treatment:

> When you take off your clothes, and, and, and are stripped to your nakedness, you first feel shame. Shame at how you look. At exposing what is such a private part of you. Shame at how the nurse and doctor look at you. Shame because you are not normal, not like others; and, well, because, because where else do you expose yourself to others' eyes? But the clinic nurses and doctors seem so insensitive to

how you feel. Sometimes they keep talking while I'm standing naked in front of them. ... (Quoted by Kleinman, 1988: 163–4.)

In an autobiographical story about the alienation of childbirth, the writer Margaret Coombs described vividly an experience of an induced birth at an expensive maternity hospital in London:

[The nurses] swoop on me, one from each side, pull my legs apart and hoist them into stirrups. The catches that lock my legs in the stirrups click shut like handcuffs. You are under arrest! You can't escape now! You're guilty! We're going to PUNISH you! (1988: 108) ... I lie, strapped down on this table-bed, my legs strapped apart in the air while he towers over my vulnerable body, all his attention focused on the space between my legs ... He issues instructions to the nurses in a deadpan voice that, despite its upper-class English accent, reminds me of the voice of mission control at Cape Canaveral. It is a voice that won't falter if the moon falls out of the sky, a voice completely stripped of emotion. When he uses that voice, I know I am just a piece of machinery to him, that his disinterest in my feelings is complete. (1988: 116)

An autobiographical account of an illness experience published in a newspaper provides a narrative of the disempowering experience of physical debilitation redolent with imagery of lack of control over one's body:

There were innumerable questions put to me about my health and bodily habits. People came and looked at my haemorrhoids without telling me what they were looking for or what they had found. I was frequently naked. A nurse shaved my anus. I began to regard my body as something separate, which is pretty much what it is all about. One's very concept of self changed: there is your body, and, at a little distance, your thinking self. The days in hospital belonged to my body. It called the shots: pain, evacuations, sleep. There was no point planning anything; my body was in control and seemed to relish providing surprises. 'I'm going to hurt now,' it might say in a quiet moment. 'Take me to the bathroom!' it would command. It was like being a nanny to a very bad-tempered child – and you needed the job. (Mackie, 1992: 24)

Such narratives, from diverse sources and recounted by patients hospitalized in three different western societies, highlight the alienating effect of illness upon a person, the feelings of detachment and distancing from one's own body, the shame of not conforming to the norm of physical wellness, of being forced to expose one's naked body and genital organs to the eyes of others on demand. In many accounts the feelings of helplessness, of losing control, of victimization are evident. The medical staff are portrayed as lacking humanity, as treating the patient like an inanimate lump of flesh or piece of machinery. The gap in power, authority, knowledge and agency between patient and medical staff yawns in these accounts.

When social scientists or members of the medical profession themselves fall seriously ill and are admitted to hospital, the experience provides them with the opportunity to reflect upon the nature of the illness experience and the medical encounter. Susan DiGiacomo, an anthropologist, developed Hodgkin's disease, a cancer of the lymphatic system, and was admitted to hospital for tests, surgery and radiation treatment, followed four years later by further surgery and chemotherapy. DiGiacomo comments that behaving as an ethnographer as well as a patient during her hospitalization and treatment served to impose 'order, pattern and meaning on a life that had suddenly taken on a frighteningly random character, and so made it possible to manage the fear' (1987: 316). In terms of the illness experience, she observed that:

> In the hospital, my identity was assailed. It is difficult to be anything but what a total institution makes of you, and it is doubly difficult when the heavy symbolic charge of cancer is added to institutional requirements ... Identity, however, seemed to be the one area in which I could retain some control. I certainly could not control my body; that was now in the hands of my doctors. (1987: 319–20)

For medical practitioners who become ill, the clash between two roles – as a patient and as a fellow member of the medical profession – provides an interesting viewpoint into how patienthood is engendered and experienced. In his review of the writings of doctors who have become patients, Hahn (1985a: 89) notes that several of such individuals found acceptance of the role of patient as deeply troubling, tending towards denial of their symptoms and diagnosis. Prominent in the transition is:

> ... the shift from the doctor's white coat, symbolizing authority, potency, and cleanliness, to the hospital 'johnny', symbolizing exposure, vulnerability, and helplessness ... These physicians commonly react to the helplessness, vulnerability, and dependency of the patient role with unequivocal, antagonistic emotions and certain, urgent needs. There is shock, fear, dread, and anxiety, but also anger, rage and mistrust. (1985a: 89–90)

Indeed, for some, it is only the maintenance of the physician role that provides a measure of security. As one doctor-turned-patient remarked:

> I discovered to my surprise, that I liked presenting my case. It felt appropriate and safe when I discussed my chest growth from a clinical point of view. The familiar role kept my anxiety at bay and allowed me some comfort in spite of the life-shattering diagnoses we invariably discussed. As long as I could play doctor to my disease, I learned I could at least partially protect myself from the anxiety and feelings of helplessness that accompanied my new status. (Quoted by Hahn, 1985a: 91.)

Another doctor who had experienced a stroke similarly noted that after the scan which confirmed the diagnosis:

> ... the puzzle was over. I was happy. My fear of multiple sclerosis, which had been referred to as inflammation, disappeared. It was replaced by the thought

that I had a diseased bit of body and the rest was all right. The stroke became an 'it' which troubled the rest of my body. (Goldberg, 1993: 216)

In his autobiographical book *A Leg to Stand On*, Oliver Sacks (1984) writes about the experience of becoming a patient from the perspective of a physician who, by virtue of a leg injury, finds himself crippled and hospitalized for a long period of time. Here he describes the 'systematic depersonalization which goes with becoming-a-patient':

One's own clothes are replaced by an anonymous white nightgown, one's wrist is clasped by an identification bracelet with a number. One becomes subject to institutional rules and regulations. One is no longer a free agent; one no longer has rights; one is no longer in the world-at-large. It is strictly analogous to becoming a prisoner, and humiliatingly reminiscent of one's first day at school. One is no longer a person – one is now an inmate. (1984: 28)

While confined to his hospital bed, Sacks' perspective on the world becomes reduced to his small room, as he is institutionalized and alienated from the world by degrees, as his existence is 'shrunk down':

There had been, for me – and perhaps there must be for all patients, for it is a condition of patienthood (although, one hopes, one which can be well- and not ill-handled) – two miseries, two afflictions, conjoined, yet distinct. One was the physical (and 'physical-existential') disability – the organically determined erosion of being and space. The other was 'moral' – not quite an adequate word – associated with the reduced stationless status of a patient, and, in particular, conflict with and surrender to 'them' – 'them' being the surgeon, the whole system, the institution – a conflict with hateful and even paranoid tones, which added to the severe, yet neutral, physical affliction a far less tolerable, because irresolvable, moral affliction. (1984: 122)

Such writings explicitly and vividly describe the illness experience from the perspective of who are used to being in control, to maintaining order over the recalcitrant human body and being the one in authority in the medical setting. These accounts suggest the powerful emotions engendered in illness and the patient role, where even doctors who are trained to deal 'objectively' with the illness of others succumb to uncertainty and anxiety when it is their own bodies that are failing. When doctors themselves are ill, they may have the most difficulty of all in accepting the helplessness of the patient's role because they are so accustomed to approaching the medical encounter from the other side. For many of these physicians, the disruptive experience of being ill dramatically changes their perspective on their own medical practices and their cosmology. As one doctor whose daughter had been hospitalized with a serious illness commented: 'My experience has changed the way I practise medicine. It is important to try and understand the predicament and fears of patients. Some relief can be provided by trying to understand what is going on for them' (Wiener, 1993: 661).

The 'potential sick role'

The body has historically been the site at which reasons for illness were interpreted. The sick body is a meaningful text; its signs and symptoms present a map for understanding. In pre-modern times, the sick body vividly presented itself as suffering the mortifications of the flesh. In the Middle Ages, little was known of the internal effects of disease, so that the body was viewed above all as an 'envelope', out of which pustules, sores, blood, loathsome fluids, odours and exhalations mysteriously erupted or seeped (Herzlich and Pierret, 1987: 76). The body as text of illness has changed since the emergence of medical science. The body has generally ceased to bear witness to disease (the disfiguring marks of Kaposi's sarcoma associated with HIV/AIDS is a notable exception). The horrific bodily signs of medieval epidemics have disappeared or become rare. Once viewed as symbolic of sin, the literal embodiment of evil, the sick body in contemporary society must now be interpreted by medical technologies (1987: 82). Modern pathology is marked by silent illnesses which often remain hidden until the disease has progressed too far for effective treatment.

As medical technology is employed in more and more contexts, the emphasis upon 'discovering' hidden disease in the body has intensified. Early diagnosis of asymptomatic disease is the cornerstone of preventive medicine (Daly, 1989: 100); both medical and lay literature are explicit on the value of early diagnosis. The current popularity of testing and screening procedures to diagnose disease in its early stages involve the redefinition of notions of health and illness. Most screening programmes encourage well people to attend in the interests of detecting 'hidden' disease or the signs of impending disease: HIV antibodies, tiny breast lumps, high-lipid cholesterol levels, hypertension, pre-cancerous cervical cells, genetic markers for disease. The process requires that anxiety levels be raised high enough in people who have experienced no symptoms so that they seek testing. In so doing, it requires that individuals question the veracity of their own assessment of their health, and rely upon medical intervention (usually facilitated by high technology) to detect the invisible signs of disease.

A medical test is automatically seen as the solution to containing disease (Nelkin and Tancredi, 1989). The very word 'test' is redolent with meanings associated with 'failing' or 'passing', of measuring up to a pre-ordained standard. There is therefore the risk that those who 'fail' the test are treated as deviants who have failed to reach the set standard. As it has been asserted with regard to screening for cervical cancer, 'what may be a routine procedure for the health professional involved can be a major incident in the life of the patient' (Quilliam, 1990). This is true whether the test result is positive or negative. Having undergone a medical test, previously well people enter a liminal state where the integrity of their bodies is questioned and left dangling while they await their test results, where the notion of a mysterious disease, which has silently invaded the body and lies in wait, is engendered. Crawford (1980: 379) calls this state of anxiety 'the potential sick role', in which societal expectations are imposed on behalf of prevention and early diagnosis, and failure to act preventively 'becomes a sign of a social, not just individual, irresponsibility'.

When a test result comes back positive, then the label of sickness is bestowed, and 'even before the body has spoken, the individual knows that the illness is or will be there' (Herzlich and Pierret, 1987: 94). As a result, panic and fright in the face of horrible bodily signs of illness have given way to a no less debilitating fear of the silent illness lurking within (1987: 87). That hidden illness must be decoded and exposed by experts, using high-technology equipment and advanced knowledge, takes the agency away from the individual, and detracts from the reality of disease, making it, in some ways, harder to accept. For example, Posner and Vessey found that for women undergoing further examination for cervical cancer, the meanings ascribed to the treatment they received related to the fact that the abnormal tissue involved was on the inside rather than the outside of the body, and thence was unseen, unknowable, lurking in the depths of the body, threatening a part vital to the woman's sense of identity' (1988: 42).

For some people, the lack of defining boundaries around their experience of illness can cause anxiety, confusion and distress. Infertility is one example of a condition which is treated and diagnosed by medicine, but yet is not conceptualized as 'a disease' and is deemed to exist by the absence of events (conception and birth) rather than the presence of symptoms (Greil et al., 1989; Sandelowski et al., 1990). Infertility has a liminal status in that it is not recognized as a problem until couples begin to make attempts to conceive, even though the problem may have existed for a long time. It is an open-ended and indeterminate condition. Many couples interviewed by Sandelowski et al. (1990) believed that infertility was not 'proven' until their reproductive spans are over, or reasoned that if it cannot be explained by medical science, then it does not really exist. Once the condition is recognized, however, there is social pressure for couples to seek medical help, specifically assisted conceptive technologies such as fertility drugs and IVF or donor insemination, rather than accept their fate using philosophical or religious interpretations.

The study conducted by Sandelowski et al. (1990) found that some people still thought of themselves as infertile even after an assisted conception had occurred; they were infertile without medical treatment but fertile with it. Other women experienced infertility as a chronic illness, affecting their views of themselves in other spheres of life. Developments in infertility treatments challenge the ability of people to accept their infertility fatalistically and get on with their lives:

Explanations that rely on such concepts as 'God's will' cannot be convincing when we believe as strongly as we do in the human ability to pull ourselves out of our condition through technical know-how. To accept the kinds of answers theodicy [religious belief] can give implies a spirit of resignation. Such a spirit of resignation does not currently exist in the pursuit of treatment of infertility … As our ability to deal with health problems in technical terms increases, we may lose the ability to deal with them at the level of meaning. (Greil et al., 1989: 226–7)

Having a potential, hidden or liminal illness is therefore as equally challenging and distressing as a 'real' illness, and is in some ways more anxiety-provoking simply because it is not clearly defined. For many people the process of undergoing exploratory investigations, with all their uncertainties, is worse than receiving a negative diagnosis, for there is no opportunity for action or psychological adjustment. Health becomes a simulacrum, a floating signifier with manifold and changing meanings, reified as an end in itself, symbolic of morality, subject to continued anxious measurement and scanning (Kroker, 1992).

Causes of disease and illness from the lay perspective

Although most patients do not have free access to biomedical knowledge, they do not necessarily come to the doctor–patient encounter as empty vessels passively awaiting the wisdom of the doctor. People's understandings of illness, disease and good health states are dynamic and sometimes incoherent, changing in response to personal experience and circumstances such as emotional states. Most individuals develop health beliefs derived from folk-models of illness, alternative forms of medical practice, the mass media and 'common sense' understandings derived from personal experience or from consultation with friends and family, and continue to subscribe to these beliefs while consuming orthodox health care. These well-established beliefs may underlie patients' refusal to comply to doctors' instructions and contribute to misunderstandings between doctor and patient if the former is not aware of the existence of these beliefs. McCombie (1987) gives the example of the lay understandings of the 'flu' among residents of a county in the south-western United States. Most people, she argues, have a much wider definition of flu than do doctors and epidemiologists. They include, for example, nausea, vomiting and diarrhoea as defining symptoms, thereby contravening the medical definition. This lay definition often results in misclassification of illnesses which poses problems for epidemiologists seeking to document patterns of disease.

The more common and the less serious the illness, the more likely it is that lay theories of causation and treatment draw upon traditional folk-models of illness. Helman (1978) discussed the folk-models of respiratory tract infection among an English suburban community based on his experience as a general practitioner. He noticed that lay models of illness tended to explain chills and colds as being due to the penetration of the environment across the boundary of the skin into the individual, caused by such environmental factors as damp, rain, cold binds and draughts. Cold thus entered the body, bringing with it illness, and indeed, causing 'a cold'; therefore bodies had to be kept protected by wearing warm clothing and shoes, avoiding getting wet or damp. The feet and the head were considered the most vulnerable to penetration; hence exhortations not to get one's feet wet or go to bed with damp hair. Sudden changes in body temperature, going from a hot room to the cold outdoors, changes in season and changes in geography were considered the putative agents of colds and chills. Colds were therefore seen as the result of losing the battle against the environment, of dropping one's guard, and hence one's responsibility for not taking proper precautions. By contrast, 'fevers' were viewed as caused by 'germs', 'bugs' or 'viruses'. Germs were conceptualized as entering the body through its orifices, particularly the mouth, nose or anus, hence crossing the body boundaries through their natural breaks. The person infected by a germ was not held responsible because there is no defence against them, as they exist whenever there are human relationships: 'the Germ has its own volition, and cannot be directly controlled by its host' (1978: 120). Helman noted that patients tended to ask if there is a 'bug like mine going around', taking comfort in the idea that there is a 'community of suffering' of which they are part, and are not an isolated case. He further observed that the spread of the germ theory of disease has affected attitudes to relationships: people have become more cautious about interaction with others because of the threat of infection (1978: 124).

Heart disease or high blood pressure are also commonly subject to lay interpretations of cause and treatment that differ rather markedly from orthodox medical explanations. A study carried out in a rural area of Virginia among patients attending a medical clinic found that several patients presented with the complaint they called 'high blood', described by them as a chronic condition in which viscous blood is thought to clog up the upper body or rise suddenly to the head. The respondents believed that diet was important in the cause of the disease, especially eating too much red meat, rich food or salt, which were believed to thicken or 'dry up' the blood. Emotions such as excitement, worry or anxiety were also believed to trigger 'high blood'. Treatment involved 'thinning' the blood and keeping calm. Other patients complained of suffering from 'weak 'n' dizzy', or feelings of vague emotional and body stress and tiredness, 'nerves', causing a disturbance of sleep patterns, tiredness and anxiety attacks, and 'sugar' or 'sweetblood', caused by eating too much sugar (Nations et al., 1985).

Since the early 1980s, a number of qualitative studies involving depth interviews with people living in various parts of Britain have uncovered patterns in the way that people conceptualize the causes of illness based on notions of individual responsibility. In a study of young Welsh working-class women, the most frequently advanced reason for the main cause of illness followed the germ theory model, implying that the women thought of illness as a short, acute episode rather than as the outcome of ageing or a chronic condition. Individual behaviour was also stressed by about half the women interviewed, including the importance of food, hard work and mental attitudes in maintaining 'resistance' to disease, while a smaller proportion discussed heredity as a putative factor. Blame was imputed for illness if people delayed going to the doctor or put themselves at risk through carelessness, stupidity or lack of foresight, but otherwise the women tended towards a non-punitive approach to illness causation (Pill and Stott, 1982).

Other studies suggest that there are important social class differences in the way that ill people are viewed and the manner that sickness is experienced. A study was conducted interviewing women from both middle-class and working-class backgrounds in London. It was found that the middle-class women, in describing concepts of health, were more likely to talk about engaging in exercise, being fit and active and eating the right food, while the working-class women tended to emphasize the importance of getting through the day without feeling ill as being central to feeling healthy. Both groups emphasized that being healthy meant not having to take time off, or not needing to visit the doctor (Calnan and Johnson, 1985). Similar research amongst a group of middle-aged working-class women living in a Scottish city (Blaxter, 1983) found that the interviewees had a very stoical, puritanical and fatalistic attitude to illness, viewing illness as a weakness, as 'giving in'. The women tended to speak about infectious disease as an 'it', a malevolent entity residing outside the person waiting to attack (supporting Cassell's and Helman's findings described earlier in this chapter). In terms of putative agents of illness, the Scottish women mentioned infection, followed by heredity or familial tendency, and agents in the external environment, such as the climate or damp housing, and stress or worry were also frequently mentioned. Causes such as ageing, neglect, inherent susceptibility and individual behaviour were less often mentioned.

The stage of the life-cycle that people have reached seems also integral to shaping their beliefs about the importance of 'lifestyle' modification to prevent against illness. Young people who have not yet settled down and had children may have the time and resources to engage in regular exercise, while people with small children, especially women, have different priorities. For example, as mothers of young children, the women interviewed by Pill and Stott (1982) put forward the belief that they themselves 'did not have time' to be ill; it was part of their role as responsible wife and mother to carry on despite illness. In a study of both men and women from middle-class families resident in Edinburgh, respondents spoke of how their lives had changed as they entered different stages of the life-cycle; one man with a young family, for example, said that he had given up contact sport for fear of serious injury (Backett, 1992: 262).

Discourses on the moral nature of illness seem pervasive in people's accounts. For example, Backett found that '[o]ften a confessional mode was adopted when relating supposedly unhealthy practices; "conscience" and "guilt" were regularly mentioned. One woman even said that her children treated their grandmother who smoked "like a leper"' (1992: 261). Interviews with elderly men and women in Aberdeen, Scotland, identified the common belief that constitutional strength was viewed as a moral matter, as well as being based on heredity and past illnesses, for it depended on will and a sense of responsibility (Williams, 1990). However, people are not always willing to emphasize personal responsibility for illness, sometimes preferring to privilege explanations that revolve around fatalistic concepts of 'chance'. For example, when people living in South Wales were interviewed about their beliefs concerning heart health, the researchers found that their informants, while believing that heart disease was to some degree preventable, also tended to hold the view that death from heart attack could strike anyone without warning, regardless of their everyday habits or physical condition. It was extremely common for people to refer to luck and randomness: 'The fat "Uncle Norman" figure who has survived into a healthy old age, despite extremely heavy smoking and drinking made an appearance in the discourse of all age, gender and class groups' (Davison et al., 1992: 682–3). Such findings provide an alternative perspective to research carried out among American respondents, where the notion of personal responsibility for one's health appears to have been more strongly embraced by the lay public (see Crawford's and Saltonstall's research described in Chapter 2).

Conclusion

The lay perspective on the illness experience, hospitalization and the causes of illness and disease has often been neglected. However, recent studies by historians seeking to uncover the voice of the patient, physicians' writings about their own experiences on the other side of the medical encounter, and ethnographic research undertaken by sociologists and anthropologists eliciting the narratives of people undergoing medical treatment or investigating lay knowledges of health and illness have produced a rich body of interpretive research illuminating these dimensions. Such empirically-based investigations have demonstrated the ways in which bodies may become inscribed by dominant discourses in the public sphere, how relations of power are exercised and reproduced in everyday activities as well as by and through medical practices, and how medical and public health ideas are incorporated into lay knowledges of health and illness. That is not to say that people simply absorb dominant discourses passively and without question; indeed, when engaged as participants in sociological research they may be responding to the researchers' questions with responses they know to be socially correct, rather than revealing their 'true' beliefs and behaviours. It is worthy of note that strong evidence was present in many of these studies about the resistance of people (especially some working-class people) to official discourses on health, including the fatalistic response to the advice that one should maintain control over one's lifestyle to ensure good health. The following chapter discusses this notion of resistance in more detail.

5

Power Relations and the Medical Encounter

This penultimate chapter examines doctor–patient interaction from a socio-cultural perspective. The chapter is predominantly concerned with exploring the issues of the power differential and 'competence gap' between doctors and patients, medical dominance, the vulnerability of patients and their capacity for resistance. The focus on the patient's perspective is extended from the previous chapter, but the present chapter also examines the doctor's and nurse's perspective to provide a rounded view of the medical encounter from both sides of the sick bed.

The functionalist perspective on power

For functionalist theorists, power is not the property of institutions, groups or individuals but is a generalized social resource flowing through the political system, given by general consensus to those who have earned it through their contribution to society. Power is thus based on legitimate authority rather than coercive, shared and accepted as just by members of a society for the rewards it brings, including its achievement of collective goals. Differentials in power and social stratification are viewed as necessary to serve the interests of society as a whole, allowing the most able to perform the most highly skilled roles and benefiting both sides of a power relationship. Thus, as noted in Chapter 1, the functionalist approach does not see the doctor–patient relationship as the product of conflict, or struggles for power. Rather, it views the medical profession as a beneficent institution that performs a needed service, and whose members are justly rewarded by high prestige, status and power for their caring and altruism, their expertise and the long years of training they have completed to gain their qualifications. Medical dominance, or the authority held by the medical profession both in the medical encounter and in the broader public sphere, is viewed as the desirable method of maintaining a social distance between the doctor and the patient, allowing the doctor to take control and perform the healing function successfully, and thus ultimately serving the best interests of the patient.

From this perspective, there are a number of explanations for the continuing power differential between doctors and patients which militate against the patient achieving agency. According to Parsons' 'sick role' (described in Chapter 1), it is incumbent upon the ill to seek medical advice so as to alleviate the potential state of deviance incurred by illness. It is only when they do so, and their illness is legitimized, that the ill temporarily escape social expectations and responsibilities. After seeking medical help, the ill must attempt to follow their doctor's directions, investing their trust and faith in medical expertise. A differential in power is therefore vital to establish the authority of the doctor and encourage compliance on the part of the patient. Indeed, according to the sick role model, doctors must strive to maintain a social difference from patients in order to meet their obligations as objective professionals. Parsons (1987/1951: 153–5) asserted that in response to the rights and obligations of the individual entering the sick role, doctors must maintain a stance of permissiveness towards the patient, suspending normal social expectations of the patient and 'making special allowances'; support the sick person, affirming his or her worth and maintaining a considerate attitude; maintain a detachment or reserve within the relationship, abrogating the expectation of reciprocity inherent in most social relationships; and reinforce normative components of the patient's motivation through approval based on medical authority and undermine deviant components through disapproval.

Furthermore, from the functionalist perspective, the state of illness is such that many patients have a psychological need to leave the decision-making to the doctor in order to absolve themselves from any responsibility for the management of their illness (Mechanic, 1979: 42). It is argued that patients are often unable to weigh alternatives rationally, and would rather place their trust in the doctor's competence and judgement as a qualified member of the medical profession, for '[d]eep in patients' unconsciousness, physicians are viewed as miracle workers, patterned after the fantasized, all-caring parents of infancy. Medicine, after all, was born in magic and religion, and the doctor–priest–magician–parent unity that persists in patients' unconsciousness cannot be broken' (Katz, 1984: 40).

Added to the distress of pain or discomfort is the element of uncertainty in clinical decision-making. If a disease is life-threatening, debilitating and subject to a number of different therapies, such as breast cancer, the patient's need to rely upon medical authority will be greater than if the disease or condition is relatively minor, such as a broken leg. Furthermore, '[w]hen patients are invited to share responsibility, they are often facing problems without clear medical solutions, mixed as they often are with social difficulties and moral dilemmas' (Maseide, 1991: 555). In such situations, many patients rely upon their faith and trust in doctors to cope with illness, preferring to hand over responsibility for the management of the illness to the doctor. For these reasons, it may be suggested that the complex relationship between patient and doctor is like that between parent and child, with patients relying upon doctors to tend to their physical and emotional needs, to nurture and protect them and to take control of a frightening and anxiety-provoking situation.

In many ways the functionalist approach is a product of its time: the 1950s and 1960s, in which the social revolutions and movements such as Marxism and feminism that disrupted expectations and power structures in the 1970s had yet to gather force. At the time in which Parsons was writing, medical practitioners were regarded as part of an elite profession that deservedly wielded power and held prestige because of its members' specialized knowledge and authority.

As noted previously, a problem with functionalist analyses of power in the medical encounter has been their tendency to focus on the micro-properties of the interaction between doctors and patients without analysing the social and political context in which such encounters take place. The research therefore generally fits into the category of social research which attempts to assist members of the medical profession to perform their job more efficiently, centring on the doctor's need to convey information to his or her patients effectively while maintaining the patient's trust and good faith and ensuring compliance. While pointing to the existence of a power imbalance between doctors and their patients, as demonstrated by domination of the encounter by doctors, these studies tend not to explore the role of medical power at the structural level. Even those research efforts which recognize that there may be negative aspects of medical dominance tend to suggest that it is only a matter of inducing a consumerist orientation in patients to challenge the power of doctors. They thus incorporate a simplistic model which views dominance in the medical setting as control over communication rather than a product of wider discourses, ideologies and practices which support power differentials. Such an approach rarely questions the ways in which medical care is organized and delivered, but accepts that the biomedical model of illness and treatment is the most appropriate. As Strong describes this perspective: 'Patients want to be cured, staff wish to cure them. Most conflict or dissatisfaction is viewed as a product of misunderstanding or mistaken technique and not of anything more fundamental' (1979: 5).

The political economy perspective on power

As discussed in Chapter 1, political economists, drawing on Marxist thought, have challenged the consensual model of the doctor–patient relationship. They argue that the relationship is characterized not by agreement and mutual benefit but by a conflict of interests between the doctor and the patient. The political economy approach views medical dominance as the outcome of a power struggle among a number of different interest groups, each intent on achieving high status and power. According to this perspective, it is occupational control that is the basis of medical power, not the inherent socially valued skills or expertise of the profession. Medical practitioners have power because of their professional status and autonomy over their work, which is maintained by their control over medical knowledge (Freidson, 1970; Starr, 1982; Willis, 1989).

As I explained in Chapter 4, the emergence of scientific medicine was an important factor in changing the relationship between patient and doctor, for the power of the medical profession became based in part upon its ability to make claims successfully about the scientific value of its work (Turner, 1995: 217). Political economists assert that the monopoly doctors have over the provision of medical services is legally supported and controlled by the state, operating through a system of licensing, and accounts for much of the power of the profession (Freidson, 1970: 83). Entry into the medical profession, and the attendant knowledge of medical practice and procedure, is strictly controlled; the number of qualified doctors is regulated by placing a quota upon entry into medical schools and by strict registration laws. It is therefore the patronage of the state that gives the medical profession the right to its monopoly over expert knowledge and practice.

For more radical commentators, the role of medicine is to obfuscate the social and political determinants of ill health by rendering illness as individual, thus supporting rather than challenging the capitalist status quo leading to much ill health: 'certain features of doctor–patient encounters "medicalize", and therefore depoliticize, the social structural roots of personal suffering' (Waitzkin, 1984: 339). It is argued that in their position of relative dominance over patients, doctors are empowered to make statements which reinforce dominant capitalist ideologies by directing patients' behaviour into non-threatening channels. For example, patients suffering from stress or depression are routinely counselled to alter their lifestyle by taking up jogging or meditation, or are prescribed mood-altering drugs, strategies which tend to direct attention away from the socioeconomic factors causing the condition. Hence medicine helps to legitimize and reproduce social class structure and the economic system. It thereby maintains the position of dominant interests, and in the process, achieves power for its members.

Critics adopting the political economy perspective point out that on many occasions doctors are called to make authoritative judgements for the legal system, employers and other social authorities; for example, when examining an employee for superannuation purposes or sick leave certification, or when assessing the extent of disability of the disabled, or when pronouncing death (Starr, 1982: 14–15). Doctors have the power to certify whether a person is physically able to work or not, and to decide when a patient should return to work. Thus doctor–patient interaction may reinforce the definition of health as the ability to work, for 'the healthy person is the person who produces' (Waitzkin, 1984: 340).

The political economy perspective argues that power relations in the western medical encounter are related to the dominance of the corporate and middle class in positions of influence in the medical system (as medical professionals, researchers, medical board members and managers) over the lower middle class and working class, who comprise the bulk of patients and lesser-skilled workers in the health care system and who have little control over their medical treatment or work conditions (Navarro, 1976; Waitzkin, 1981). While commentators such as Freidson and Starr recognize that professional authority is often essential to fulfil the demands of the therapeutic process, they argue that medical authority has gone far beyond this level, encroaching into areas for which medical judgement and expertise are inappropriate, demanding too many resources and exercising too much control and political power over health care delivery. Critics argue that in the United States in particular, where medicine has historically been privatized, the quest for profit is increasingly becoming a major influence upon the quality of care provided to patients, and health care professionals are encouraged not to spend too long with each patient (McKinlay and Stoeckle, 1988). The ideology of capitalism therefore prevails (Navarro, 1976; Doyal, 1983; Baer et al., 1986), even while patients continue to expect medical care based on altruistic motives. The effects of capitalist ideology upon the medical encounter work to constrain the choices available to health care professionals and their patients, and frustrate attempts to change and improve the system (Waitzkin, 1984: 343).

From this perspective, the process of strict regulation and 'professionalization' of medical practitioners has the beneficial effect that it ensures a certain minimum standard of medical expertise in persons entitled to practise as medical doctors, and to some degree protects patients against 'quacks'. However, the continuing control of the medical profession over medical knowledge ensures an asymmetry of information between the doctor and patient. The restricted entry into the profession, and the maintenance of an esoteric body of knowledge which requires considerable interpretation, results in the patient having little basis on which to judge the quality of medical service or advice. By virtue of their lack of access to orthodox medical knowledge which is maintained by monopoly, patients are forced to defer to doctors to take over the decision-making process to a large extent, leaving little room for judgement or agency on their part.

It is argued by political economy commentators that the 'competence gap', which is maintained by the medical profession's monopoly on knowledge, serves to support the profession's powerful position by maintaining patient dependency (Freidson, 1970; Johnson, 1972; Waitzkin and Stoeckle, 1972; Starr, 1982). While members of the lay population of contemporary western societies may be exposed to more sources of information about health and medical matters than previously, due largely to increased coverage by the mass media, the publication of popular books about health and illness, and, in recent times, the use of the Internet to disseminate information, the treatment of illness still relies upon the interpretation as well as the possession of the appropriate knowledge. Medical expertise, and clinical decision-making, is not simply the possession of relevant facts and figures, but is based on implicit 'intuitive' clinical competence which is developed over time and which cannot easily or rationally be explained (Atkinson, 1981; Gordon, 1988b). In that way, medical expertise is more an 'art' than a 'science', passed on through oral culture, apprenticeship and the case method. New physicians must learn to use their textbook knowledge to recognize meaningful patterns and recognize what information is salient: 'The use of the body and its senses and feelings are intimately involved in clinicians' expertise' (Gordon, 1988b: 277).

Hence, even if lay people had access to the same medical textbooks, professional journals and lectures as medical students, their knowledge would not be supported by that intangible 'apprenticeship' training which comes from practical experience over a long period of time in the clinical setting. It is this expertise based on experience that underpins the professional nature of medicine (Atkinson, 1981: 110–14). The emphasis on faith neutralizes threats to the physician's status, for it removes the need for justification based on logic and ensures that the body of knowledge remains esoteric (Freidson, 1970).

While functionalist analyses of the doctor–patient encounter have not often critically considered issues of social class, political economists argue that there is a social class schism between doctors and patients which acts to preserve power on the side of doctors in the medical encounter. Doctors in western societies invariably come from the ranks of the privileged classes, with only a minority of working-class origin. Their background and life experiences therefore tend to prevent them from taking due cognizance of the social structural roots of their patients' ill health (Starr, 1982: 12; Waitzkin, 1984: 343–4). The world of the surgery is overwhelmingly formal and middle-class, including the language, manner and accent of the doctor. It is therefore probable that middle-class people may feel more comfortable, more on an equal footing with doctors than do people of low social class, who may feel at worst alienated and at best intimidated by the doctor's air of authority and omnipotence.

The evidence from qualitative interviews with lay people of different social classes carried out in parts of Britain certainly suggests that people of higher social class may feel more empowered and qualified than people of low social class to evaluate the services of the doctor, and to change to another if they are displeased. For example, a study of economically disadvantaged Scottish women (Blaxter and Paterson, 1982) found amongst the older women 'characteristic attitudes of deference, gratitude, and a remarkable trust' (1982: 161) towards their general practitioner, with a marked reluctance to change doctors. While the younger women were less deferential and some did report exercising active choice and control over the health services they utilized, most women, although feeling that their interaction with doctors was unsatisfactory, did not have the confidence or sense of power to take steps to change their doctor. These women 'lacked the skills, education and stable social environment which would have made dealing with the system easy' (1982: 195).

In another study, the interaction of Scottish women patients with doctors in consultations relating to reproductive health was examined (Porter, 1990). Although the women complained at length about waiting times, having to undress and being practised on by medical students and receptionists, they were most unwilling to comment negatively on what the doctor had said or done, even when their doctor had been provocative. In the medical encounter itself, these women tended to passively accept the statements of doctors, showing no signs of annoyance or even surprise. This silence was not due to deference to the medical profession in general, because the women respondents expressed criticisms of other doctors. Some women may not have been personally concerned with the middle-class tenets of good doctor–patient relationships. For others it was simply not in their best interests to acquiesce with the doctor's statements because they may have received worse treatment if they questioned the doctor's authority or behaviour. Furthermore, the women may not have felt 'qualified' to argue with or criticize the doctor, especially as most doctors are expert in providing good reasons for their advice and actions against which it is difficult to argue if one is not medically trained. Indeed, in family planning clinics women were sometimes requested to play an active part in decision-making, and often found this hard to do.

To summarise, from the political economy perspective there is an imbalance of power in the doctor–patient relationship. Members of the medical profession have the upper hand because of the status given to their knowledge and professional standing, their position in the class structure as highly educated, wealthy and middle-class, and their control over medical credentials. As such, they are able to dominate not only the medical encounter, but also are disproportionately powerful in broader society, in terms of being able to represent problems as medical issues (rather than caused, for example, by social inequalities) and claiming authority over these problems. Patients, particularly those who are poorly-educated, come from the working class or are disempowered by virtue of their ethnicity or age, are placed in a passive position when dealing with doctors. Political economists believe that this imbalance of power leads to inequities, leaving many patients unable to challenge doctors' decisions and those from disadvantaged backgrounds receiving poorer care and less choice. At the political level, political economists claim, members of the medical profession enjoy an unfair advantage in shaping decisions related to issues that they have defined as medical, and social inequalities causing ill-health remain unchallenged.

The poststructuralist and postmodern perspective on power

The Foucauldian scholar David Armstrong (1987b: 69–70) critiques the Marxist analysis of power relations in the doctor–patient relationship as simplistic in conceiving of the doctor as like a sovereign power exercising control over patients' bodies. He suggests that such a model of power examines only the overtly visible elements of medical power and has little explanation for the taken-for-granted moments in which patient and doctor collude to solve the illness problem: 'Look at the lines of medical surveillance: "What is your complaint?" "How do you feel?" "Please tell me your troubles." See the routine clinical techniques: the rash displayed, the hand applied to the abdomen, the stethoscope placed gently on the chest. This is the stuff of power. Trivial perhaps but repetitive, strategies to which the whole population at times must yield' (1987b: 70).

Contemporary theory of the medical encounter based on Foucault's insights argues that the clinical examination, which dates from the end of the eighteenth century, is one of the apparatuses of disciplinary power, in which the body 'is both the target and effect of power' (Armstrong, 1982: 110). In medical and other examinations, individuals are 'located within a field of visibility, subjected to a mechanism of objectification, and thereby to the exercise of power' (Smart, 1985: 87). Each individual is marked as a 'case', and thus the individual is constituted as the subject as well as the object of knowledge. From a Foucauldian perspective, medical dominance is an inappropriate term and it is neither possible nor desirable to specify who is subjecting or dominating whom (Fisher, 1991: 177–8). For this perspective then, the exhortations of political economists and others that patients be encouraged by doctors to talk more about their lives, and to site their symptoms in the context of their everyday activities and life stresses, provide an even greater opportunity for the medical gaze to be directed towards the patient, opening the way for more subtle, individualized means of surveillance and social control (1991: 180).

Foucauldian approaches stress that power in the context of the medical encounter is not a unitary entity, but a strategic relation which is diffuse and invisible. Power is not necessarily a subjugating force aimed at domination which itself is vulnerable to resistance, but rather is closer to the idea of a form of social organization by which social order and conformity are maintained by voluntary means. Power is therefore not only repressive, but also productive, producing knowledge and subjectivity. Discipline acts not only through punishment, but through gratification, with rewards and privileges for good conduct. Both the doctor and the patient, for example, subscribe to the belief of the importance of medical testing, constant monitoring and invasive or embarrassing investigative procedures in the interests of the patient. Explicit coercion is generally not involved; patients voluntarily gives up their bodies to the doctor's or nurse's gaze because that is what people are socialized to expect. Of course, there are instances where surveillance of bodies may occur violently, such as in prisons, police stations and psychiatric institutions, but control also takes place through less openly aggressive means, through cultural and personal values and norms (Grosz, 1990: 65). The Foucauldian notion of medical power thus extends the medical dominance thesis of the political economists by viewing power relations in the medical encounter as even more pervasive, and even more subtle, simply because power is 'everywhere', enforced as much by individuals' unconscious self-surveillance as by authority figures.

Scholars adopting a social constructionist stance influenced by Foucault have examined encounters between medical and other health professionals and their patients for the use of language and practices in attempts to take control of the situation and silence resistant discourses. They describe the range of shifting subject positions taken up by both patients and health professionals at various times in the medical encounter, examining the ways in which these subject positions may involve the selection of various discourses to serve specific purposes. From this perspective, power relations are dynamic and constantly negotiated and re-negotiated between the participants in medical interactions as they serve to define their identities.

For example, Silverman (1987: Ch. 9) examined the discourses used by doctors in encounters with adolescent diabetics. He showed how, even in the context of encouraging patient participation and responsibility for one's own illness management, as is the case with diabetes treatment, doctors practise surveillance over their patients. They do so by reviewing their blood test results, questioning the thoroughness of their own management using a moral framework which implies guilt and punishment on the part of the patient who lapses, and directing patients as to the most desirable ways to behave. Patients are not 'pounded into submission' by the doctor, but rather 'incited to speak' (1987: 226), allowing invisible power relations to take place within a framework in which the patient is encouraged to take responsibility for his or her own behaviour.

When discussing power in the medical encounter, the functionalist and the Foucauldian perspectives therefore overlap to some degree. In understanding power relations as productive rather than coercive, Foucauldian theory restates the assertion of classic functionalism that medical dominance is *necessary* for practitioners to take control in the medical encounter to fulfil the expectations of both parties, rather than being a source of oppression, as is argued by the political economists. In this view, detachment, reserve, responsibility for the patient's well-being and an authoritarian stance must be maintained by the doctor, and the notion of patients being 'empowered' to take control in the encounter makes little sense, for such a change in the relationship calls into question the reason why the very encounter exists.

Another perspective on power in the medical encounter is that offered by writers taking up the postmodern theorizing of Deleuze and Guattari. The notion of the 'body-without-organs' (introduced in Chapter 2) incorporates the idea that although this body may be territorialized by the discourses and practices of such dominant institutions as biomedicine, there is always potential for resistance. The 'body-without-organs' is reflexive and dynamic, constantly defining and redefining itself, and is able to be reterritorialized by drawing on alternative discourses. This perspective emphasizes agency and capacity for resistance, an openness to change and becoming other (Fox, 1993, 1997, 1998, 2002). Interestingly enough, although Foucault's work on medicine and the clinic tends to suggest a passiveness on the part of the body under medical care, a subjugation to the dominance of medical discourses and practices, in his later writings Foucault began to move towards a similar notion of resistance as that presented in Deleuze and Guattari's oeuvre (see, for example, Foucault, 1988). In his notion of the care of the self, Foucault began to address the ways in which the project of identity and embodied selfhood is agential rather than simply passive, and how struggles over power are enacted at the site of the body (Lupton, 1995).

Patients' resistance to medical dominance

There have certainly been some signs over the past 30 years that at least some patients, at least some of the time, attempt to challenge the power of medicine. For those who believe that the medical profession has too much power, evidence of a growing movement directed towards encouraging patient assertiveness is accepted as a sign of a diminishing of medical dominance. Several sociologists have asserted that the growth of the ethos of consumerism in the 1970s, in association with an increasing corporatization of medicine, has made an impact upon the professional status of medical practitioners. For example, McKinlay and Stoeckle (1988: 191) allege that Freidson's notion of professional dominance, based on the power engendered by control of knowledge, is no longer valid in the case of doctors in the United States and other western countries. They contend that 'the industrial revolution has fully caught up with medicine' (1988: 203), for there is now a trend towards the deskilling of doctors, the growth of bureaucratic organization limiting their autonomy, their payment by salary rather than fee-for-service, and the fragmentation of doctors because of the increasing number of sub-speciality societies. These factors, they argue, combined with a continuing over-supply of physicians, have contributed to the erosion of the traditional power of doctors and an increase in their economic vulnerability and alienation in the workforce.

That the medical literature is so obsessed with persuading patients to comply with doctors' directives certainly implies that patients' decisions not to follow 'doctor's orders' occur reasonably frequently. Indeed, this approach to seeking medical care is encouraged by the ideology of individualistic voluntariness which underpins late-capitalist economic and political systems, especially that of the United States. Thus, it has been argued, 'Although there is some social expectation that he [*sic*] will look after himself, especially if ill, what a person does about his health is largely up to him. He has a great range of autonomy in regard to lifestyle and the kind and amount of health services used' (Gallagher, 1976: 217).

Although the power relationship within the doctor–patient relationship is weighted towards the doctor, it is the patient's decision whether to seek a doctor's opinion at all, whether to continue seeking advice and whether to comply with the treatment regimen (1976: 216).

The power relations of the doctor–patient relationship are only really challenged if the impetus for more control over the encounter comes from patients rather than medical professionals (Silverman, 1987: 203). Resistance may emerge from various quarters; for example, the patient visiting a private clinic rather than a public clinic, and who is therefore more aware of 'paying' for a 'service', is more likely to challenge the efficiency of the doctor, as is a patient who is chronically ill and 'knows the ropes', or patients who themselves are medically qualified, the patient who is terminally ill and who therefore is accorded greater consideration and power, and the patient who is of a higher social class or educational level or who is related to a member of the medical profession (1987: 131–2).

In a similar argument, Singer asserts that '[t]o attend solely to the power of the powerful and thereby lose sight of resistance and struggle by the oppressed is itself an act of unintended expropriation and enfeeblement, and an act of social distortion as well' (1987: 251). He interviewed a woman who sought medical attention for a suspected ectopic pregnancy over the course of her medical treatment. He observes that the woman's expectations in her medical encounters were shaped by a variety of factors, including her lay biomedical world-view and her familiarity with the technology and procedures of modern medicine; her exposure to the feminist critique of biomedicine; her fears generated from the experience of a previous ectopic pregnancy; her strong desire to have children; and her sense that as a client who had paid for the treatment that she had a right to satisfying health care. When she was dissatisfied by the medical treatment offered her, the woman sought help from her social support network, including a medical student, a pregnancy researcher and a nurse, who supplied her with information and medical journal articles. She then questioned her subsequent treatment and made demands of the health professionals she consulted. Singer (1987: 259–60) concludes that while this woman demanded more (and better) medical treatment, evidence of a propensity towards biomedicalization, she was not passive; rather, she was active and resourceful, prepared to make demands and question medical judgement.

It seems that it is not always members from more privileged backgrounds who resist medical authority. While they may not demonstrate equal assertiveness in the medical encounter, patients from less privileged backgrounds may react to their position of powerlessness by becoming non-compliant, uncooperative or helpless, or by exercising small acts of defiance. For example, a study of pregnant Puerto Rican women attending an American clinic found that they commonly resisted medical judgements, procedures or doctors' behaviour they disliked by missing appointments, telling doctors what they wanted to hear and refusing to speak English in subsequent interactions (Lazarus, 1988: 47).

One study (Bloor and McIntosh, 1990) looked at the extent and types of resistance offered by the female, working-class clients of health visitors and patients receiving treatment in four therapeutic communities, including a house for disturbed and mentally handicapped adolescents, a psychiatric day hospital and two half-way houses for disturbed adolescents. It was found that while attempts at surveillance and monitoring were intrinsic features of health visiting and therapeutic community practice, the clients/patients they studied were highly aware and resentful of this, and resisted surveillance in varied ways. The working-class women challenged the legitimacy of the health visitors, regarding their personal knowledge based on experience as superior to the theoretical knowledge of the latter, engaged in covert non-cooperation by assuring the health visitor that they were following prescribed ways of behaviour which, in fact, they had no intention of carrying out, and concealed practices they knew were frowned upon, such as weaning babies early. Patients in the therapeutic communities took part in overt non-cooperative behaviour, escaped and also engaged in concealment to resist the health professionals' gaze.

It is evident that patients do not always take their doctors' advice. Williams (1990) found that for many of his Scottish respondents, from both working-class and middle-class backgrounds, conflicts of judgement between patient and doctor were commonly interpreted as a sign that the doctor was wrong, based on lay health beliefs which conflicted with medical advice: 'Many people felt they ought to obey the doctor, but did not expect always to do everything they ought to do, and indeed expected at times to enjoy not doing it' (1990: 174). Gabe and Calnan (1989) suggest that the doctor–patient relationship is characterized not by medicalization, but by the 'deferential dialectic' in which patients are often deferential to doctors because of self-imposed constraints, yet maintain an active role in the relationship, evaluating medical practice from their own point of view.

Such findings suggest there is potential for people to resist the passive patient role. However, it should be emphasized that while the current orthodoxy is to promote the 'consumerist' role of patients, exhorting them to challenge doctors' authority, there are limits constraining the extent to which patients can do so (Lupton, 1997b). Patients may well not want or be able to conform to such a role. The health problem of the patient for which she or he is seeking treatment has an obvious impact on the extent to which the patient may feel empowered or wish to take control in the encounter. For some minor illnesses or conditions, patients may prefer a brief consultation in return for a prescription; for others, impersonality may be a requirement if an intimate examination is involved, such as a gynaecological examination. If the illness is particularly severe, complex, disabling or chronic, patients may be so ill or anxious or both that they are desperate to put their treatment into the hands of someone else deemed competent to deal with the problem and willing to spend time with them. In some situations, patients may not wish to know the full details of their illness, treatment or prognosis (Rier, 2000).

Such factors as the emotional dimensions of the encounter and the patient's accumulated bodily experiences also serve to influence the extent to which patients may seek to take on the 'consumerist' approach. Many patients want to be able to invest trust and faith in their doctor, to allow them to make decisions on their behalf (Lupton, 1997b). Trust, indeed, may be a central requirement for very ill patients to cope with their situation and to assist their survival (Rier, 2000).

As discussed above, social class, age, ethnicity and gender may also influence patients' motivations to challenge their doctors and resist medical dominance. Those who are socio-economically disadvantaged have less access to education, resources and such publications as consumer guides compared with people of greater socio-economic advantage. While middle-class patients may be more willing to challenge the power of members of the medical profession, the notion of the 'good' patient may act as a constraint. The 'good' patient does not question the authority of doctors; if patients attempt to do so, the penalty may be a put-down such as 'Where did you go to medical school?', outright rejection such as 'You'll have to find someone else', or black-listing of a patient among other doctors (Ehrenreich and Ehrenreich, 1978: 59). Many patients depend upon doctors to give them immediate relief from their symptoms, or at least to 'solve' the problem, allowing transference of their problems to the doctor: 'it is a manifestly benevolent relationship: disobeying a teacher or boss might be seen as gutsy, but disobeying a doctor can only be construed as irrational' (1978: 61). It is therefore doubtful that the new breed of patient described in consumer guides – armed with medical knowledge and ready to challenge the doctor's authority or even to litigate if things go wrong – is in the majority.

One example of a highly educated, well-motivated patient who attempted to 'take control' of her illness is the anthropologist Susan DiGiacomo, whose experiences with cancer treatment and hospitalization were mentioned in Chapter 4. In the attempt to maintain control over the situation and participate actively, DiGiacomo read medical journal articles on her disease, and approached doctors as colleagues rather than as superiors. She found surprise, disapproval and conflict eventuated as a result of her active challenging of medical authority. One doctor told her that 'I don't think it's wise for you to try to become an expert on your own disease. It could be very damaging for you psychologically' (1987: 321).

While she resented such statements, DiGiacomo also found that being allowed to participate in decision-making bore with it its own problems, including sharing in the medical practitioner's worries. She concedes that while the doctor seeks to hold power over the patient, there is sometimes a need for this: 'power is particularly important in securing co-operation with forms of treatment – chemotherapy – that are arduous, extremely unpleasant, and dangerous, and possibly even lethal. The doctor emerges as omniscient and omnipotent, and the ambiguity inherent in the relationship between treatment and prognosis is, if not eliminated, substantially reduced' (1987: 339). DiGiacomo further comments that the medical profession's attempts to disguise the uncertainty of some treatments when dealing with seriously ill patients has misfired, for patients come to expect a perfect outcome, and if disappointed, are seeking redress in ever larger numbers by suing their physician for malpractice (1987: 340).

While political economists call for reform, arguing that patients should be given more agency by the medical profession if medical dominance is to be tempered, Foucauldian theorists assert that the medical profession has already absorbed the ideology of greater patient participation into its praxis, which ideology serves to enlarge the field of power of medicine rather than constrain it (Arney and Neill, 1982; Armstrong, 1983: Ch. 11; Silverman, 1987). They call into question the notion, espoused by those commentators calling for greater patient participation in health care delivery, that medical power should be reduced, by pointing out that the medical encounter depends on a differential of power and knowledge between doctor and patient. Both the roles of the 'doctor' and the 'patient' are constituted by the discourses and practices of medicine, which rest on the doctor remaining in the position of expert. Therefore, to challenge the medical profession's expertise, to make attempts to reduce the knowledge gap between doctor and patient, simply destroys the purpose and role of medicine. Why should people seek medical advice if doctors do not have a greater degree of expert knowledge than they? How can the doctor–patient relationship exist if patients continually call into question the knowledge, judgement and clinical skills of doctors? What purpose would be gained if lay people were forced to acquire expert medical knowledge for themselves and how would/could that occur? Whose interests would ultimately be served? As Silverman suggests:

> To ask of medicine that it should cease to survey objectified bodies or give up its search for hidden truths concealed in organic processes is to demand that medicine should dissolve itself. This, of course, would be unacceptable not only to doctors, but also to lay people who demand of medicine precisely that it should provide such truths. (1987: 224)

Further, in response to the Foucauldian notion of the power of the clinical gaze, it has been contended that the new emphasis upon 'knowing' the patient in medical and nursing discourse in fact provides patients with a greater locus of power, for '[u]nlike the "truth" of the disordered body, visible through examination or biochemistry, the truth of the subject cannot be exposed without the explicit permission of the subject concerned' (May, 1992a: 600). In other words, the patient cannot be forced to speak; he or she has the ability to remain silent, or to lie.

As noted above, for this perspective the maintenance of such a power differential is not necessarily considered a negative part of the medical encounter; power is viewed as necessary to facilitate the needs and expectations of both patient and doctor. While power may be used abusively in the medical encounter, it is also used positively (Maseide, 1991; Lupton, 1997b; Rier, 2000). Those patients who choose to invest their trust and faith, to relinquish decision-making to their doctors, need not necessarily be viewed as passively acceding to their doctors. Rather, they may be regarded in a more positive light as choosing to engage in a practice that they consider is vital to their own emotional and physical well-being. They may decide that the 'good patient' is a role that they wish actively to take on, even if at other times they may choose to engage in the role of the more challenging 'consumerist' patient. Both the 'passive' and the 'consumerist' patient position, therefore, may be a conscious and deliberate response to a personal investment individuals may have to present themselves in a certain manner, consonant with their social and embodied position at the time at which the medical encounter takes place. Alternatively people may respond to their doctors on a highly unconscious level of engagement, behaving in hostile or assertive ways because of an inherent fear of dependence, or else seeking a trusting relationship that echoes that of the child–parent relationship because of the emotional comfort it offers. Neither response need be mutually exclusive: the same person may experience both these types of emotional investments, leading perhaps to ambivalence about their dependence on doctors (Lupton, 1997a).

The doctor's view

In discussing the ways in which doctors approach the medical encounter, it is important to understand the socializing processes by which individuals achieve the official credentials to practise medicine. Medical training engenders a set of beliefs and a system of knowledge which structures the ways in which doctors diagnose illness and respond to patients. The training is based upon the positivist scientific method, centring on the rapid accumulation of 'facts' with little space devoted to consideration of human communication or the history and epistemology of medicine. Medical students are taught that there is a diagnosis for every condition, and that every condition has a defined set of treatment strategies. When medical students go to a busy hospital for further training, there is little room for uncertainty or prevarication. The good student doctor is expected to be able to make instant judgements and get the job done quickly, and learns to view patients as diseases, easily categorized into unidimensional stereotypes. Spending a long time with patients and encouraging questions is not valued in the hospital or public clinic setting (Atkinson, 1981; Lazarus, 1988; Stein, 1990). Medical students must learn to deal with delicate, embarrassing situations involving intimate touching or emotionally upsetting events such as death, responding with matter-of-fact neutrality and behaving as if it is 'routine' (Atkinson, 1981: 44–5).

When it comes to practising as a fully-fledged medical practitioner, depending upon whether doctors are general practitioners in solo practice, residents in busy hospitals or in 24-hour clinics, in rural practice or in the city, or medical specialists, the demands of the workplace will differ. If they are working in a hospital, they must cope with staff relationships, personal uncertainty over their skills (especially if they are still training or have little experience), disputes over jurisdictional boundaries and other power struggles within the hierarchy of the medical and nursing professions (Gallagher, 1976; Gerson, 1976; Stein, 1990). The management of time is of utmost importance for the medical and nursing staff, who are in the position of having to deal with many patients in a short space of time, but is also used as a strategy of maintaining authority.

Hahn (1985b), an anthropologist, spent five months accompanying a medical specialist on daily hospital rounds, consultations at a hypertension clinic, occasional office visits and night and weekend calls, so as to construct a participant-observation study of the specialist's working world. Hahn notes that time management was integral to the specialist's working day: 'Barry [the specialist] is oppressed by two sorts of temporal constraints. Too much to do in the allotted time, and the urgency of action imposed by what are too often literal "deadlines". Time is differently shaped accordingly: excess draws it out, imminence intensifies every moment' (1985b: 62). The situation thus often demands that doctors contain the extent of personal interaction in favour of professional detachment, that patients are treated as 'cases' rather than people, despite the needs of many patients to be treated more as an individual person than as a generic patient.

As discussed above, according to the functionalist and Foucauldian perspectives, power enables doctors to act in the competent role demanded of them by most patients, and which is legally and professionally prescribed. Thus doctors are not necessarily behaving in a deliberate attempt to oppress their patients and subordinate staff; they are behaving in a way which is expected of them by their co-workers and their patients, and cannot easily 'decide to break the frame of their professional game' without serious consequences (Maseide, 1991: 552). Doctors themselves are subject to the field of power that constitutes institutionalized norms of behaviour in medical practice, while patients expect such behaviour as necessary and rational (1991: 553). Thus, '[m]edical discourse cannot simply be understood in terms of unnecessary or causal forms of convenient domination or arrogance, in the form of interruptions, control of turn-taking or information deficiencies' (1991: 554). From the moment the patient walks into the waiting room or hospital, it is up to the medical staff to take control. As the 'experts' in the medical encounter, doctors and other health professionals must advise patients how to behave in the encounter, direct their bodily movements in clinical examinations, prepare them for surgical procedures and advise them on behaviours relating to their health problem and treatment regimes, for as 'non-experts' the majority of lay people simply do not know what to expect or do.

Analyses of the doctor–patient encounter using ethnomethodological techniques often provide illustrative accounts of the way in which authority and depersonalization is functional for both medical professionals and patients. Emerson's (1987/1970) account of the processes by which a gynaecological encounter is negotiated examines the social construction of reality. She analysed the way in which the examination of a woman's genitals, a potentially embarrassing and sexually sensitive encounter, is negotiated by patient, doctor and nursing staff. Emerson notes that the doctor takes the initiative in guiding the patient through the encounter, giving cues that 'other people go through this all the time'. The major definition which must be sustained is that the touching of the woman's genitals is taking place in a medical setting, and is thus unerotic and not threatening, but rather is therapeutic, routine and in the patient's best interests. If this definition is followed, then it is assumed that 'no one is embarrassed' and 'no one is thinking in sexual terms'. To save embarrassment on both sides, the medical staff's demeanour assumes that the encounter is matter-of-fact and totally socially acceptable. For this to be sustained, the patient must be viewed as a technical object rather than an individual: 'It is as if the staff work on an assembly line for repairing bodies; similar body parts continually roll by and the staff have a particular job to do on them' (1987/1970: 218). The medical definition of the situation gives the staff the right to perform their invasive and often painful procedures without fear of accusations of sexual assault or cruelty: 'The patient needs the medical definition to minimize the threat to her dignity; the staff need it in order to inveigle the patient into co-operating' (1987/1970: 219). The use of medico-scientific language is a major part of sustaining the definition, helping to depersonalize and desexualize the encounter; for example, the doctor or nurse refers to 'the vagina' but not 'your vagina', while the vulgar directive to 'spread your legs' is generally replaced by the more genteel and formal 'let your knees fall apart' (1987/1970: 221).

It is also important for doctors to follow certain rules of behaviour in the medical encounter, some of which will limit patients' agency, to avoid being sued for malpractice, especially in the case of an uncertain outcome: 'A doctor may be wrong, but his or her fault should be institutionally defendable' (Maseide, 1991: 556). For example, a participant-observation study of the manner in which specialist doctors disclosed information to their patients about a positive diagnosis of breast cancer (Taylor, 1988) observed that despite demands from consumer groups on the part of patients for more information, and research which suggests that patients are dissatisfied with the amount of information given to them by doctors, the situation demands that doctors be careful in the information they disclose. A breast cancer diagnosis is catastrophic news for the patient. The specialist is aware that the patient's prognosis is not entirely linked to the specialist's technical skill: even if a cancerous lump is removed successfully, the patient could still die within a few months, and is more likely than not to die within five years. In addition, there is no single treatment of choice. The specialists are thus obliged to tell women that while they must have immediate surgery with possible removal of the breast, there is uncertainty as to which procedure is best and indeed as to the effectiveness of any surgery, and no permanent cure can be guaranteed.

In such a situation, most specialists coped with the trauma by choosing not to share the knowledge of the uncertainty of the treatment with their patients when they were suffering from shock and fear, and evading direct questions. When specialists did try to emphasize the uncertainty of the procedures, patients often responded badly, as in the following exchange:

> *Doctor:*   We really don't know which surgery is best. We do not have any real answers. We are collecting data to help us with these questions. Let me tell you about this clinical trial ...
>
> *Patient:*   Doctor, I am asking YOU what you think is best for me. For God's sake you are a doctor ... I don't want my breast taken off ... but then ... I want to live ... I've got three kids you know ... (Quoted by Taylor, 1988: 449.)

Despite the emotional difficulties of communicating uncertainty, some specialists in this study said that they feared malpractice suits if the patient had not been informed of all possible treatment options and had not been told that she had breast cancer. Others used the strategies of euphemisms and vague statements in the attempt to soften the blow, believing that patient trust was an important part of the treatment process: 'Despite continuing personal discomfort, the Clinic physicians preferred to develop techniques and policies to reduce their tension rather than confront the issue directly' (Taylor, 1988: 460).

Non-medical criteria are integral to the medical decision-making processes of surgeons, in ways which have serious implications for their patients. For example, factors such as surgeons' concerns about the hospital organizational structure, competition between specializations, personal income, working relationships with other surgeons and the need to participate in research trials may all influence medical decisions, but the decision-making process tends to be obscured through such strategies as the surgeons not acknowledging they are making a decision, by denying that they have an option in making the decision, and by embedding the decision in irrelevant information (Katz, 1985). For example, in one study, surgeons who wanted their breast cancer patients to participate in a clinical trial feared that their patients would not want to participate if given the full information. The surgeons therefore dealt with the situation by presenting the information about the research at the same time as they announced that the patient may have a diagnosis of breast cancer. The patient thus was confronted with an anxiety-provoking and information-laden situation, in which the information about the clinical trial was carefully embedded so as to maximize consent (Katz, 1985).

Another study of the medical management of menopause suggests that over the years physicians develop their personal working model for the problems that are encountered regularly as part of medical practice (Lock, 1985). In the management of menopause, the model is constructed from such factors as the personality of doctors and their attitudes towards women and sexuality; the doctors' ages, gender, stage of development in the life cycle and level of experience; their chosen sub-speciality; the type of training they received (oriented towards the psycho-social or the biomedical model of illness); their level of contact with teaching hospitals, house staff and medical library facilities; their familiarity with the latest professional literature; the socio-demographics of their patient population; the impact of the mass media coverage of the disease on the doctors and their patients; and the economic and political organization of the health care system within which doctors operate (1985: 125–6). Other factors may be added: the type and quantity of clinical information available to the physician (general practitioners receive different information from senior hospital specialists); the audience (for example, whether medical or lay); the type of condition (for example, whether straightforward or more complex); time factors; the position that the clinician occupies in the professional hierarchy; and the 'pet' theories of the clinician about the condition (Helman, 1985: 310). In the menopause study, among the gynaecologists and general practitioners who were interviewed there were marked differences in attitudes connected with menopause, resulting in different therapies being offered to patients. As this suggests, the 'construction of clinical reality' is shaped in many ways which affects patient care, due in part to the ambiguities which surround the biomedical information available to doctors which is amenable to numerous interpretations (Lock, 1985).

The nurse's perspective

Just as patients and medical students and practitioners are socialized in certain ways according to the institutionalized norms and needs of the clinic and the hospital, nursing students and nurse practitioners are subject to demands and constraints shaping their interaction with patients and colleagues. While they are equally subject to time constraints and the need to retain professional detachment, nurses have the added strain of being far lower in the medical hierarchy than doctors, often treated by both doctors and patients as little more than servants. Nurses working in hospitals must deal with professional conflicts over responsibility for the patient, negotiate struggles over power with physicians and contend with sexism and paternalism on the part of both doctors and patients. While nurses are given primary responsibility for the care of patients, they are also subject to bureaucratic rules and the imposition of medical authority which often militate against their potential to exercise professional autonomy (May, 1992b: 475).

The power differential between nursing staff and doctors in the clinical setting is due to differences of gender, social class and status as well as the nature of the tasks performed. Nurses are overwhelmingly female, while medical practitioners have tended to be mostly male. While more women have entered medical training over the past two decades, few men have taken up nursing, and positions of power in the medical hierarchy – the specialists and surgeons – are still occupied by far more male than female doctors. An indication of the uneasiness felt by male surgeons about their power over *male* nurses is demonstrated by their tendency to suggest that the nurse is homosexual: 'The male nurse is therefore reduced to the role of honorary woman, by the fallacious equation of male nurse = gay = effeminate = woman' (O'Hara, 1989: 93). The female domination of nursing is related to its low status, as is the hitherto lack of tertiary qualifications required to be a practising nurse (although in numerous countries many nurses now complete a university degree), both of which have contributed to the poor conditions of employment of nursing, including far lower pay than other health workers, low autonomy and lack of a career structure.

There is currently very little published research on the socio-cultural aspects of the power relationship between nursing staff and medical practitioners, or between nurses and patients, evidence of the tendency of even sociologists and anthropologists to neglect consideration of the role of nurses in the medical setting. One interesting account of the operating theatre as a degradation ritual from the perspective of a student nurse (O'Hara, 1989) made observations about the way in which the institutional practices of the medical setting define the status and identity of doctors, patients and other medical staff such as nurses. O'Hara noted that the regime in operating theatres acts to privilege the doctors' demands over both nurses and patients. For example, although surgeons routinely arrive for operations late, when the procedure begins nursing staff are expected to rush to fulfil their demands: 'Nurses rightly must arrive on time, and those on the lowest grade, auxiliaries, clock in like ancillary staff, yet surgeons occupy a different time-zone. They can routinely arrive as late as they want every day, particularly in the morning, with absences ranging from half an hour upwards, without a word of explanation or apology asked for or given' (1989: 88).

The sheer mobility of both medical and nursing staff in the hospital and the physical geography of medical and nursing work disrupts the distribution of nurses' knowledge about their patients' bodies (May, 1992b: 475–6). This often leads to a chaotic, stressful and inefficient working environment, in which 'nurses come to "know" about the patient as a biological entity in the context of their relations with a powerful group of medical actors who define the state of the body and project its career' (1992b: 477). However, the ideology that positions nurses as empathetic, striving to 'know the patient' as an individual, as a 'whole person' rather than as just a set of symptoms, can be interpreted as an explicit exposition of surveillance and disciplining of patients' bodies. For nurses, the clinical gaze is extended from the external features of the patient's body to the private thoughts, feelings and everyday lives of patients, in the quest to find the patient's 'real' or 'authentic' character in a way which may be considered even more intrusive: 'Through being "known" and through "talking and listening", the patient is encouraged to give voice to her [*sic*] private and authentic concerns – and so to produce and expose her own truth' (May, 1992a: 597). As one nurse commented: 'As a nurse you get very intimate – not only physically intimate [with patients]. You're catching somebody while they really are down ... – I guess you could say some nurses believe they're seeing people at their very base, the very element of their – ... You see them at their most vulnerable' (Lawler, 1991: 157).

Yet, despite this potential source of power, the social position of nurses in relation to patients is more complex than that of the doctor–patient relationship. The tasks carried out by nurses as part of their working day are central to their lack of social status, and contribute to the differential of power between doctors and nursing staff. Nurses must perform 'dirty work' tasks traditionally viewed also as 'women's work', including washing patients' genitalia, assisting them with bedpans, dealing with symbolically contaminating and emotionally revolting bodily fluids such as blood, saliva, pus, phlegm, vomit and faeces, and participating in the preparation of corpses (Lawler, 1991; Wiltshire and Parker, 1996). Nurses deal with bodies that transgress boundaries, that are broken down and violated by illness and medical treatment, and must use their own bodily capacities to assist them, as well as emotionally support them. As such, nursing work is often emotionally exhausting and draining, and nurses often feel that they cannot talk about their work with others who are not nurses (Wiltshire and Parker, 1996).

Nurses are constantly positioned as submissive 'helpmeets' rather than authoritative agents in the medical setting, assisting doctors and carrying out their orders and responding to patients' requests in ways that are never demanded of doctors: for example, a student nurse in an operating theatre is expected to be 'socially invisible' but also 'asked to materialize at any moment to fulfil a humdrum task' (O'Hara, 1989: 80). Indeed, it has been argued that the intimate bodily functions carried out by nurses for patients render them as primarily sexual beings: 'having seen and touched the bodies of strangers, nurses are perceived as willing and able sexual partners. Knowing and experienced, they, unlike prostitutes, are thought to be safe – a quality suggested by the cleanliness of their white uniforms and their professional aplomb' (Fagin and Diers, 1984: 17). This interpretation provides an explanation for the prevalence of sexual harassment suffered by nurses at the hands of male medical staff and patients, and for the stereotypical image of the young, attractive female nurse as available sex object or the male nurse as homosexual. The strong linking of nursing with values routinely represented as ideally 'feminine', such as altruism, caring, gentleness, nurturance and empathy, serves to reinforce the nursing profession as the domain of women, and hence its continued low status and its members' lack of power in the medical setting.

Moral values in the medical encounter

While medicine is predicated on scientific principles of objectivity and the ethical tenet of altruism, moral values are suffused throughout the medical encounter. In doctors and other medical professionals' interaction with patients, it is not only the biomedical model and the imperatives of time which shape medical judgements, but value judgements about the patient based on gender, social class, ethnicity, age, physical attractiveness and the type of illness (for example, whether it is 'deserved' or not).

As noted earlier in this chapter, doctors and other medical staff have models of a 'good' or 'bad' patient which they use to make judgements about patient care. There is an 'unofficial, moralistic taxonomy of types of patients' (Stein, 1990: 98) which operates to influence the ways in which patients are treated in the hospital setting. 'Good' patients do not bring the disease or illness upon themselves, are not responsible for its control, respond quickly to treatment, do not question the treatment and are compliant; that is, they affirm the self-image of the doctor, who wants to view him- or herself as successful, competent and confident, a '"winner" in the battle against disease' (1990: 98). Conversely, 'bad' or 'difficult' patients are held responsible for their disease, do not respond well to treatment, refuse to approach their illness stoically, are querulous and non-compliant, are too demanding, are hostile, seek to control the doctor and question his or her authority and competence, and therefore make the doctor feel unsuccessful, out of control and a 'loser' (1990: 98). Such patients are tagged by medical staff with names which ridicule them, such as 'troll', 'wimp', 'jerk', 'problem patient', 'cry-baby' and 'whiner' (1990: 71), which transfers the fault for the lack of progress from the doctor to the patient.

In an American hospital emergency ward, which treated mainly people of low socio-economic status and non-white and non-Anglo ethnicity, staff applied cultural concepts which differentiated between the 'deserving' and the 'undeserving' of treatment or care. For example, the young were considered more deserving than the old and 'welfare cases' were viewed as not deserving of the best care compared with people of high social status. These moral categories were reflected in the names given to 'undeserving' patients by nurses, doctors and other staff: 'garbage', 'liars', 'scum', 'deadbeats', people who 'come out from under the rocks'. Moral judgement was also reflected in diagnoses and subsequent medical treatment and care: men who were labelled 'drunks' and women who were diagnosed as having 'pelvic inflammatory disease' were so-labelled not only because of symptoms, but also because of other factors, such as their race or ethnicity, their state of dress and their manner of speech (Roth, 1981/1972).

Hahn (1985b: 75) observed that Barry Siegler, the specialist he accompanied for some months in his participant-observation study, possessed a deep sense of moral certainty which was demonstrated in the attitudes he had towards patients, such as his ambivalence about the treatment of an alcoholic, as well as his presumption that he knew what was best for his patients. There were three axes that Siegler used to make distinctions between patients; one of medical interest, a second of personal pleasant-ness and a third of strength and interest of character (1985b: 99–102). If patients were categorized as 'nice', Siegler was pleased when they did well and troubled when they suffered. 'Interesting' patients were those who presented problems which were sufficiently complex to be intriguing and good teaching material but which were soluble, or patients who had striking but inoffensive personalities. If patients were disliked, they were described as 'turds', 'son of a bitch', 'bitch', 'nut', 'a crock', and were treated by the doctor with impatience. Patients fell into this category if Siegler judged that they were non-compliant, or morally or socially offen-sive because of their 'promiscuity' or poverty, or if they had brought the illness upon themselves.

Alternative therapies and self-help groups: challenging medical dominance?

Since the 1970s, alternative therapies (also known as holistic or natural therapies) have been embraced by a growing number of people who feel disaffected by the strictures of scientific medicine or who have conditions which have not been successfully treated by biomedicine (Cant and Sharma, 2000). The discourses of these therapies constitute a rejection of the dualisms of nature/culture, individual/society, mind/body and subject/object which have characterized orthodox medicine. They seek to recon-nect the bodily and social worlds and often to effect social transformation (Scott, 1999). Alternative therapists claim that their approach offers a viable, non-alienating, more 'natural' and less invasive way of promoting health and curing ills. Illness is seen as an imbalance between the indi-vidual and his or her environment, a view which contrasts with the bio-medical model of disease as invasion from an external pathogen. In a climate where concerns about iatrogenic disease, the self-serving financial interests of orthodox doctors and the high costs of medical technology have been placed prominently on the agenda for public discussion, alter-native therapies appear a refreshing and radical alternative which offer a sensitive, caring attitude and personal contact with healers.

In some ways they do fulfil their promise. Most alternative therapies eschew the use of high-technology and laboratory reports in diagnosing and treating illness and disease. They offer instead treatment which depends upon the sensitivity of the patient and practitioner relationship, and simple, non-technical, non-invasive methods (for example, hypnosis, massage, medi-tation, nutritional therapy, herbal remedies, heat treatment, acupuncture) to effect a cure. The alternative therapies therefore appear to offer a solution to the growing domination of high-technology, with all its impersonality and expense, in the health services. By rejecting the Cartesian duality which splits mind and body, alternative therapies take the perspective that the 'whole' person must be considered when physical health is the issue. The emphasis upon the individual's life-history and the combining of the mental, the spiritual and the environmental with the physical dimensions of health address many people's dissatisfaction with the mechanical, fragmented body image of biomedicine and their need to conceptualize their health in a holistic manner which deals with the context of their everyday lives.

Alternative therapies ascribe the causes of ill health to more than just the purely biological, and encourage individuals to take responsibility for their own health by rejecting the disempowered role of the submissive patient. The emphasis is upon the perception of health as a value in itself, and upon the individual actively participating in the continuing maintenance of good health (Berliner and Salmon, 1980; Patel, 1987; Cant and Sharma, 2000). Unlike biomedical medicine, alternative therapies can provide satisfactory explanations for the questions 'Why me?' and 'Why now?', 'replacing the sterile world of biologic facts with a readily understood moral system' in which the right attitudes and behaviours are rewarded with good health (Crawford, 1980: 374). People may also be attracted to alternative therapies not only because of dissatisfaction with conventional medicine, but also because of the mythology of nature and health which underpins such therapies. 'Nature' has a powerful symbolic meaning in late-capitalist society, related to virtue, morality, cleanliness, purity, renewal, vigour and goodness (Coward, 1989: 16–17). Its use as the dominant element of alternative therapies' ideology is a major attraction for clients, for '[n]ature by implication is that which is safe, gentle and has inherent properties which will benefit individuals' (1989: 19).

However, critics of this approach argue that the use of the symbol 'nature' in alternative therapies is selective; for example, defining synthesized drugs as 'artificial' and 'chemicals' (and thus bad for the health), while herbs are represented as natural and non-chemical, and therefore safe, even though many naturally occurring substances can be toxic, and many chemicals are derived from naturally occurring substances (Coward, 1989: 20–1). More importantly, critics contend that the ideology of alternative medicine differs little from scientific medicine by placing undue emphasis upon the individuals' responsibility for the maintenance of their health (Scott, 1999). Most alternative therapies, while rejecting the philosophical tenets of orthodox medicine, do not offer a political critique of health service practices (Coward, 1989: 10–11). It is claimed that the alternative therapies often join scientific medicine in not sufficiently acknowledging the important link between an individual's health and the broader social milieu in which he or she lives (such as the impact of social class), and thereby serves as merely one facet of the institution of medicine's role in legitimizing and obscuring the prevailing social inequalities leading to ill health.

The re-emergence of the alternative therapies as serious competitors in the medical market place has resulted in a power struggle between alternative and orthodox practitioners over whose body of medical knowledge is the best to treat illness. Although orthodox medicine has had difficulty claiming more success in treatment than alternative medicine, it has always been able to cite its 'scientific' basis as a selling point (Willis, 1978: 17). 'Unscientific' concepts of spirituality and vital forces which are assumed in holistic therapies are not readily accepted by biomedicine, for they do not conform to the doctrine of specific aetiology and illness as a result of an external pathogen (McKee, 1988: 780–1).

As discussed in Chapter 4, orthodox medicine has been legitimized under the rubric of a scientific discipline and has been able to have the scientific paradigm of medical care accepted as 'the' paradigm, accusing alternative practitioners of invoking 'magical' beliefs without scientific basis. The irony here is that for most users of orthodox medicine the symbols and rituals of medical care are just as mysterious as those used in alternative therapies. Most patients have little understanding of the bio-scientific basis of a diagnosis or why a certain drug or treatment is prescribed: for them, it is simply a matter of faith, of belief in the 'magic' of medicine and the credentials of the practitioner.

In response to allegations of 'witch-doctor' fraudulent behaviour from traditionalists, alternative practitioners have attempted to legitimize their practices by introducing standardization and licensing. Many universities now offer degree courses in such therapies as acupuncture and chiropractic. Just as traditional medicine has controlled a monopoly of specialist knowledge in order to sell it at a high price as a commodity, so too the struggle by alternative practitioners to have their practices legitimized is an attempt to have control over knowledge (Willis, 1978: 17). This movement towards credentialism may offer protection to the consumer by the assurance of the attainment of a minimum level of knowledge and skills. The corollary, however, is that alternative medical practitioners, by emphasizing the 'professional' aspects of their craft, are more likely to approach the doctor–patient model of treatment prevailing in biomedicine, in which the patient is generally submissive and the doctor dictatorial. Given that it is this very approach which so alienates many of the people who turn to alternative medicine, holistic practitioners may well be in the process of diminishing one of their main attractions. In their struggles for legitimacy, therefore, alternative therapies are steadily weakening the boundary between the traditional and the holistic approaches to health care and thus losing any potential they may have had to offer an alternative to scientific medicine.

Indeed, many of the practices of alternative therapies may be regarded as commodifying alienation, for '"personal" problems are temporarily relieved as a particular practice tends to adjust the individual to the society from which the pathology has arisen' (Berliner and Salmon, 1980: 143). The enthusiasts of alternative therapies are overwhelmingly from the middle class, and therefore the movement seems to have little to offer people of low socio-economic status (Crawford, 1980: 365). Economically disadvantaged people suffer a greater level of morbidity and early mortality than people of high socio-economic status, and seemingly derive the least benefit from the orthodox medical system. They are more likely to be alienated by the middle-class world of traditional medical care, and have fewer choices about how to conduct their lives. As payment for most treatment by alternative practitioners is rarely reimbursed by public or private health insurance schemes (except in the case of the more accepted practices such as acupuncture and chiropractic), the barrier of even greater financial cost to the patient serves as an effective limitation of the services of alternative practitioners to the more wealthy.

Critics argue that in its quest for 'perfect', 'total' or 'positive' health, which encompasses all aspects of a person's life and which is seen as much more than simply the absence of disease or discomfort, in many ways alternative medicine only adds to the medicalization of western culture, and further extends jurisdiction over patients' autonomy (Coward, 1989; Scott, 1999). Just as the ideology of nursing, in its interest in the 'whole' person, may be viewed as extending the medical gaze into the personal lives of patients, so too a similar focus on all aspects of a patient's life as championed by alternative therapists may be interpreted as an extension of power.

The discourses of alternative therapies seek to recast the imagery of the body and disease by moving away from aggressive military metaphorical conceptualizations of the body (as discussed in Chapter 3) to depicting the body as 'natural', as self-regulating and part of a wider ecological balance, with the words 'balance', 'harmony', 'regulate', 'spirit' and 'energy' prevailing. However, moral judgements are still not avoided, for such language serves to position the body as a metaphysical essence, and in doing so makes judgements based on what is 'good' and what is 'bad' for the body (Montgomery, 1991: 355–8). Moreover, the use of production/ mechanical metaphors to explain the body's workings is evident in the discourses of alternative therapies, particularly the use of the word 'energy', conforming to capitalist ideologies of production: 'Especially when energy appears in the context of ideas of balance or harmony of bodily energies, it suggests efficiency, a metaphor of the body as productive, not wasteful or static, but in tune with its environment and expanding in productive possibilities' (Coward, 1989: 57).

As a result, it may be contended that alternative therapies retain most aspects of medical ideology: notions of health and illness still have a medicalized and functional meaning (Crawford, 1980: 370). Even more so than biomedicine, many alternative therapies place an onus on individuals to take responsibility for their health, thus directing attention from the social and political causes of ill health: 'If natural health is locked within us, waiting to be released, then it lies within the individual power to achieve health' (Coward, 1989: 42). While apparently 'demedicalizing' patients' lives by propelling them away from orthodox medical therapies, the discourses and practices of alternative therapies simultaneously 'remedicalize' them by emphasizing the importance of lifestyle, modes of thought, emotions and spirituality to health states (Scott, 1999; Cant and Sharma, 2000). Alternative therapies thus do little to challenge the medical paradigm, for they are more concerned with practice and procedure than symbolic meaning. Indeed, they may be regarded as all the more insidious because they overtly offer an alternative to the prevailing model of health care while covertly legitimizing social inequality.

Since the 1970s, self-help and support groups became a popular strategy of resistance for those disaffected by medical dominance. Such groups offer the opportunity for people who feel isolated and alienated from others because of their illness to join together with like sufferers. Groups such as Alcoholics Anonymous have formed to provide mutual support, to demystify medicine and to gain control of services. Self-help women's clinics sprang up in the 1970s, in which, with the help of female health workers, women discussed their medical histories in small groups and shared breast and cervical self-examinations, the fitting of diaphragms and intra-uterine devices, and pregnancy testing and prenatal care in the group setting (Ruzek, 1981; Broom, 1991).

Like alternative therapies, the self-help movement has been subject to criticism for its middle-class orientation, its general failure to question the structural reasons for ill health, and the continued emphasis upon individual responsibility for health, without confronting the barriers to individual change. It has been argued that self-help groups continue to direct attention towards expanding the provision of health care rather than questioning the dynamic nature of the discursive constitution of illness and the body (Broom, 1991: 148–9). Moreover, the Foucauldian perspective sees self-help groups as extending the normalizing gaze, this time through the judgements of the members of the group, who replace medical professionals in maintaining constant surveillance over themselves and each other (Silverman, 1987: 230), often via use of the public confession (especially in such groups as Alcoholics Anonymous and weight-control groups).

Health advocacy and activist groups such as ACT UP, whose activities were described in Chapter 3, also pose a challenge to medical dominance by drawing the public's attention to instances of discrimination, inequity and poor treatment. However, such groups often demonstrate a paradoxical relationship with scientific medicine; on the one hand, decrying medical dominance and seeking greater control over the treatment process, but on the other, calling for increased access to medical treatment. ACT UP groups in the United States and Australia, for example, have staged demonstrations drawing attention to the slowness at which new drugs are trialled and developed, demanding access on the part of all people with HIV/AIDS to every new drug. The contradictions inherent in demanding increasing medical treatment while resenting medical dominance have not fully been addressed by such groups.

In recent times the Internet has offered an unparalleled opportunity for self-help groups to quickly exchange and update large volumes of information and provide emotional support. This may be particularly important for people who have been rendered immobile or incapacitated by an illness or disability. Individuals also seek medical information using the Internet: one recent Australian study found that almost one in three Internet users searched for health information online (Robotham, 2002b). Real-time discussion and chat groups allow individuals with the same ailment to communicate with each other quickly and easily around the world. Computerized forums have the benefits of providing anonymity if this is desired by participants, which to some extent alleviates the surveillance aspects of the group. Members may confess or recount intimate details of their experiences without having to reveal their names. So, too, the phenomenon of the computerized 'home page', in which ill people present their illness narratives, give individuals the opportunity to recount detailed accounts of their illness experiences for the edification of others who may be going through or facing the same experiences. These accounts, which may be highly critical of orthodox medicine or individual treatments or certain practitioners, allow patients to move from being the consumers of health care information to the producers of resources such as information and advice for others (Hardey, 1999, 2002).

The Internet health advice and support network blurs the boundaries between orthodox medical knowledge, consumer knowledge and alternative medical knowledge (Hardey, 1999, 2002). As such, this network has the potential to allow lay people to mount a challenge to the medical profession's control over information and resources, the full implications of which have yet to reveal themselves. Here again, however, issues of access to the technology are important in influencing the extent to which lay people can use it as an alternative source of information and support.

Conclusion

This chapter has presented a number of different major theoretical approaches used to analyse the role and function of power relations in the doctor–patient relationship. All these approaches acknowledge the existence of a differential of power in the medical encounter, but they vary in the extent to which they view medicine as oppressive. Medicine, from the functionalist perspective, is viewed as a means of alleviating deviance, a benevolent way of restoring patients to normality, and thus of maintaining social order in a consensualist society. In the eyes of political economists, medicine is largely an instrument of domination used by the ruling classes to maintain their powerful position, and should be replaced by self-help and community-led initiatives for health care. For those who have taken up the insights of poststructuralist and postmodernist theory, illness and disease are products of specific historical and political circumstances, with medical practices also responding to these circumstances. Some writers adopting these approaches recognize the need for a power imbalance to fulfil the expectations and needs of both doctors and patients, and therefore lean towards the functionalist perspective. Others conform more to the political economy perspective in seeing a struggle for power in the medical encounter with patients being controlled and oppressed by doctors. Yet others have identified a capacity for resistance and change opening up in the struggles for power over the body and the interstices between dominant discourses that occur in the medical encounter.

Interview studies and observations of doctors, nurses and other health professionals' behaviour and attitudes in settings such as the clinic and the hospital provide an alternative perspective on medical dominance to contrast with that of the patient. They show, for example, that doctors are forced to deal with patients' expectations of their omnipotence and often their desire not to share the uncertainty of their treatment, the need to reduce embarrassment, their own need to perform well, to progress in their career and avoid litigation, as well as institutional demands to deal with patients quickly, efficiently and without making too much of an emotional investment. They demonstrate, too, that rather than being uniformly oppressive and manipulative, the maintenance of medical dominance is frequently necessary to deal with these competing demands.

It may be concluded that to view power relations in the medical encounter as simply abusive and oppressive of patients' rights and agency, or by contrast as universally beneficent and mutually co-operative, is too simplistic an understanding of the complex nature of this social interaction. Power in the medical encounter may be both productive and oppressive; both patients and doctors have expectations and needs related to the encounter which may at times demand that the doctor take an authoritative stance. While there is limited scope for patients' resistance, to challenge this authority calls into question the whole nature and rationale of the medical encounter. Critics thus need to look more closely at the alternatives available to the traditional doctor–patient relationship.

6

Feminisms and Medicine

For at least two decades, feminist writing has been an important commentator upon medicine as an agent of social control and the social construction of gender in medical discourse. Feminist critiques of medicine have frequently gone to the heart of issues concerning the body, the illness experience, the changeable nature of disease categories and their use for social control, and relations of power between patients and medical professionals. However, as noted in Chapter 2, there has been a constant tension in feminist writings about the body and medicine between recognition of the uniqueness of women's embodied experience and the desire to deny that any such uniqueness exists. On the one hand, the capability of women to bear and breast-feed children and the changes in their bodies associated with menstruation, pregnancy and menopause have been valorized as constitutive of femininity, as evidence of women's specialness and power, as experiences to be enjoyed and welcomed as essential to femininity. On the other hand, concern about the ways in which such phenomena have historically been defined by patriarchy as the basis for women's inferiority and their exclusion from the public and economic spheres has led some feminist writers to deny women's embodiment, to seek to reduce differences between the sexes and to view women's physical experiences as purely social constructions constituted by medical and scientific discourses.

The rise of the second-wave feminist movement in the 1970s was accompanied by a trenchant critique of the ways in which biomedicine differentiates between social groups and supports hegemonic ideologies defining gender roles, as well as those dealing with social class and race. This critique highlighted the ways in which medical discourses have historically constituted a site of sexual discrimination, using medico-scientific justification for differentiating women from men on the basis of biology and anatomy and to provide 'scientific evidence' to prevent women from entering public life. More recently, some feminists have argued that the medicalization thesis adopted by many feminists writing about health in the 1970s, which tended towards viewing women's 'authentic' understandings of their bodies as being 'tainted' by medical discourses, is overly simplistic (Bransen, 1992). It has been pointed out that while the medical system has been a source of women's oppression, it has also contributed to their liberation. For example, some feminists argue that biomedicine has offered women greater control over their fertility due to developments in contraceptive technologies and has contributed to the dramatic reduction in the proportion of deaths attributable to childbirth in the space of a century.

Ehrenreich and English have lucidly articulated the difficulties of feminist political standpoints on biology:

> Say that menstruation is painful and distressing, and women will be arbitrarily barred from occupations that involve concentration and responsibility. Say that it is unnoticeable and that we are as consistently healthy as males are supposed to be, and all women will be required to lift the same weights and work the same long hours required of men regardless of the degree of discomfort experienced. Say that the last months of pregnancy are difficult, and we will be fired at the first signs of swelling. Say that there is 'nothing unhealthy about being pregnant', and we will be held to eight hours a day, five days a week. There are real dangers – for all of us – in either understating or exaggerating our needs as women. (1974: 88)

This chapter examines the vexed issues surrounding women's bodies and medicine in the context of feminist scholarship. In doing so, specific medical issues which have traditionally been designated as feminist concerns are discussed, including gynaecology, women's sexuality, menstruation, menopause, childbirth, contraception, prenatal screening and the new assisted conception technologies. The tension between the competing claims of biology and society/culture in moulding women's bodily experiences and their treatment at the hands of the medical profession is a continuing concern of the chapter, as is the historical link between past and contemporary medical discourses dealing with women's bodies.

Gynaecology, sexuality and the feminine body

Women's bodies have historically been represented and treated in medicine as especially threatening to the moral order and social stability of society, largely due to the seemingly uncontrollable and dangerous nature of their sexuality (Turner, 1995: Ch. 5). For centuries women have traditionally been defined as the Other in medical discourse, the 'sick' or incomplete version of men: as weaker, unstable, the source of infection, impure, the carriers of venereal disease or the source of psychological damage to their children (Ehrenreich and English, 1974: 6). Thus twin paradoxical ideologies have been supported: on the one hand, women as weak and defective, on the other, women as dangerous and polluting (1974: 14).

These ideologies have been expressed in the discourses and imagery of medical texts for centuries, and translated into practices. For example, contemporary anatomy textbooks designed for medical students, as did those published in the nineteenth century, still tend to portray the male body as the standard human body, against which the 'different' and 'inferior' female body is compared. The male body is described as the active agent or portrayed as more developed, stronger and firmer than the female body (Petersen, 1998). Illustrations in current medical textbooks routinely use male bodies to portray specific features shared by the sexes, making it impossible to learn female anatomy without first learning male anatomy, while comparative references to female anatomy make constant use of the terms 'smaller', 'feebler', 'weaker' or 'less developed' to demonstrate how women differ from men (Lawrence and Bendixen, 1992).

The emergence of the specialization of gynaecology provides an example of the ways in which women's and men's bodies have been viewed and treated differently by scientific medicine. Since the beginning of the nineteenth century, gynaecology has legitimated views that sexual activity and reproduction are more fundamental to women's than men's nature, and that therefore women are better suited to the domestic sphere as wives and mothers than taking part in the public arena of work, politics and commerce (Moscucci, 1990). Gynaecology identifies women's reproductive anatomy as a special field of study, for which there is no masculine counterpart. The specialization emerged with the Enlightenment and a growing interest in the 'science of man' and the need to distinguish scientifically the sexes from one another.

However, it has not always been the case that rigid distinctions have been made between the 'masculine' and the 'feminine' body. Recent histories of the human body have identified the dynamic and fluid nature of gender, strongly associating changes in perceptions of ideal femininity and masculinity with political interests evident at the time. For several thousand years before the Enlightenment, it was considered that male and female bodies were inherently the same; female genitals were considered the lesser, inverted homologues of male genitals. By 1800, however, writers were beginning to insist that the sexes were opposites, both physically and morally (Laqueur, 1987). In particular, the ovaries were identified as the 'control centres' of reproduction in female animals. This notion was translated to women: ovaries came to be regarded as 'the essence of femininity itself' (1987: 27). Women, by virtue of the menstrual cycle, came to be viewed as similar to animals experiencing sexual urges, needful of control by civilization. Claims as to the desirability of women's behaviour in the public and private spheres were predicated on the differences perceived between their bodies and those of men. This fundamental change in ways of thinking about gendered bodies may be regarded as being political and distinct of developments in scientific knowledge (1987: 4).

Schiebinger (1987) similarly argues that the first representations of the female skeleton appeared in Europe in the eighteenth century during a time in which there were attempts to define the position of women in European society: 'The interests of the scientific community were not arbitrary: anatomists focused attention on those parts of the body that were to become politically significant' (1987: 42). From the 1750s onwards, doctors in France and Germany developed an unprecedented strong interest in discovering and defining sex differences in parts of the human body, including bones, nerves and veins, so as to demonstrate the inherent deficiencies of the female sex. For example, in drawings of the female skeleton, the female skull was drawn as smaller than that of the male as proof that women's intellectual capabilities were inferior (Schiebinger, 1987). It was believed that rather than philosophy or theology, science could penetrate the dark secrets of femininity, providing conclusive evidence of the difference between the sexes based on men and women's 'natural capabilities' (Moscucci, 1990: 15).

It is worthy of note that the female body was routinely compared against the ideal of the European male body type at a time when there were mercantilist interests in promoting population growth, and hence childbearing was represented as the natural and desirable destiny of women (Schiebinger, 1987: 53). In concert with this ideology of motherhood, the uterus became valued rather than denigrated as it was previously. While women were often represented as more animalistic than men in Victorian writings, because they were controlled by their reproductive organs, they were also described as the repository of traditional wisdom and knowledge, morally superior to men, suitable for raising children and caring for the ill, hence defusing their dangerous sexuality (Moscucci, 1990: 37).

In medical writings of the time, women were portrayed as physically delicate, irresponsible creatures in need of men's protection and guardianship; in short, as incomplete adults (Moscucci, 1990: 31–2). Too much development of a woman's brain was said to atrophy the uterus, hindering the very function for which women were designed by nature. For example, in a work entitled 'Concerning the Physiological and Intellectual Weakness of Women', the German scientist P. Moebius wrote: 'If we wish woman to fulfil the task of motherhood fully she cannot possess a masculine brain. If the feminine abilities were developed to the same degree as those of the male, her maternal organs would suffer and we should have before us a repulsive and useless hybrid' (quoted by Ehrenreich and English, 1974: 28). The Harvard professor Edward Clarke opposed women's entry to higher education on the grounds that intellectual work would reduce the supply of nerve-energy to the female reproductive system, producing 'monstrous brains and puny bodies; abnormally active cerebration and abnormally weak digestion; flowing thought and constipated bowels' (quoted by Moscucci, 1990: 104). Similarly, the 'evidence' that women's pelvises were larger than men's was used to support arguments that they were designed for child-bearing and should be confined to that role.

In the nineteenth century, medical writings on the dissection of women's bodies for the purposes of furthering anatomical knowledge positioned doctors as explorers of the mysterious dark recesses of the feminine body, entering unknown territory like colonialists penetrating the wilds of Africa. Medical discourses portrayed doctors and anatomists as conquering heroes in the quest for treasure and power. The penetration of surgery into women's bodies in the name of anatomy provided a way for the male members of the medical profession to 'know' the female sex as completely as possible, to open up and expose her mysteries (Showalter, 1990: 129–31). By contrast, the inside of men's bodies seemed not to hold such mystery, overtly perhaps because the male genitalia are outside the body and are therefore 'visible appendages rather than mysterious orifices' (1990: 133). However, at the deeper ideological level, the dissection and examination of the innards of the woman was a substitute for self-knowledge, symbolizing the gaining of control over a threatening femininity (1990: 134).

With the development of women's hospitals in England in the nineteenth century, gynaecology became centralized in these institutions, eventually excluding general practitioners and establishing gynaecology as a recognized specialist practice. These hospitals provided the opportunity for male practitioners to expand their knowledge of women's diseases, for they were, in effect, 'a gallery of female types as well as a living museum of pathology' (Moscucci, 1990: 101). The introduction of the speculum for vaginal examinations in the mid-nineteenth century promoted disquiet and controversy in medical circles, for it was believed to incite sexual interest in young unmarried women and 'blunt' women's modesty (Moscucci, 1990; Dally, 1991). Discourses on the use of the speculum alluded to the sexual nature of its use, using the metaphor of medical science as rape by referring to the undesirability of penetration, the flouting of moral virginity and the loss of innocence caused by its introduction into the body. For example, one experimental physiologist argued in the British medical journal *Lancet* in 1850 that 'the female who has been subjected to such treatment is not the same person in delicacy and purity as she was before' (quoted by Moscucci, 1990: 115).

In the nineteenth and early twentieth centuries menstruation and pregnancy were treated as abnormal and as sicknesses rather than normal bodily functions. Women were seen as being controlled by their uterus and ovaries: doctors found uterine and ovarian 'disorders' behind almost every female complaint, from headaches to sore throats and indigestion (Ehrenreich and English, 1974: 29). Medical procedures such as removal of the ovaries, hysterectomy and clitoridectomy were used to treat all types of illnesses and mental states, including what was regarded as being an inappropriately high libido (Wertz and Wertz, 1981: 167). In the mid to late nineteenth century and early twentieth century, women of the upper classes were constricted by their clothing and social customs into invalidism, spending their lives indoors sewing, sketching, reading and supervising servants and children. It was considered acceptable and fashionable to retire to bed with 'sick headaches', 'nerves' and other mysterious ailments (Ehrenreich and English, 1974: 17–18).

Admittedly, the risks of childbearing at the time were comparatively high: in the United States in 1915, 61 women died for every 10,000 live babies born, compared with two per 10,000 in the 1970s. Tuberculosis was also a health problem: in the United States, for every 100 women aged 20 years in 1865, more than five would be dead from tuberculosis by the age of 30, and more than eight would be dead by the age of 50 (Ehrenreich and English, 1974: 19–20). However, even physically healthy upper- and middle-class women were cast in the roles of perpetual invalids based on their feminine physiology, encouraged to see themselves as ill whenever they menstruated, and to avoid exercise and most activities. As both menstruation and pregnancy were cast in the medical literature as 'medical problems', all women became potential patients subject to the surveillance and ministrations of male members of the medical profession (Turner, 1995).

The emergence of the condition of 'hysteria' in the nineteenth century is a clear example of the manner in which medically defined and documented illnesses are embedded in social, political and historical conditions. The condition is the apotheosis of the way in which women at that time were defined as invalids, ruled by their reproductive organs. Hysteria was an illness that affected upper- and upper-middle-class women almost exclusively in the nineteenth century. Its name comes from the Greek word for uterus, and it was seen as a disease of this organ, and therefore a condition peculiar and unique to women. The symptoms of hysteria included fits and fainting, loss of voice, loss of appetite, coughing or sneezing, hysterical screaming, laughing and crying. It had no organic cause, and seemed resistant to medical treatment. As the tendency to hysterical behaviour seemed particularly common among young single women, old widows, divorced women or women who were unmarried and pursuing careers, the conclusion was made in medical discourses that the condition was caused by women's failure to pursue 'normal' sexual activity with their husbands and childbirth, with the implication that women could only resist the illness of hysteria by conforming to societal expectations of respectability (Turner, 1995: Ch. 5).

Likewise, the 'rest cure' which was fashionable for privileged women may be viewed as stereotyping women as delicate and unsuitable for demanding activities, and thus constraining their potential for active resistance to their social confinement. The 'rest cure' was frequently administered by medical practitioners to women during the late nineteenth century if they displayed severe nervous symptoms, including patients diagnosed with hysteria but also with hypochondria, neurasthenics and physical complaints such as cardiac, renal, gynaecological and neurological disorders. Such women were advised to relinquish control to their physicians and to desist from any kind of mental or physical activity or stimulation. They were confined to bed for periods from six weeks to two months, secluded from company, fed continuously and administered with vaginal douches and rectal enemas by a nurse. Some women were not permitted by their doctor to sit up, sew, write or read for up to four or five weeks. Patients were also subjected to 'moral re-education', involving the use of various psychotherapeutic approaches on the part of the doctor, including teaching the patient principles of philosophy, patience, resignation and consolation using suggestion, logical argument, support of the patient's willpower and the management of her emotions (Bassuk, 1986).

While the identification of hysteria in privileged women in epidemic proportions and the fashionability of administering of the 'rest cure' may be regarded as evidence of oppressive medical dominance and constrictive of women's freedom, viewed from the Victorian woman's perspective the hysterical fit may have been the only acceptable outburst possible for women in a society in which illness was expected of privileged women (Ehrenreich and English, 1974: 39–41). Similarly, the rest cure enabled women to avoid responsibilities or the sexual demands of authoritarian husbands in a socially acceptable way, providing them with the opportunity to avoid confronting their own sexual feelings and conflicts at a time in which women were beginning to question traditional domestic roles (Bassuk, 1986: 147–8). In the Victorian era there were very few outlets for women's frustrations and rage at being socially and physically confined; hence, frustration expressed in the form of a hysterical fit or neurasthenic symptoms became an act of rebellion, even while such behaviour was shaped by the prevailing expectations of appropriate womanly behaviour.

Unfortunately, such behaviour ultimately perpetuated the stereotypes of femininity; women's dependency on men was fostered by medical discourse, and the attempts women made to rebel against their role were medicalized, seen as 'proof' of women's need for a confined and secluded life (Bassuk, 1986: 147). Medical attention directed towards women became surveillance in detecting the first signs of rebelliousness and interpreting them as symptoms of a 'disease' which had to be treated and cured: 'The more women became hysterical, the more doctors became punitive toward the disease; and at the same time, they began to see the disease everywhere themselves until they were diagnosing every independent act by a woman, especially a women's rights action, as "hysterical"' (Ehrenreich and English, 1974: 42).

The socially constructed nature of these illnesses is demonstrated by the fact that at the same time as wealthy women were positioned as dependent, fragile invalids unsuited for physical activity, working-class women were working long hours in crowded factories or sweat shops, with the constant danger of fatal or disfiguring industrial accidents, or as domestic labour or prostitutes. While privileged women were encouraged to retire to their beds when menstruating, working-class women were not given time off by employers for pregnancy or recovery from childbirth, and there were few doctors willing to attend women who could not afford their services (Ehrenreich and English, 1974: 4–8). Working-class women, like working-class men, were seen by the upper classes as agents of contagion, spreading disease from their homes in the slums (1974: 62).

The historical legacy of the medical profession's fear of the female sexual body is evident in discourses on gynaecology in modern times. For example, Scully and Bart (1981) analysed the contents of general gynae-cology texts published in the United States during the mid to late twenti-eth century. They found a persistent bias towards greater concern with the patient's husband than with the patient herself, and that women were represented as anatomically designed to reproduce, nurture their infants and keep their husbands sexually satisfied. In the 1940s and early 1950s, women were described as sexually unresponsive in the textbooks, but encouraged to feign enjoyment for the sake of their husbands. In the Kinsey era (1953 to 1962), despite the findings of Kinsey, gynaecologists continued to cling to the notion of the vaginal orgasm and labelled those patients who did not experience it as 'frigid'. In the mid to late 1960s and early 1970s, at least half the textbooks examined still maintained that pro-creation was the major function of sex for women, and Masters and Johnson's findings concerning the greater intensity of the female libido compared to that of the male went largely unreported.

Laws (1990) examined six commonly used contemporary medical text-books on gynaecology and a number of recently published articles in medical journals. She found that the value of the womb to women was praised in medical textbooks in almost mystical terms as the seat and symbol of women's femininity. Dysmenorrhoea, or menstrual pain, was frequently treated in medical textbooks as often exaggerated by women, and represented as common to women who are sexually frustrated, single or neurotic, indulge in an 'unhealthy lifestyle' or do not have the 'right' atti-tude towards menstruation. In the gynaecology texts, discussion about pre-menstrual tension was patchy and incomplete, with little clarity about what defines the difference between 'all women' and 'pre-menstrual tension sufferers' (1990: 201f). It may be argued, therefore, that the condition of 'pre-menstrual tension' inhibits women's recognition and public discussion of any negative changes around menstruation, for it reinforces the notion that women are ruled by their reproductive organs and provides a means by which women can be discredited publicly and privately (1990: 214).

Contraception and abortion

Contraception and abortion are focal points of societal ambivalence about the feminine role, the right of women to take control over their bodies and their reproductive destinies, and the subsequent impact upon their poten-tial for emancipation. Controversies over the provision of contraception and safe methods of contraception to women have revolved around notions of the ideal of motherhood for all women and the desire of the medical profession to maintain control over women's reproduction.

It is interesting to note that historically the contraceptive pill was a belated development in the technology of birth control. The basic scientific and technical prerequisites for its development existed 13 years before any drug company began research or development work aimed at producing the pill, and it was 22 years before it was first sold to women (Walsh, 1980: 182). While World War II may have been one reason for this delay, the main reason was the strong antipathy of the medical profession towards research into new forms of contraception. Doctors argued against birth control on both medical and moral grounds (1980: 184–5). At the end of the nineteenth century, when the first-wave feminist movement began to campaign for the right to effective and safe birth control, doctors claimed its effects included 'galloping cancer, sterility and nymphomania in women; mental decay, amnesia and cardiac palpitations in men; in both sexes the practice was likely to produce mania leading to suicide' (quoted by Walsh, 1980: 184).

In the 1920s, contraception was still considered 'distinctly dangerous to health', sterility and 'mental degeneration in subsequent offspring' being among the alleged effects (Walsh, 1980: 184). In 1925, the editor of the *Journal of the American Medical Association* asserted that there were no safe and effective birth control methods (Gordon, 1978: 152). Yet it seems that at the same time as male doctors were decrying the use of birth control for others, seeing it as a threat to their learned authority and professional status, they were among the earliest to use birth control to limit the size of their own families (Walsh, 1980: 184–5).

Although in the early twentieth century contraceptives continued to be associated with promiscuity, vice and prostitution, fear of overpopulation gave credence to research on contraception, and a rise in living standards in the western world and the beginnings of the feminist and human rights movements served to give greater respectability to its use (Gordon, 1978: 176). However, eugenic concerns began to predominate over the concerns of the early feminist movement for women's emancipation from incessant child-bearing, and eventually dominated the birth control debate in the 1920s (1978: 170). For example, one of the leading proponents of birth control in the United States, Margaret Sanger, wrote in 1919: 'More children from the fit, less from the unfit – that is the chief issue of birth control' (quoted by Gordon, 1978: 170). While motherhood continued to be affirmed as the main source of women's fulfilment, family planning activists argued that small families offered economic and health benefits (Gordon, 1978: 177). Population control was seen as a cure for poverty (Wajcman, 1991: 76).

When members of the medical profession eventually began to accept these arguments, they maintained that contraceptive advice should only be given to women whose life or health was in danger, thus providing for continuing control over the regulation of women's reproduction by preserving the sole power to prescribe or fit contraceptives (Walsh, 1980: 186–7). Even today, there are relatively few novel, safe contraceptive choices for women, and nearly all of them involve consulting a medical professional. The development of contraceptive technologies in the twentieth century was firmly oriented towards heterosexual men's definition of sexual activity. The contraceptive pill allows men to avoid responsibility for contraception, and solves the problem of the diminishment of pleasure associated with condoms. For women, the freedom from worry about contraception provided by the pill and the associated potential for sexual enjoyment comes at the cost of long-time medicalization and potential health-threatening side-effects (Wajcman, 1991: 77–8). Decisions about research into and the marketing of contraceptive technologies are routinely made by male-dominated management in international drug companies, research teams and national governments. Although there are well-documented medical side-effects of using the contraceptive pill, especially for those women who smoke cigarettes, corporate and professional interests militate against its replacement in the global market by an alternative product (Newman, 1985: 136; Wajcman, 1991: 76). Drug companies have routinely used women living in rural areas of developing countries for the testing of new drugs, including the controversial Depo Provera injectable steroid (Newman, 1985: 136).

Ambivalence about the role of the contraceptive pill in freeing women to enter the workforce is reflected in the tendency of the news media to devote dramatic headlines to the health risks of the pill, while at the same time drawing an association between the choice of a career over motherhood and the risk of developing cancer. This tendency was noted in an analysis of the 1983 'Pill Scare' in the British press, in which a moral panic about the dangers of taking the pill was generated, with overtones of retribution for 'promiscuous' sexual activity which did not lead to motherhood (Wellings, 1985). In a study I carried out of representations of breast cancer between 1987 and 1990 in the Australian press (Lupton, 1994b), I found that the linking of breast cancer with reproductive choices was apparent in several news items about breast cancer. Articles reported on numerous occasions that if women chose to delay having children or 'failed' to have children they put themselves at much higher risk of developing breast cancer. This was linked with evidence showing that 'affluent', 'professional', 'yuppie', 'single' or 'career' women were at greater risk. The latent message conveyed in such statements suggested that women who refuse to adopt the traditional feminine maternal role and choose instead a professional, well-paid career are courting disaster and bodily punishment for not fulfilling their biological destinies.

The development of a new orally administered drug, RU486, for use as an early abortifacient technology inspired much controversy in the late 1980s and early 1990s. Techniques of abortion have historically attracted contention, based on moral and ethical issues concerning the right of the foetus to life versus the right of pregnant women not to give birth to an unwanted child. The introduction of the drug RU486, used in conjunction with a progesterone injection or suppository to trigger the shedding of the uterine lining up to the eighth week of pregnancy, has engendered multiple constructions according to the key groups either advocating or opposing its use. For the scientists involved in developing RU486, the drug represents progress, a new solution, career success, the triumph of technological medicine. Family planning and population control organizations see RU486 as a relatively safe and effective way to allow women to control the size of their families, and the problem for them is lack of access. For pharmaceutical companies the drug is assessed in terms of its profitability and the risk of litigation or negative public response, while medical groups tend to view RU486 as a wonder drug whose provision is thwarted by politicians intent on limiting medical autonomy. Anti-abortion groups view RU486 as cheapening human life, making abortions an easier choice for women and potentially dangerous for women who take it, while feminist pro-choice groups see the drug as a breakthrough discovery that renders abortion a more dignified, less invasive, safer procedure, and offers women from developing countries the possibility of legal abortion (Raymond et al., 1991; Clarke and Montini, 1993).

Yet some women's health movement groups have been wary of the uncritical acceptance of the drug, noting its disadvantages which include the necessity of multiple medical visits, the possibility of severe cramping and bleeding and unknown side-effects and long-term consequences of the dose of hormones involved. They argue that the drug should only be offered to women after rigorous clinical testing, and then should only be presented as one choice among several abortion technologies, and that women should only choose it having been provided with full information about the drug (Raymond et al., 1991; Clarke and Montini, 1993). There is thus a constellation of competing discourses and perspectives on RU486, very few of which actually attempt to consider the views of women users themselves as the individuals directly affected by the introduction of the technology (Clarke and Montini, 1993: 64–6).

Menstruation and menopause

While menstruating women may no longer necessarily be viewed as automatic invalids in contemporary western societies, it is evident that menstrual rules and taboos serve to mark out the woman as Other, as different, whether she is represented as contaminating or as vulnerable and needful of protection. Drawing upon Douglas' (1980/1966) work on symbolic cultural rules about dirt and pollution, menstrual discharge may be regarded as matter 'out of place' in that it breaches the boundaries of a body that normally contains blood unless there is injury (Buckley and Gottlieb, 1988; Koutroulis, 2001). The potent symbolic meanings of blood, relating to death, pain, loss of control and warfare – that is, general bodily and societal disorder – and the regular emergence of menstrual blood from the uterus and vagina – parts of the body which are themselves considered dirty and contaminating – combine to render menstrual blood as a highly meaningful and anxiety-provoking fluid. The socio-cultural anxieties around the possible contaminating nature of menstruation is demonstrated in television and magazine advertisements for tampons and napkins, in which these products are referred to euphemistically as 'feminine *hygiene* products' and the capacity of such products to provide 'protection', 'freedom from worry' and 'cleanliness' for their wearer is constantly reiterated.

Yet menstruation is also linked to positive notions of femininity, the achievement of sexual maturity, fecundity, lack of pregnancy, normality, bodily order and good health, and is a symbol of bodily renewal (Lee, 2002). The ceasing of menstruation among anorexic women, for example, is generally represented in the medical and popular literature as a sign of ill health and bodily dysfunction rather than as a blessing, while the ceasing of menstruation in menopause can be regarded as both a welcome relief and a mourned loss of femininity. Consequently, amenorrhoea (temporary lack of menstruation) is regarded in western societies as abnormal and pathological, even though in other historical times and in other contemporary cultures the regular menstruation of the 'normal' western cycle was not experienced by the majority of women, because of constant pregnancy or undernutrition (Buckley and Gottlieb, 1988: 44–5). Even in contemporary western societies, many women experience temporary amenorrhoea or irregular and unpredictable menstruation. The regular, 28-day 'menstrual cycle' as it is commonly perceived in western societies may thus be considered culturally constructed.

The gendered nature of western societies is such that the social meanings of menstruation are inherently political, especially in a society where men have greater power than women and notions about 'nature' are used to justify this power. The inextricable cultural link of menstruation with child-bearing and thence to femininity means that women who do not menstruate are regarded as less than fully female (Laws, 1990: 3–5). Hypothesizing that men's attitudes towards menstruation are the source of women's feelings, Laws chose the unusual strategy of interviewing British men rather than women about their attitudes to menstruation. Based on her research, she speculates that the pollution beliefs which some men express about the uncleanliness of menstrual blood is evidence of their powerful position over that of women: 'Dirt represents lack of self-control, and those whom the powerful wish to control are expected to be eager to demonstrate their compliance' (1990: 36).

Many of the men interviewed in this study perceived menstruation as disgusting, expressed in jokes and narratives about tampons and sex during menstruation. The men did not readily tend to make the link between menstruation and the reproductive process, while in medical texts this link was made emphatically: 'The jokes and talk which go on in men-only groups, when they mention menstruation, focus on what men see as the sexual significance of periods, never on its reproductive meaning' (Laws, 1990: 105). Men talked about how it affected their sexual access to women. By comparison, gynaecologists writing about menstruation in medical texts expressed ambiguous ideas, emphasizing on the one hand the 'normality' of the process and on the other, drawing upon discourses of disorder and disease related to menstruation. For example, in three medical texts the shedding of the uterine lining was described as 'necrosis', or the death of cells (1990: 137).

Among women themselves there are paradoxical beliefs and concepts about the symbolic role of menstruation in their lives. Women interviewed about their feelings and beliefs concerning menstruation articulated three genres of explanation (Bransen, 1992). The first was the genre of emancipation, characterized by an active, self-assured and responsible 'me', controlling and coping well with any distress associated with menstruation. The second, the objective genre, conceived of the body and the menstrual cycle as an object belonging to certain experts, such as doctors. The menstrual cycle was seen as having a valid function – preparation for bearing children – but was largely regarded as negative. Finally, there was the natural genre, a more positive conceptualization in which the menstrual cycle was viewed as an object of Nature, an essential part of being a woman, giving signals and advice to the woman and cleansing the body of its 'poisons'. While there are important differences between these conceptualizations, in all three genres of explanation the menstruating body is largely viewed as separate from 'me', from subjectivity. While the women's accounts were not simply repeating medical images of menstruation, fragments of medical theories were undoubtedly present, and all three genres allowed space for a doctor to intervene in the case of disorders of the menstrual cycle (see Lee, 2002, for similar findings).

Like menstruation, menopause is a process which is rarely mentioned publicly by those experiencing it, and until very recently, has attracted little attention from feminist scholars. However, with the publication in 1991 of Germaine Greer's controversial book, *The Change: Women, Ageing and the Menopause*, in which she criticizes the use of hormone replacement therapy (HRT), menopause began to receive a greater level of public attention and debate, and also sociological investigation. Menopause is a process which is idiosyncratic, indeterminate and open-ended, and is subject to contested definitions, often centring around its status as a disease which requires treatment (Lock, 1986; Kaufert, 1988; Kagawa-Singer et al., 2002; Green et al., 2002). In westernized countries, menopause has become medicalized in the medical literature, treated as a deficiency disease which may be 'corrected' by HRT and defined as a generalized abstract concept which is independent of individual women's social, cultural, racial and economic backgrounds and personal experiences (Kaufert, 1988). The menopausal woman, in both medical and popular discourses, is represented as deficient, out of control, no longer fully feminine and therefore not sexually desirable. The valorizing of HRT (and 'natural' alternatives such as phyto-oestrogens) presupposes that oestrogen defines femininity, and that a lack of it must be treated with replacement hormones (Lupton, 1996; Harding, 1997).

Research has shown that, like menstruation, menopause is subject to a wide degree of interpretation on the part of women who have experienced it, and is not necessarily subject to medical definitions. For example, Kaufert's (1988) interviews with Canadian women found that they tended to define themselves as menopausal if there had been a change in their accustomed pattern of menstruation, and did not wait until menstruation had stopped entirely (which is the medical definition of menopause). For these women, then, menopause was not an *event*, but a *process* based on their own perception of what was normal for them. Indeed, some women who were experiencing hot flushes called themselves menopausal regardless of the status of their menstrual cycle. Another investigation of the meanings of menstrual loss among a group of pre- and post-menopausal women living in a small village in South Wales (Skultans, 1988) found that women's attitudes towards their own menstrual periods fell into one of two categories. Some women wished to avoid the loss of menstrual blood, while others desired it and thought menstruation beneficial to their health. The first category believed that menstruation was an unwanted occurrence, physically damaging and weakening, and hence looked forward to the transition and were eager to reach menopause as soon as possible. Women in the second category regarded menstruation as vital to their well-being, as rejuvenating, viewing blood loss as correcting sluggishness, and insisting on the value of 'a good clearance' to 'right the system'. For these women, menopause was conceived of as a 'threat' to their feminine identity (Skultans, 1988: 142–4, 159). Such research further demonstrates that there are conflicting discourses among women themselves concerning the value and importance of menstruation, and subsequently menopause, to their self-identity.

Like menstruation, menopause may have many positive as well as negative meanings. Particularly for women in Anglo/European cultures, for example, the bodily symptoms of menopause may be perceived as distressing and embarrassing, requiring medication such as HRT, and menopause as consonant with the negative meanings of ageing, loss of control over bodily processes (as in 'hot flushes') and loss of fertility (Lupton, 1996; Green et al., 2002; Kagawa-Singer et al., 2002). For many other women, however, menopause may be regarded positively as signalling the beginning of a new phase in their lives, one in which, as older women with grown-up children, they are able to become more independent and free to focus on their own needs rather than those of dependants. This is the dominant view, for example, of women of Japanese ethnic background (Kagawa-Singer et al., 2002).

Unlike menstruation and menopause, pre-menstrual syndrome has been accorded much publicity in the mass media, especially following trials in Britain in 1980 in which two women charged with murder used diminished responsibility due to pre-menstrual syndrome as a defence. The roots of contemporary discourses on the pre-menstrual syndrome have been traced back to those on hysteria in the late nineteenth century

(Rodin, 1992). Both groups of discourses refer to the irrationality, lack of control and madness of women ruled by their reproductive cycles and organs. Such discourses serve to reduce the behaviour of women to the functioning of their bodies, making them personally responsible for their behaviour, and removing consideration of the social context of women's lives. Indeed, Laws (1990) found in her interviews with men that a number of them expressed the belief that 'at that time of the month' women were moody and unreliable, at the mercy of their hormones.

It has been asserted by some commentators that pre-menstrual syndrome has emerged as a social problem in the political context of women's entry into the paid labour force and the arguments of the second-wave feminist movement for greater equality and increased opportunities for women, inciting debate about the 'appropriate' position of women in late twentieth-century society (Rittenhouse, 1991: 413). One study found that debates about pre-menstrual tension in the American news media and medical literature came to revolve around the assessment of the ability of women to participate fully in the public domain. The most recent shift in discourse, emerging at the end of the 1980s, represented a modification of previous views on pre-menstrual syndrome in the medical literature and less focus on the unpredictability of pre-menstrual women in the popular literature. Feminist challenges have appeared to have shaped popular and medical discourses to some extent, providing evidence that medicine is not necessarily the ultimate determinant of dominant discourses on the body (Rittenhouse, 1991).

Another study of articles on pre-menstrual syndrome appearing in magazines published in the United States between 1980 and 1987 (Chrisler and Levy, 1990) found that articles tended towards reporting negative menstrual cycle changes, presenting a confusing array of symptoms and contradictory treatment recommendations. Negative changes mentioned in articles included bloating/swelling, depression, chest pains, ringing in the ears, numbness/tingling in the hands and feet, cold sores, bruising easily, cold sweats, eye problems and poor judgement, hot flushes, emotional outbursts, muscle spasms, oily skin and hair, low energy, increased thirst, lack of appetite, feelings of worthlessness, panic attacks, alcoholic bouts ... the list goes on. While some positive changes were mentioned, such as heightened sensitivity and self-esteem, good concentration, increased creativity, sense of well-being, bursts of energy, euphoria and increased libido, these represented only 15 per cent of all changes mentioned. The articles referred to the menstrual cycle as 'the cycle of misery', a 'cascade of chemical changes', 'the monthly monster', the 'inner beast' and the 'war being waged by the body's hormones'. Pre-menstrual women were described as 'prisoners of our hormones', 'cripples', 'handicapped', 'raging beasts' and 'raging animals' (1990: 98). The reliance on the nineteenth-century notion of women as controlled by their menstrual cycle as if they were lower-order animals on heat is evident in this contemporary use of language in popular texts.

These studies demonstrate that language and discourse are particularly important in constructing notions of wellness and disease in relation to women's bodies. As discussed in Chapter 3, Martin (1987, 1990b, 1991) has exposed the ways in which medical literature refers to menstruation as wasteful, a loss, failure, the ovum as passive, while the male reproductive system is described in ways which emphasize production, dynamism, aggression, success. Menopause is commonly described in medical texts as failed production, a breakdown of the system, decay, a pathological state, while childbirth is represented using the mechanical/capitalist metaphor, in which '[t]he woman's body is the machine and the doctor is the mechanic or technician who "fixes" it' (1987: 54), while the product of her 'labour' is the baby. Alternatively, the uterus is portrayed as a machine that produces the baby, with the doctor in charge as the supervisor or foreman of the labour process (1987: 63).

A dominant metaphor used in medical textbooks to describe women's reproduction was that of a signalling system, in which the hormones were portrayed as 'communicating' to tissues or organs, while the hypothalamus 'gives directions' to the pituitary gland. This metaphorical system mimics the dominant hierarchical form of organization in western societies. The system of communication is presented as being geared to production: of female hormones, ova and ultimately, a foetus. As a result, when this ultimate outcome does not eventuate, the female reproductive cycle is portrayed negatively, as wasted production, death and failure (Martin, 1987: 40–5). As one medical textbook claimed: 'When fertilization fails to occur, the endometrium is shed, and a new cycle starts. That is why it used to be taught that "menstruation is the uterus crying for lack of a baby"' (1987: 45).

The propensity of medical discourses to view menopause as a pathological, abnormal state may therefore be viewed as stemming not only from the negative stereotypes of ageing women in western societies, but from the metaphor of the properly functioning human body as an information-processing system like a computer (Martin, 1987: 42) (see Chapter 3 for a detailed discussion of this metaphor of the body). In menopause, this signalling system is represented as malfunctioning, breaking down the system of authority because of lack of response on the part of the ageing reproductive organs in response to the 'messages' sent by the pituitary gland. This lack of production is a horror for post-industrial society, as is out-of-control production (for example, the way that cancer cells are viewed as proliferating wildly, to the detriment of the body's functioning). Hence the negative representations of menstruation, which 'fails to produce' a foetus, and the medical depiction of the female reproductive system at menopause as a nightmare of industrial chaos resulting from organization members who no longer perform their designated functions to order (1987: 43).

Childbirth and the struggle for control

The changing nature of childbirth over the past two centuries demonstrates the increasing control of the medical profession over women's bodies. Up until the close of the seventeenth century, attendance at childbirth had always been the preserve of women. Midwives assisted women in labour, while the labouring woman's close women friends and relatives attended and assisted. Their experience and knowledge about birthing was passed from one generation of women to the next. Throughout the eighteenth century a struggle took place between female midwives and the emerging male-dominated medical profession over the control of intervention in the birth process. The use of forceps, which enabled the delivery of live infants in cases where previously either mother or child would have died, became the exclusive domain of physicians and surgeons, and was associated with the emerging (male-dominated) profession of medicine. The introduction of the forceps gave these men the edge over female midwives who were adept at the manual delivery of babies and who had all the practical knowledge about birth and birthing (Wilson, 1985; Moscucci, 1990; Wajcman, 1991: Ch. 3). According to custom, midwives were not allowed to use instruments as an accepted part of their practice. Therefore, if the birth was obstructed, a male practitioner was sent for: 'The task of the midwife was to deliver a *living* child, the task of the male practitioner was to deliver a *dead* one' (Wilson, 1985: 137, emphasis in the original).

Midwifery resisted the pressure of the male medical profession for many years, but became vulnerable with the rise of scientific medicine during the nineteenth century. Due to increasing medical regulations and municipal ordinances designed at excluding women from obstetrics, from the early Middle Ages women were forced out of attending births. Female midwives were discredited and marginalized. Attempts to professionalize medicine led to competitiveness amongst physicians, surgeons, barbers and midwives to establish control over fields of medical practice. Scientific knowledge became valorized over experiential knowledge, and women midwives were denied access to medical training. Midwifery became associated with superstition and witchcraft (Ehrenreich and English, 1973; Brighton Women and Science Group, 1980; Wertz and Wertz, 1981; Oakley, 1987; Blumenfeld-Kosinski, 1990: Ch. 3). The 'man midwife' came into being in the middle decades of the eighteenth century, and treatises of midwifery began to be written for male practitioners, which, from 1750 onwards, criticized the female-dominated ceremony of childbirth (Wilson, 1985: 140).

Because of its technological and surgical nature, caesarean birth was among the first obstetrical procedures to be lost to the control of midwives and placed under the aegis of male practitioners. Blumenfeld-Kosinski (1990: 90) notes an increasing presence of male attendants at caesarean births in illustrations from the fourteenth century, when midwives had exclusive control over the birth and no men were portrayed as participating at the scene, to as early as the fifteenth and sixteenth centuries, when midwives were excluded as active participants in such births, and male surgeons were depicted as performing surgery on the labouring woman. Thus technical intervention rapidly became the hallmark of male medical practice and a means of excluding women.

The emergence of the male medical profession's treatment of the diseases of women related to childbirth has been linked to concerns about the reproduction of the population and the quality of the labour force in the late eighteenth century (Moscucci, 1990: 11–13). As a result of these concerns, medical men began to address themselves to the standards of midwifery practice, the diseases of child-bearing women and those of infants. Midwifery practices were criticized for the high level of infant and maternal deaths, with the ideology of the rationality of science viewed as providing the answer. Moreover, the issue of professional rivalry was integral to the increasing domination of men over childbirth. The social background, training and career patterns and aspirations of men in gynaecology contributed to the clinical and institutional development of the specialization. These included the professional marginality of male midwives and their attempts to gain higher status within the medical profession, and the centrality of midwifery and gynaecology to nineteenth-century general practice, which meant that the regulation of gynaecology was believed to be an important part of the organization of medical practice as a whole (Moscucci, 1990; see also Dally, 1991).

Since the late nineteenth century, pregnancy and childbirth have become progressively medicalized and the pregnant woman cast as a patient. While hardly any women received prenatal medical care in the United States in 1900, by the end of that century almost all received such care regularly. Over that time in the medical literature, pregnancy became portrayed as more pathological and pregnant women as therefore requiring close medical surveillance (Barker, 1998). There is currently a lively debate about the necessity for having all births attended in hospital, and the safety of home births. Before World War II the majority of women gave birth at home, attended by midwives and possibly their general practitioners. In 1927, only 15 per cent of infants were born in hospitals or other institutions in Britain. However, by 1985, 99 per cent of all deliveries occurred in hospitals in Britain (Stanworth, 1987: 10). In the mid-twentieth century, the trend grew towards the routine use of anaesthesia, the resort to forceps, the artificial induction of births, the standard practice of the episiotomy and caesarean sections.

In the 1970s and 1980s, feminist commentators began to examine the treatment of labouring women by the medical profession, and questioned the ideologies underlying medical discourses on childbirth. Feminist critiques contended that the desire to create better, safer facilities for labouring women had turned into a system whereby women were processed through pregnancy and after, according to some 'average' pattern. Some commentators argue that most women have an uneventful labour, and would not be better off giving birth in hospital. Rather, the inexorable move towards hospitalizing women at confinement suits the requirements of the medical profession, by locating all women in the same place (Oakley, 1987: 52).

Critics assert that there have been two main effects of transporting birth into the hospital: first, the emphasis is on curative medicine, on the pathological problems of illness, their discovery, measurement and cure; second, women, at an extremely vulnerable time in their lives, are put into a system which has very little to do with them as individuals but is concerned only to process the greatest number of women through birth without incident. In the process, the woman is placed in a position of compliance with expert advice throughout her pregnancy and delivery, and her personal needs and wishes tend to be ignored. Birth is increasingly seen as something that cannot be left alone, that must be interfered with, monitored and 'helped along'. The mother is expected to fit into given images and concepts and to comply with doctors' instructions. The emphasis is usually on the needs of the baby rather than the mother. The situation encourages the pregnant woman to be distant from the process, to hand over control of her body to others and to take advice, which may make it difficult to take back control after the birth, when she may have no real knowledge of her own feelings or of her baby. It is argued that, not surprisingly, on returning home from hospital many women are overwhelmed by anxiety and many suffer post-natal depression (Brighton Women and Science Group, 1980; Oakley, 1980, 1984, 1987).

The natural childbirth movement has been a response to these criticisms. It largely rejects medical technology and often conceptualizes birth as a mystical experience. This movement sought to re-establish the importance of pain as part of the birthing experience, arguing that the individual situation and subjectivity of the woman should be recognized as influencing the meaning and experience of pain, including her relationships, her past experiences and her attitude towards pregnancy (Arney and Neill, 1982). Over the past four decades there have been progressive moves on the part of obstetricians and hospitals to accommodate the desires of women to 'demedicalize' childbirth and make the experience more 'natural'. However, recent commentators have pointed out that such a shift in discourse and practice has not necessarily liberated women to enjoy freedom and agency while in childbirth, and indeed continues to deny them choice based on individual needs. The emphasis on 'natural' childbirth, involving as little drug intervention as possible, has resulted in a situation in which women feel constrained to request pain relief (Porter, 1990: 192). Women who subscribe to the ideology of natural childbirth may feel cheated and 'unfeminine' if they are forced to accept medical intervention during pregnancy or labour, such as a caesarean section. The emphasis is upon women taking control over their own pregnancies; yet there is little recognition of the larger social context in which women are rendered powerless (Evans, 1985: 122).

It has been asserted that a middle-class, rationalist economic ideology underlies natural childbirth discourses. The movement emphasizes control over birth, which in turn emphasizes informed consumer choice: 'This model is one of the individual in the marketplace of birth options; a woman becoming as informed as possible, and exercising relatively free choice among these options ... the buyer (the birthing woman) seems in control because she can take it or leave it' (Martin, 1990b: 308). Martin (1990b: 310) points to a social class difference in the attitudes of women to control in childbirth. She suggests that middle-class women tend to value personal control over all spheres of life, which translates into resisting medical control while courting personal control in childbirth, including refusing pain relief during labour. Some working-class women, in contrast, are less concerned about engaging in 'out-of-control' behaviour during labour, perhaps resisting the middle-class ideology about the desirability of always being in control.

The problem with the middle-class model is that the opportunity for women to relax and relinquish control is lost. Indeed, it could be argued that such movements place greater pressure on women to be 'natural mothers', as if such a thing is biologically inherent, to experience birth in the 'natural' way untainted by the use of pain-relieving drugs. The natural childbirth movement has been criticized for drawing a distinction between 'natural' and 'artificial' childbirth, and for championing the view of women as simple, instinctive, close to nature, while men are seen as rational and scientific (Coward, 1989). The objectification and symbolizing of women's bodily parts, which is commonly a feature of feminist discourses on natural childbirth, is problematic for some (1989: 175). Furthermore, while medicalization of the experience of childbirth has been the subject of trenchant critique, it is worthy of note that the same critics have rarely questioned the medicalization involved in prenatal screening technologies or the vast medical resources consumed by post-delivery care for low birth-weight infants (Crouch and Manderson, 1993: 61).

It is also a moot point whether the medical profession's acceptance of women's demands for natural childbirth is evidence of a relinquishing of its control over childbirth. Arney and Neill (1982) argue that as a result of obstetric practice changing to embrace the tenets of natural childbirth, including less use of anaesthesia and the provision of constant support, medical control over the patient has been maintained and intensified rather than diminished. Adopting a Foucauldian perspective, they argue that patients have become more highly visible, subject to constant surveillance in the interests of 'support'. For example, childbirth preparation classes may be seen as constituting women as objects in an enlarged field of medical visibility, by encouraging them to air their concerns and fears publicly in a form of confessional. The turn towards natural childbirth in the late twentieth century, with its emphasis on the holistic experience, resulted in women surrendering not only childbirth to the control of the medical profession, but their personal thoughts, their experiences and their subjective selves.

The natural birth movement could therefore be regarded as furthering medical dominance over childbirth, by directing intense medical attention on the individual woman's behaviour and self-control during labour and incorporating obstetrical treatment unproblematically into its ideology without questioning the structural aspects of power in the medical encounter. Feminist self-help movements are more radicalized, actively considering and critiquing the social context of childbirth, including resisting the power relationship between women and their doctors (for example, the *Our Bodies/Ourselves* women's health handbook written by the Boston Women's Health Collective). They emphasize participation in health care and holistic approaches to health, and encourage women to treat themselves and each other rather than seek recourse to male medical practitioners. However, the radical women's health self-help movement has made slow progress, and remains the domain of politicized, largely white and middle-class women (Evans, 1985: 124).

Prenatal screening technologies

The introduction of prenatal screening techniques to monitor foetal development has sparked a range of critiques which question their ultimate benefit and future purpose. The most commonly used techniques include the taking of ultrasound images of the foetus in the uterus, providing a visual record of foetal development, and screening of the pregnant woman's blood serum for alpha-foetoprotein levels, which indicate risk factors for Down's syndrome, congenital nephrosis or neural tube defects. Chorionic villus sampling, which involves drawing a sample of tissue from the placenta, and amniocentesis, or the drawing of amniotic fluid from the uterus, provide genetic material which are used to identify a range of genetic abnormalities. These more physically invasive but also more accurate tests tend to be offered only to those women aged in their late 30s or older, when the risk is greater of the foetus having a genetic abnormality.

The proportion of women experiencing such testing has dramatically increased since the 1970s, particularly for ultrasound, which has now become almost universally applied to pregnant women at around the 18 weeks' gestation mark. There is very little questioning of the necessity of these procedures. Many women undergo such tests simply because they believe them to be 'routine', and therefore necessary, safe and reassuring procedures (Rowland, 1992; Santalahti et al., 1998). Women are often not made aware that abnormalities, both major and minor, may be discovered via the procedure and that the findings may be inconclusive. Providing such information may cause needless worry and distress for women during their pregnancies (Robotham, 2002a). In the case of serum testing, which has a high rate of false positive results, women are also often not prepared for the consequences should they receive such a result, in which case they must face the possibility that their baby has an abnormality and must decide in a state of high anxiety whether to undergo a more invasive procedure such as amniocentesis to determine whether or not there is such a problem (Santalahti et al., 1998).

The intensified focus in the medical and popular literature on the 'risks' to which foetuses may be exposed as they develop *in utero* – posed by such actions as the food and drinks consumed by the mother, the level of stress they experience, the drugs they ingest, as well as factors such as maternal age – also contributes to pregnant women's anxiety and accompanied desire to undergo tests to alleviate this anxiety by showing that there is 'nothing wrong' (Lupton, 1999). While the opportunity to ensure that the pregnancy is going well and allay anxieties concerning the health of the foetus appears eminently desirable, some feminists have pointed out that the decision to have an amniocentesis, for example, is in fact not clear-cut. While amniocentesis provides information about genetic abnormalities and conditions such as Down's syndrome, spina bifida and muscular dystrophy, allowing the choice for the parents to abort the foetus, it is not viable until there is enough amniotic fluid to be drawn, and there is a risk (almost 1 per cent) that spontaneous abortion will follow the procedure, compared with an overall rate of about 2 per cent that there will be a genetic defect (Rapp, 1985).

Waiting for the results of tests such as amniocentesis for up to two weeks can be an immensely anxious time for many women and their partners:

> While we are all told that 'no news is good news', it's a hard period to endure. Caught between the late date at which sufficient amniotic fluid exists to be tapped (sixteen to twenty weeks), the experience of quickening, when the woman feels the foetus move (roughly, eighteen to twenty weeks), and the legal limits of abortion (few abortions are performed after twenty-four weeks in the USA), we all have terrible fantasies, and many of us report distressing dreams. (Rapp, 1985: 318)

Should the results indicate the presence of a genetic abnormality, women are advised to undergo an abortion. Late second-trimester abortions involve injecting saline solution or urea to induce labour, so that the woman must undergo labour to deliver a dead foetus. Another option is dilation and evacuation of the uterus, which involves the dismemberment and removal of the foetus and the amniotic fluid (Rapp, 1985: 320–1). Following the abortion, women must adjust to post-pregnancy without a child.

Prenatal screening affects the way women conceptualize their pregnancies; decisions to undergo interventions affect how 'real' the foetus becomes to the woman and the time at which the foetus becomes 'our baby' (Hubbard, 1984). The emergence and routinization of tests such as amniocentesis have incited the need to confront more decisions about whether to carry that particular pregnancy to term. These decisions, of course, are structured within social expectations concerning what is a valid and acceptable decision. The twin use of ultrasound and amniocentesis works to confront women with an emotional dilemma: 'ultrasound makes the foetus more our baby, while the possibility of abortion makes us want to keep our emotional distance in case the pregnancy isn't going to end up with a baby after all' (1984: 335). The availability of the amniocentesis test partly serves to attract attention away from researching the reasons why chromosomal abnormalities occur, including environmental, occupational and social class factors (1984: 339).

The health effects of irradiation with ultrasound have also been raised as an issue by some critics (Holland and McKenna, 1984: 415; Rowland, 1992: 69–70). Although there is evidence that ultrasound can have adverse biological side-effects, there have been few efforts made to systematically test the procedure using randomized control trials, as drugs and other medical procedures are often tested. Another method of antenatal screening, chorionic villus sampling, was promoted as an earlier and less risky method of screening for genetic defects. However, this technique has been linked with birth defects such as limb deformities if carried out too early in the pregnancy (Saul, 1993).

There are noticeable differences in the ways that the women participating in prenatal screening procedures conceptualize the procedure and articulate their feelings compared with the medical discourses surrounding the procedures. Rapp (1990) discussed the medical discourses surrounding prenatal diagnostic tests such as amniocentesis and ultrasound in the context of patient–counsellor consultations in a screening clinic. Her interviews and observations during the field study noted a tension between the universal, abstract language of biomedicine and the individualized narratives provided by women of their experiences. Women found themselves conceptualizing of their pregnancy in medical terms, even while they expressed ambivalence about their desire to undergo testing. One woman said that following amniocentesis, 'I cried for two days after I had the test. I guess I was identifying with universal motherhood, I felt like my image of my womb had been shattered. It still feels like it's in pieces, not like such a safe place as before' (quoted by Rapp, 1990: 31).

Yet many other women welcome the chance to undergo prenatal screening. Petchesky (1987), although a critic of screening, concedes that many pregnant women (those whose pregnancies are wanted) enjoy the imaging process for its provision of reassurance, control and feelings of intimacy with the foetus. She concludes that '[w]e have to understand the "market" for the pill, sterilization, IVF, amniocentesis and high-tech pregnancy monitoring as a more complex phenomenon than either the victimization or the male-womb-envy thesis allows' (1987: 72). While women may see in foetal imaging what they are told they ought to see, women's reproductive consciousness is not only a product of dominant discourses, but is intimately linked to their age, past reproductive experiences, ethnicity, sexual preference, health status and desire for a child. Those women who have experienced difficulties in pregnancy, and who may have suffered miscarriages or are older than average, will find ultrasound more reassuring and more of a positive experience than women who have had no difficulty with fertility, who may resent the incursion of the ultrasound into their domain (1987: 76). Such women cannot be regarded as 'victims' of reproductive technologies. Indeed, for many women the ultrasound image has been appropriated as a domestic icon, part of the 'family' album collection of images representing kin-networks and relationships (1987: 74–5).

It seems clear that there exist disparate discourses concerning the desirability of medical technology used in prenatal testing among both feminist commentators and women experiencing pregnancy. One researcher (Evans, 1985) interviewed 200 women about their experiences of pregnancy and giving birth. The study found that women felt ambivalent about medical intervention and the use of technology. While many women resented doctors' actual behaviour, they continued to believe in their medical competence and the importance of seeking prenatal help. Women expressed the desire for more personal control over their pregnancies, while simultaneously desiring more use of medical technology. This seemingly contradictory finding can be explained if women's attitudes are seen as the product of the history of struggle over childbirth in which men assumed power over obstetrical procedures, and of the confused representations of pregnancy and motherhood which accompanied this change. Women's deference to the 'doctor knows best' ideology may be related to the asymmetry of information between doctors and patients, socialized respect for professionals with specialized training and for the men in general.

Dependence on medical intervention on the part of the expectant mother is not necessarily counter-productive. For example, the use of techniques designed to detect abnormalities can be seen as a palliative for the confused mother-to-be who feels neglected by the doctors in whom she is expected to place so much trust, allowing her to feel more confident about her pregnancy (Evans, 1985: 120). Nonetheless, a distinction should be drawn here between monitoring techniques such as prenatal screening, which has the potential to provide peace-of-mind for an anxious and uncertain pregnant woman, and the wider use of interventionist technology during childbirth, where the issues are more complex (1985: 119).

Feminist critics of the burgeoning of prenatal screening in western societies have identified another potential oppressive use of such technologies; that is, the increasing burden placed on the pregnant woman to undergo all possible lifestyle modifications, screening procedures and medical assistance in childbirth in the interests of the foetus. As prenatal screening becomes more and more expected and accepted as routine, the birth of a disabled child implies fault on the part of the mother, with the possibility of legal action against a woman should she refuse to be tested while pregnant. 'Foetal rights' have begun to take precedence over maternal rights (Hubbard, 1984: 344–5; Rose, 1987: 166–7).

There have already been cases where adult children have successfully sued their mothers for negligence. In one Australian incident in the early 1990s, a woman with severe cerebral palsy won a court case in which she claimed that her mother had been driving recklessly while pregnant and as a result had become involved in an accident allegedly causing damage to her foetus ultimately leading to cerebral palsy. A local newspaper article reporting this case was headlined 'Unborn babies can sue – mums warned' (*Sunday Telegraph* (Sydney), 13 June 1993) and was illustrated by a photograph of a foetus encased in its amniotic sac, seemingly floating in space, a self-contained and apparently self-sufficient individual separate from the maternal body. The discourses concerning the desirability of a 'perfect' baby, the placing of the onus on the mother to take every precaution to ensure her infant's health, including *in utero*, and those on maternal-child bonding become incompatible at this point. The pregnant woman is increasingly portrayed as separate to and the adversary of her own pregnancy/foetus, by presenting a 'hostile' maternal environment or refusing proposed medical intervention (Petchesky, 1987: 65).

Research was carried out on public reaction to cases in which American women were charged with 'perinatal endangerment', or endangering their newborn infants during, or due to, labour without medical assistance. It was found that engaging in unassisted childbirth attracted characterizations of women which drew upon moral narratives that represented them as 'calculating criminals', 'unnatural' and 'callous murderers', in sources as diverse as interviews with legal and medical workers and journalists, newspaper articles, police reports, court files and psychiatric, medical and probation records. Discourses surrounding maternal behaviour intersected with a number of contemporary debates in the United States (and elsewhere in the developed world) on abortion, child abuse, infant welfare and the medicalization of childbirth. The criminalization of unassisted birth and the construction of the 'anti-mother' drew from each of these discourses, as well as that of the vulnerability and preciousness of the newborn infant. The crimes of the 'anti-mother' included using unauthorized drugs during pregnancy, disregarding doctor's orders, choosing vaginal delivery over a court-ordered caesarean delivery, and appearing 'cold' when questioned about her infant's death (Tsing, 1990).

The discourses surrounding these cases privileged the need to keep troubled young mothers from engaging in child abuse or infanticide for the infant's sake rather than the needs of the women themselves: 'Their own vulnerability did not mean that they deserved more services, more rights, or a better society. Instead, it situated them more clearly as objects of social control' (Tsing, 1990: 289). As this suggests, women giving birth are charged with the sole responsibility for taking care of the infant, yet this responsibility is also negatively portrayed as dependency on the medical system.

These findings echo those of an earlier study of the discourses on maternal behaviour in textbooks and newsletters written for paediatricians in the 1970s (Howell, 1978). This study found a strong tendency for paediatricians to describe their work as 'rescuing' children from those who would harm them. Parents were singled out in particular, and mothers were disparaged as contributing to the ill health of their children through neglect or ignorance, or on the other hand for being unduly alarmed over minor illness (1978: 204). Few texts looked at external causes of ill health, such as car accidents and environmental poisoning, or the impact of poverty upon malnutrition, but rather focused attention on the ways in which mothers neglect their children's health, by allowing them too much sugar, for example.

It would thus appear that the discourses on 'good' mothering which have been evident in medical writings and the popular media in the past few decades have been extended to the moment of conception and even before. Women are now advised not to drink alcohol or smoke cigarettes from the time they realize they are pregnant, and some doctors and popular medical advice books even suggest that a woman *planning* to fall pregnant should be responsible and prepare her body by giving up alcohol and smoking, losing weight and engaging in regular physical exercise. Those women who choose to ignore such advice, or who simply cannot, for one reason or another, give up cigarettes or alcohol, are routinely portrayed as selfish, irresponsible and uncaring (Lupton, 1999). Once again, the primary emphasis of such discourses is upon the health and well-being of the foetus. The term 'foetal abuse' has even been used to describe the mother's 'chemical assault' of the foetus through alcohol, nicotine or other drugs, accompanied by predictions that women found 'guilty' of such assault will be forced to give up their child to the state's care (Rowland, 1992: 128). The reasons why women may find it difficult to follow such advice, such as their use of cigarettes or alcohol to counter and cope with low social support, social isolation, unemployment, high levels of stress, poverty, the burdens of child-rearing and lack of other available pleasurable options to relax (Graham, 1987; Oakley, 1989), are rarely considered or acknowledged as appropriate in such forums.

Assisted conception technologies

As the above discussion has emphasized, female reproduction in the late twentieth and early twenty-first centuries has been subject to a number of complex, and often contradictory and contesting, discourses. The advent of the new assisted conception technologies, including IVF, embryonic transfer, surrogacy and ova and embryo donation, has provided a focal point for political struggles between feminism and medicine, and has incited heated debates within the ranks of feminism itself.

Many of these debates centre on the culturally constructed meaning of 'motherhood' and 'childbirth'. As suggested earlier in this chapter, one dominant feminist perspective celebrates the essentially female power of being able to bring forth children, as expressed in the natural childbirth movement which celebrates the collective, supportive female experience of birth. Another rejects the notion that childbirth should be the preserve of women, and indeed argues that the linking of reproduction with women and too great an emphasis on the mother–child bond serves to disempower women and restrict their social and economic mobility. This latter perspective seeks to deny rather than celebrate the material bodily experiences of childbirth and breast-feeding. The two perspectives make uneasy bedfellows. The contemporary confusion expressed in feminist and other discourses about motherhood has been described in the following terms: 'Motherhood is woman's greatest hope and greatest anxiety: it is pathogenic, pathological, but it is the ultimate romance. Nothing could be more confusing' (Manion, 1988: 186).

With the advent of the new assisted conception technologies, the term 'mother' has been subjected to changing and multiple meanings. Some phrases circulating in the popular media and medical texts to demonstrate the lack of an essentialist notion of motherhood include 'egg mother', 'birth mother', 'name mother', 'surrogate mother', 'gene mother', 'biomother', 'adoptive mother', 'foster mother', 'legal mother', 'organ mother', 'nurturant mother' and 'earth mother'. As this suggests, there is no 'true nature' or 'real meaning' or 'definitive definition' of childbirth or motherhood; the discursive processes by which the terms are used, and the historical and social settings in which they are used, determine their meaning and, indeed, ontology (Treichler, 1990: 130). For example, even a brain-dead woman who was kept alive until the (assisted) birth of her child was called a 'mother' in the American news media, implying that motherhood can be reduced to the passive incubating of a foetus alone, with no human consciousness required as part of the role (Hartouni, 1991: 32–3).

Some radical feminists have argued that reproductive technologies are beneficial to women, for they have the potential to free them from the constraints of childbirth. Shulasmith Firestone, for example, asserted in the 1970s that women should be freed from the 'tyranny of reproduction by every means possible' (1972: 193). However, other feminists emphasize women's lack of choice in the face of male control over the new reproductive technologies. For some critics writing from this position, the processes by which the new assisted conception technologies take place reduce women's bodies to reproductive commodities, removing women's agency in the interests of patriarchal control (Arditti et al., 1984). These writers also point to the paradox that while the new reproductive technologies are hailed in public forums, abortion rights are under attack, there is still no safe contraceptive available for women (or men), infant mortality rates remain high among the underprivileged and welfare for existing children and their mothers remains vastly underfunded (1984: 3–4). Similarly, the development of new assisted conception technologies has been interpreted as a logical continuation of men's desire to take control over pregnancy and childbirth (Rowland, 1992). In taking over responsibility for conception via their domination of medical technologies, men overcome their feelings of alienation, inadequacy and jealousy of motherhood by symbolically becoming 'both mother and father to the in-vitro-created child' (1992: 11). In surrogacy arrangements, it is claimed, men buy women's wombs for themselves, rendering women subordinate slaves in the process (1992: 12).

Such critics have documented the embarrassment, disappointment, physical discomfort, depersonalization and humiliation felt by women undergoing medical treatment for infertility. They have also drawn attention to the possible side-effects of the drug therapies, involving super-ovulation to encourage the production of ova, to treat infertility which seldom receive publicity in public forums. These include birth defects, the increased chance of multiple births, dizziness, visual problems and nausea, the development of ovarian cysts, thrombosis and cancer, and the medical drawbacks of surgery involved in ovum collection (Rowland, 1992: Ch. 1).

Popular discourses on IVF tend to reinforce the notion of the infertile woman as unhappy and unfulfilled, and routinely represent it as the technological saviour of such women, offering a 'medical miracle' as a solution. In the mass media, especially newspapers, television news and documentaries and women's magazines, male scientists and doctors are commonly portrayed as active, expert and rational, the 'producers' and 'fathers' of 'test-tube babies', while women are represented as desperate for children, passive, reacting emotionally to their chance to experience the joys of desired motherhood. Critiques of IVF from feminist or other quarters and discussion of its failures or side-effects are rarely given attention in such coverage (Franklin, 1990; Hartouni, 1991; Noble and Bell, 1992; Rowland, 1992: Ch. 6).

Franklin (1990: 217) identified three major discourses organizing media and medical representations of infertility: the discourse of social loss, the discourse of biological destiny and the discourse of medical hope. In stories of childless couples or women, narrative closure was achieved to the problem of desperateness for children by the introduction of the new reproductive technologies as the ultimate and obvious 'solution', thereby normalizing them, with little recognition of the low success rates, the cost involved, the traumatic procedures undergone by the woman and the substantial moral and ethical questions raised by the new technologies (1990: 216). Further, media and medical accounts of childlessness invariably positioned it as being related to biological infertility on the part of married, heterosexual couples, while reasons related to social structural causes such as unemployment, low income, lack of child-care facilities, disability, sexual preference or marital status were not included within the frame of childlessness. The 'cure' for infertility was thus routinely portrayed as medical treatment, not social change (1990: 220–1).

Feminist critics have argued that the language of 'reprospeak' in media and medical texts frequently reduces women to depersonalized, dismembered body parts, described as walking incubators using such phrases as 'uterine environments' and 'gestational carriers' (Rowland, 1992: Ch. 6). Such language is regarded as translating into practice, obfuscating the effect that drugs and surgery have upon the woman's whole body, and rendering women's bodies as accessible, manipulated and opened, increasingly visible and controlled by medical science: 'Thus, practitioners can unselfconsciously *speak* of disembodied parts of women – "the ovaries , ripe eggs", and of "recovering" these parts even as they *materially* scrutinize, alter or remove these parts of women's bodies' (Steinberg, 1990: 86, emphasis in the original).

However, the wave of feminist writings strongly against assisted conception technologies that dominated the early 1980s began in later years to be challenged by a further poststructuralist feminist perspective. Some feminists called into question the essentialist nature of such critiques, arguing that in their 'patriarchy as conspiracy' approach to understanding the nature and meaning of the new reproductive technologies, ideology and power are positioned as external to, rather than constitutive of, the female body, and that such writings represent women as passive victims rather than as active agents (Bowe, 1987; Reiger, 1987; Stanworth, 1987; Caddick, 1992). It is contended that such a perspective implies that women have no real choice, constrained and seduced as they are by patriarchal definitions: 'On the one hand, women are told that they are the dupes of patriarchal ideology; on the other, we find that bodies, with their needs established in a secondary relationship to their contexts, remain distinctly separated from the technologies which can only "intrude" into them' (Caddick, 1992: 115). The poststructuralist feminist approach subsequently rejects the notion that the 'real female body' is acted upon, but instead views it as being inscribed and constituted by discursive processes. For this perspective, the new reproductive technologies are themselves regarded as producing subjectivity rather than as 'false consciousness'.

Still other feminist writers reject the determining power of discourses, arguing that there is capacity for change which is addressed by a feminist 'body politics', allowing women to speak about their bodies in their chosen way and resist scientific discourses (Jacobus et al., 1990: 7). According to this perspective, it should be women's right to choose how they should use, or reject, the new medical technologies. Feminism is critiqued for largely failing to recognize the possibility of using medical technology as a resource (Bowe, 1987). It is suggested that the experience of unwanted menstruation each cycle for an infertile woman is just as alienating as undergoing medical procedures: 'Women know their bodies, and infertile women who want pregnancy know them with anguish' (1987: 151). There is a struggle over the meaning of reproduction between different interest groups. For obstetricians, the prime focus is overcoming technological difficulties and achieving success in pregnancy rates, which further advances their field and enhances their professional prestige. While the psychological and social burden of infertility is often referred to, the financial, emotional or physical costs of undergoing treatment are rarely discussed in the medical literature. By contrast, patients view the problem as the inability to have children 'of their own' rather than a biological problem, perceiving a loss of control over their own bodies (Strickler, 1992).

Depth interviews carried out with people experiencing infertility have found that infertile women express feelings of 'loss of control' over their bodies, grief for the child they have never had and disappointment at failing expectations. Yet, because of the possibility of assisted fertility treatment, infertility is an open-ended state, allowing hope but also deferring final acceptance of infertility (Greil et al., 1989; Steinberg, 1990).

In one study (Modell, 1989), health professionals and clients of an IVF programme were interviewed. It was found that the concept of 'odds', or statistical chances, was a constantly used rhetorical strategy in conversations about IVF, used to organize and condense various statements about the individual chances of becoming pregnant, the rate of pregnancy in the programme as a whole and the probability attached to technological intervention. The health professionals involved tended to use a statistical meaning of odds, even comparing the procedure to a gamble equivalent to a roulette wheel stake. In contrast the patients used the term in a more subjective context, as applying to their own chances of success in a last-ditch attempt to achieve a pregnancy. In the clients' speech there was a recurring tension between the 'natural' and the 'artificial' in the IVF procedure, with the tendency to emphasize the former over the latter so as to confirm the desirability of seeking technological intervention for parenthood. This research indicates that people participating in procedures such as IVF actively seek to frame the experience in a positive way by the selective use of language; in doing so, they 'normalize' the experience for themselves, and come to see it as an acceptable alternative.

In the culture of individualism and achievement which obtains among many members of the middle class in particular, not being able to have a child at the right time, as planned, is difficult to accept and seems 'unfair'. As a result, infertile couples seeking treatment seem to have a 'love-hate' relationship with assisted conception technologies; while the technologies offer hope of a child, self-fulfilment and a greater degree of control over their destinies by pursuing all available options, they also involve a battery of tests, surgery, expense, discomfort and prolonged uncertainty (Strickler, 1992). It should also be acknowledged that there are constraining factors linked to women's social class, age and ethnicity which limit their access to medical technologies, or render them more vulnerable to medical domination and societal pressures to undergo procedures such as amniocentesis to determine the gender or genetic makeup of their foetus or surrogate motherhood. The liberal, consumerist-oriented view that women should have 'a right to choose' tends to ignore such structural constraints, 'new reproductive technologies may have very different implications for Third World and First World women, within and between countries' (Wajcman, 1991: 61).

Conclusion

Early feminist writings on medicine as culture questioned the uses to which medicine was put by members of the medical profession in pursuit of the control and oppression of women, and called for women's liberation from the bounds of medical 'care'. The advent of poststructuralist understandings have challenged the notion that 'truth', 'knowledge' and the 'essential' female body can be perceived as universals, arguing on the contrary that they are susceptible to change based on political struggles and discursive representations. Poststructuralist feminist scholars now claim that women's experiences of the body cannot be separated from the discourses and practices which constitute them, that there is no 'authentic' body waiting to be released from the bounds of medicine. Some feminists further argue that rather than being positioned as passive dupes of the patriarchal system, women should be able to choose as individuals the extent of medical intervention offered them in relation to such experiences as childbirth and conception. The differing political positions evident among feminists in their evaluation of the benefits offered to women by medical techniques and treatments reflect the struggles over meaning present in all areas of social life affected by biomedicine. Feminist commentaries and critiques of medicine as it affects women's lives not only highlight the competing theoretical claims present in the contemporary humanities and social sciences, but crystallize the ambivalence that permeates modern attitudes to medicine in western societies.

Conclusion

As medicine continues to dominate other social arenas, the paradox of its benevolence, its ability to save lives and its miraculous properties versus its capacity to support social inequities, to cast villains and victims and to entrench power differentials, becomes ever more evident. These contradictions are constantly apparent when discussing the role played by medicine in society, and have been particularly pertinent for women and other marginalized groups, to whose social position medicine has historically contributed. In this book I have attempted to depart from the approach to medicine and culture that tends to view non-western societies' discourses and practices as socially constructed, but which fails to recognize that the biomedical model dominant in western societies is equally a product of social relations. I have demonstrated that in western societies, as in all other societies, issues of health, illness, disease and death are inextricably interlinked with social processes; that is, the biological dimensions and medical understandings of these phenomena cannot easily be extricated from the socio-cultural settings in which they are known and experienced.

The recent renewed attention to ways in which the body is constituted by medical discourses and practices has brought to the fore one of the most contentious and important debates in social theory: that which examines the respective roles of structure and agency in the lives of individuals (Turner, 1992: 159). Macro-theorists in the sociology of health and illness, particularly those embracing the political economy approach, have traditionally emphasized structure over agency when analysing the role played by medicine in the lives of people. In contrast, other social theorists who have taken a micro-perspective, such as the phenomenologists, have emphasized individual agency in the medical setting, or the ways in which people can shape their own destinies and give meaning to their lives. This book has argued for a bringing together of these theoretical perspectives in ways that maintain a recognition of the distinctive contribution made by each approach while at the same time acknowledging the points at which they merge. Although the poststructuralist understanding of the integral contribution of language and discourse in shaping notions of reality has sometimes been criticized for reducing the agency of social actors under the power of language, this book has demonstrated that there is the possibility of resistance as long as attempts continue to be made to access or develop alternative discourses from which individuals may construct subjectivity.

Awareness of the manner in which disease categories and treatment practices are developed and institutionalized to the exclusion of others is of critical importance to understanding the social role of medicine in any culture. In demonstrating the dynamic and relative nature of medical knowledges, such insights provide space for the resistance to dominant forms of knowledge. In exposing the social bases of medicine, health care and illness states, by showing how they are not necessarily given or 'true' but are subject to change, the poststructuralist and postmodernist perspective renders these phenomena amenable to negotiation, allowing the opportunity for alternative ways of thinking and speaking that avoid taken-for-granted assumptions and stereotypes. For marginalized groups, such challenges have assisted their quest to be heard; for example, if people living with HIV/AIDS can insist that they be considered survivors rather than passive invalids by rejecting the term 'AIDS victims', if menopausal women can successfully argue that the ceasing of menstruation is a new, libratory dimension of womanhood rather than the death of femininity, then the bodily experiences and practices around these processes can be transformed.

Poststructuralist and postmodernist writings have also had the important effect of challenging researchers in the humanities and social sciences themselves to be reflexive, to examine their own position of power and claims to truth in the research and writing process. Foucault (1984b: 74) has contended that it is the role of the scholar to expose the mechanisms by which 'truth' is constituted, and in whose interests it works, and thence to be in the position of ascertaining the possibility of a new politics of truth. Gatens argues in the context of feminism that '[i]t is important to begin the exploration of other ontologies which would be developed hand-in-hand with a politico-ethical stance that accommodates *multiple*, not simply dichotomously *sexed* bodies' (1988: 67, emphasis in the original).

This argument may be usefully extended to the context of bodies in medicine. Scholars interested in the socio-cultural dimensions of illness, disease and the body in medicine need to be aware of the potential of their writings to contribute to oppressive, constraining and stereotypical discourses that support confining dualisms such as Self/Other, masculine/feminine, sick/well, rational/irrational, active/passive, productive/wasteful, nature/culture, disorderly/controlled and moral/immoral, and to use their understanding of the socially constituted nature of knowledge to allow space for the production of novel, multiple knowledges about bodies in the medical setting that avoid either/or distinctions.

References

Ahmad, W. and Jones, L. (1998) 'Ethnicity, health and health care in Britain', in A. Petersen and C. Waddell (eds), *Health Matters: A Sociology of Illness, Prevention and Care*. Sydney: Allen and Unwin, pp. 114–27.

Allen, J. (1992) 'Frameworks and questions in Australian sexuality research', in R. Connell and G. Dowsett (eds), *Rethinking Sex: Social Theory and Sexuality Research*. Melbourne: Melbourne University Press, pp. 5–31.

Arditti, R., Klein, R. and Minden, S. (1984) 'Introduction', in R. Arditti, R. Klein and S. Minden (eds), *Test-tube Women: What Future for Motherhood?* London: Pandora, pp. 1–7.

Ariès, P. (1981) *The Hour of Our Death*. London: Allen Lane.

Armstrong, D. (1982) 'The doctor–patient relationship: 1930–80', in P. Wright and A. Treacher (eds), *The Problem of Medical Knowledge: Examining the Social Construction of Medicine*. Edinburgh: Edinburgh University Press, pp. 109–22.

Armstrong, D. (1983) *Political Anatomy of the Body: Medical Knowledge in Britain in the Twentieth Century*. Cambridge: Cambridge University Press.

Armstrong, D. (1984) 'The patient's view', *Social Science & Medicine*, 18 (9), 737–44.

Armstrong, D. (1987a) 'Silence and truth in death and dying', *Social Science & Medicine*, 24 (8), 651–7.

Armstrong, D. (1987b) 'Bodies of knowledge: Foucault and the problem of human anatomy', in G. Scambler (ed.), *Sociological Theory and Medical Sociology*. London: Tavistock, pp. 59–76.

Armstrong, D. (1997) 'Foucault and the sociology of health and illness: a prismatic reading', in A. Peterson and R. Bunton (eds), *Foucault, Health and Medicine*. London: Routledge, pp. 15–30.

Armstrong, D. (2002) *A New History of Identity: A Sociology of Medical Knowledge*. Basingstoke: Palgrave.

Arney, W. and Neill, J. (1982) 'The location of pain in childbirth: natural childbirth and the transformation of obstetrics', *Sociology of Health & Illness*, 4 (1), 1–24.

Atkinson, P. (1981) *The Clinical Experience: the Construction and Reconstruction of Medical Reality*. Guildford: Gower.

Atkinson, P. (1990) *The Ethnographic Imagination*. London: Routledge.

Backett, K. (1992) 'Taboos and excesses: lay health moralities in middle-class families', *Sociology of Health & Illness*, 14 (2), 255–73.

Baer, H., Singer, M. and Johnsen, J. (1986) 'Toward a critical medical anthropology', *Social Science & Medicine*, 23 (2), 95–8.

Banks, C. (1992) '"Culture" in culture-bound syndromes: the case of anorexia nervosa', *Social Science & Medicine*, 34 (8), 867–84.

Barker, K. (1998) 'A ship upon a stormy sea: the medicalization of pregnancy', *Social Science & Medicine*, 47 (8), 1067–76.

Barthes, R. (1973) *Mythologies*. London: Paladin.

Bassuk, E. (1986) 'The rest cure: repetition or resolution of Victorian women's conflicts?', in S.R. Suleiman (ed.), *The Female Body in Western Culture: Contemporary Perspectives.* Cambridge, MA: Harvard University Press, pp. 139–51.

Beier, L. (1985) 'In sickness and in health: a seventeenth century family's experience', in R. Porter (ed.), *Patients and Practitioners: Lay Perceptions of Medicine in Pre-Industrial Society.* Cambridge: Cambridge University Press, pp. 101–28.

Berger, P. and Luckmann, T. (1967) *The Social Construction of Reality.* London: Allen Lane.

Berliner, H. and Salmon, J. (1980) 'The holistic alternative to scientific medicine: history and analysis', *International Journal of Health Services,* 10 (1), 133–45.

Berman, B. (1989) 'The computer metaphor: bureaucraticizing the mind', *Science as Culture,* 7, 7–42.

Berridge, V. and Strong, P. (1991) 'AIDS and the relevance of history', *Society for the Social History of Medicine,* 4 (1), 129–38.

Berthelot, J. (1986) 'Sociological discourse and the body', *Theory, Culture & Society,* 3 (3), 155–64.

Birken, L. (1988) *Consuming Desire: Sexual Science and the Emergence of a Culture of Abundance, 1871–1914.* Ithaca, NY: Cornell University Press.

Blaxter, M. (1983) 'The causes of disease: women talking', *Social Science & Medicine,* 17 (2), 59–69.

Blaxter, M. and Paterson, E. (1982) *Mothers and Daughters: a Three Generational Study of Health Attitudes and Behaviour.* London: Heinemann.

Bloor, M. and McIntosh, J. (1990) 'Surveillance and concealment: a comparison of techniques of client resistance in therapeutic communities and health visiting', in S. Cunningham-Burley and N. McKeganey (eds), *Readings in Medical Sociology.* London: Routledge, pp. 159–81.

Blumenfeld-Kosinski, R. (1990) *Not of Woman Born: Representations of Caesarean Birth in Medieval and Renaissance Culture.* Ithaca, NY: Cornell University Press.

Bordo, S. (1990) 'Reading the slender body', in M. Jacobus, E. Keller and S. Shuttleworth (eds), *Body/Politics: Women and the Discourses of Science.* New York: Routledge, pp. 83–112.

Bourdieu, P. (1984) *Distinction: a Social Critique of the Judgement of Taste.* London: Routledge and Kegan Paul.

Bowe, M. (1987) 'A woman's choice? The IVF option', *Arena,* 79, 146–55.

Bradbury, H., Gabe, J. and Bury, M. (1995) '"Sexy docs" and "busty blondes": press coverage of professional misconduct cases brought before the General Medical Council', *Sociology of Health & Illness,* 17 (4), 458–76.

Brandt, A. (1988) 'AIDS and metaphor: toward the social meaning of epidemic disease', *Social Research,* 55 (3), 413–32.

Brandt, A. (1991) 'Emerging themes in the history of medicine', *Milbank Memorial Quarterly,* 69 (2), 199–214.

Bransen, E. (1992) 'Has menstruation been medicalized? Or will it never happen ...?', *Sociology of Health & Illness,* 14 (1), 98–110.

Breslow, L. (1982) 'Control of cigarette smoking from a public policy perspective', *Annual Review of Public Health,* 3, 129–51.

Brighton Women and Science Group (1980) 'Technology in the lying-in room', in The Brighton Women and Science Group (ed.), *Alice through the Microscope: the Power of Science over Women's Lives.* London: Virago, pp. 165–81.

Broom, D. (1991) *Damned If We Do: Contradictions in Women's Health Care.* Sydney: Allen and Unwin.

Broom, D. (2001) 'Reading breast cancer: reflections on a dangerous intersection', *Health*, 5 (2), 249–68.

Brown, P. (1992) 'AIDS: the challenge of the future', *New Scientist Supplement*, 18 April.

Brumberg, J. (1988) *Fasting Girls: the Emergence of Anorexia Nervosa as a Modern Disease*. Cambridge, MA: Harvard University Press.

Buckley, T. and Gottlieb, A. (1988) 'A critical appraisal of theories of menstrual symbolism', in T. Buckley and A. Gottlieb (eds), *Blood Magic: the Anthropology of Menstruation*. Berkeley, CA: University of California Press, pp. 3–50.

Bury, M. (1986) 'Social constructionism and the development of medical sociology', *Sociology of Health & Illness*, 8 (2), 135–69.

Bytheway, B. and Johnson, J. (1998) 'The sight of age', in S. Nettleton and J. Watson (eds), *The Body in Everyday Life*. London: Routledge, pp. 243–57.

Caddick, A. (1986) 'Feminism and the body', *Arena*, 74, 60–88.

Caddick, A. (1992) 'Feminist and postmodern: Donna Haraway's cyborg', *Arena*, 99/100, 112–28.

Calnan, M. and Johnson, B. (1985) 'Health, health risks and inequalities: an exploratory study of women's perceptions', *Sociology of Health & Illness*, 7 (1), 54–75.

Calnan, M. and Williams, S. (1992) 'Images of scientific medicine', *Sociology of Health & Illness*, 14 (2), 233–54.

Cant, S. and Sharma, U. (2000) 'Alternative health practices and systems', in G. Albrecht, R. Fitzpatrick and S. Scrimshaw (eds), *Social Studies in Health and Medicine*. London: Sage, pp. 426–39.

Caskey, N. (1986) 'Interpreting anorexia nervosa', in S. Suleiman (ed.), *The Female Body in Western Culture*. Cambridge, MA: Harvard University Press, pp. 175–89.

Cassata, M., Skill, T. and Boadu, S. (1979) 'In sickness and in health', *Journal of Communication*, 29 (4), 73–80.

Cassell, E. (1976) 'Disease as an "it": concepts of disease revealed by patients' presentation of symptoms', *Social Science & Medicine*, 10, 143–6.

Charles, N. and Kerr, M. (1986) 'Food for feminist thought', *Sociological Review*, 34 (3), 537–72.

Chernin, K. (1985) *The Hungry Self: Women, Eating and Identity*. New York, NY: Times Books.

Chrisler, J. and Levy, K. (1990) 'The media construct a menstrual monster: a content analysis of PMS articles in the popular press', *Women and Health*, 16 (2), 89–104.

Clark, D. (1993) '"With my body I thee worship": the social construction of marital sex problems', in S. Scott and D. Morgan (eds), *Body Matters: Essays on the Sociology of the Body*. London: Falmer, pp. 22–34.

Clarke, A. (1993) 'Modernity, postmodernity and reproductive processes, c. 1890–1992, or, Mommy, where do cyborgs come from anyway?' Paper delivered at the Sex/Gender in Techno-Science Worlds conference, University of Melbourne, 26 June – 1 July 1993.

Clarke, A. and Montini, T. (1993) 'The many faces of RU486: tales of situated knowledges and technological constraints', *Science, Technology and Human Values*, 18 (1), 42–78.

Clarke, J. (1992) 'Cancer, heart disease and AIDS, what do the media tell us about these diseases?' *Health Communication*, 4 (2), 105–20.

Clarke, J. and Robinson, J. (1999) 'Testicular cancer: medicine and machismo in the media (1980–94)', *Health*, 3 (3), 263–82.

Clatts, M. and Mutchler, K. (1989) 'AIDS and the dangerous other: metaphors of sex and deviance in the representation of disease', *Medical Anthropology*, 10, 105–14.

Comaroff, J. (1982) 'Medicine: symbol and ideology', in P. Wright and A. Treacher (eds), *The Problem of Medical Knowledge: Examining the Social Construction of Medicine*. Edinburgh: University of Edinburgh Press, pp. 49–69.

Conrad, P. (1999) 'A mirage of genes', *Sociology of Health & Illness*, 21 (2), 228–41.

Coombs, M. (1988) 'Induced and abandoned: the story of an April fool', in M. Coombs, *Regards to the Czar*. Brisbane: University of Queensland Press, pp. 100–34.

Courtenay, W. (2000) 'Constructions of masculinity and their influence on men's well-being: a theory of gender and health', *Social Science & Medicine*, 50, 1385–410.

Coward, R. (1989) *The Whole Truth: the Myth of Alternative Health*. London: Faber and Faber.

Crawford, R. (1980) 'Healthism and the medicalization of everyday life', *International Journal of Health Services*, 19, 365–88.

Crawford, R. (1984) 'A cultural account of "health": control, release and the social body', in J. McKinlay (ed.), *Issues in the Political Economy of Health Care*. New York, NY: Tavistock, pp. 60–103.

Crimp, D. (1989) 'AIDS: cultural analysis/cultural activism', in D. Crimp (ed.), *AIDS: Cultural Analysis, Cultural Activism*. Cambridge, MA: MIT Press, pp. 3–16.

Crimp, D. (1992) 'Portraits of people with AIDS', in L. Grossberg, C. Nelson and P. Treichler (eds), *Cultural Studies*. New York, NY: Routledge, pp. 117–30.

Crouch, M. and Manderson, L. (1993) 'Parturition as social metaphor', *Australian and New Zealand Journal of Sociology*, 29 (1), 55–72.

Cunningham-Burley, S. and Bolton, M. (2000) 'The social context of the new genetics', in G. Albrecht, R. Fitzpatrick and S. Scrimshaw (eds), *Social Studies in Health and Medicine*. London: Sage, pp. 173–87.

Dally, A. (1991) *Women under the Knife: a History of Surgery*. London: Hutchinson Radius.

Daly, J. (1989) 'Innocent murmurs: echocardiography and the diagnosis of cardiac normality', *Sociology of Health & Illness*, 11 (2), 99–116.

Davis, K. (1997) '"My body is art": cosmetic surgery as feminist utopia?', *European Journal of Women's Studies*, 4, 23–37.

Davis, K. (2002) '"A dubious equality": men, women and cosmetic surgery', *Body & Society*, 8 (1), 49–65.

Davison, C., Frankel, S. and Davey Smith, G. (1992) 'The limits of lifestyle: re-assessing "fatalism" in the popular culture of illness prevention', *Social Science & Medicine*, 34 (6), 675–85.

DiGiacomo, S. (1987) 'Biomedicine as a cultural system: an anthropologist in the kingdom of the sick', in H. Baer (ed.), *Encounters with Biomedicine: Case Studies in Medical Anthropology*. New York, NY: Gordon and Breach, pp. 315–46.

DiGiacomo, S. (1992) 'Metaphor as illness: postmodern dilemmas in the representation of body, mind and disorder', *Medical Anthropology*, 14, 109–37.

Douglas, M. (1974) *Implicit Meanings: Essays in Anthropology*. London: Routledge and Kegan Paul.

Douglas, M. (1980/1966) *Purity and Danger: an Analysis of Concepts of Pollution and Taboo*. London: Routledge and Kegan Paul.

Douglas, M. (1984) *Food in the Social Order: Studies of Food and Festivities in Three American Communities*. New York, NY: Russell Sage Foundation.

Douglas, M. and Calvez, M. (1990) 'The self as risk-taker: a cultural theory of contagion in relation to AIDS', *Sociological Review*, 38 (3), 445–64.

Doyal, L. (1983) *The Political Economy of Health.* London: Pluto Press.

Dreuihle, E. (1988) *Mortal Embrace: Living with AIDS.* New York, NY: Hill and Wang.

Ehrenreich, B. and Ehrenreich, J. (1978) 'Medicine and social control', in J. Ehrenreich (ed.), *The Cultural Crisis of Modern Medicine.* New York, NY: Monthly Review Press, pp. 39–79.

Ehrenreich, B. and English, D. (1973) *Witches, Midwives and Nurses: a History of Women Healers.* Westbury: Feminist Press.

Ehrenreich, B. and English, D. (1974) *Complaints and Disorders: The Sexual Politics of Sickness.* London: Compendium.

Ehrenreich, J. (1978) 'Introduction: the cultural crisis of modern medicine', in J. Ehrenreich (ed.), *The Cultural Crisis of Modern Medicine.* New York, NY: Monthly Review Press, pp. 1–35.

Emerson, J. (1987/1970) 'Behaviour in private places: sustaining definitions of reality in gynaecological examinations', in I. Stoeckle (ed.), *Encounters between Patients and Doctors: an Anthology.* Cambridge, MA: MIT Press, pp. 215–34.

Enright, D. (ed.) (1989) *The Faber Book of Fevers and Frets.* London: Faber and Faber.

Epstein, S. (1978) *The Politics of Cancer.* San Francisco, CA: Sierra Club Books.

Epstein, S. (1990) 'Losing the war against cancer: who's to blame and what to do about it', *International Journal of Health Services*, 20 (1), 53–71.

Erwin, D. (1987) 'The militarization of cancer treatment in American society', in H. Baer (ed.), *Encounters with Biomedicine: Case Studies in Medical Anthropology.* New York, NY: Gordon and Breach, pp. 201–27.

Estes, C. and Linkins, K. (2000) 'Critical perspectives on health and aging', in G. Albrecht, R. Fitzpatrick and S. Scrimshaw (eds), *Social Studies in Health and Medicine.* London: Sage, pp. 154–72.

Evans, F. (1985) 'Managers and labourers: women's attitudes to reproductive technology', in W. Faulkner and E. Arnold (eds), *Smothered by Technology: Technology in Women's Lives.* London: Pluto Press, pp. 109–27.

Fagin, C. and Diers, D. (1984) 'Nursing as metaphor', *International Nursing Review*, 31 (1), 16–17.

Fairclough, N. (1992) 'Discourse and text: linguistic and intertextual analysis within discourse analysis', *Discourse & Society*, 3 (2), 193–217.

Featherstone, M. (1987) 'Leisure, symbolic power and the life course', in J. Horne, D. Jary and A. Tomlinson (eds), *Sport, Leisure and Social Relations.* London: Routledge and Kegan Paul, pp. 113–38.

Featherstone, M. (1991) 'The body in consumer culture', in M. Featherstone, M. Hepworth and B.S. Turner (eds), *The Body: Social Process and Cultural Theory.* London: Sage, pp. 170–96.

Featherstone, M. and Hepworth, M. (1991) 'The mask of ageing and the postmodern life course', in M. Featherstone, M. Hepworth and B.S. Turner (eds), *The Body: Social Process and Cultural Theory.* London: Sage, pp. 371–89.

Fee, E. and Porter, D. (1992) 'Public health, preventive medicine and professionalization: England and America in the nineteenth century', in A. Wear (ed.), *Medicine in Society: Historical Essays.* Cambridge: Cambridge University Press, pp. 249–76.

Firestone, S. (1972) *The Dialectic of Sex.* London: Paladin.

Fischler, C. (1986) 'Learned versus "spontaneous" dietetics: French mothers' views of what children should eat', *Social Science Information*, 25 (4), 945–65.

Fischler, C. (1988) 'Food, self and identity', *Social Science Information*, 27 (2), 275–92.

Fisher, S. (1991) 'A discourse of the social: medical talk/power talk/oppositional talk?', *Discourse & Society*, 2 (2), 157–82.

Fiske, J. (1992) 'British cultural studies and television', in R. Allen (ed.), *Channels of Discourse, Reassembled*. London: Routledge, pp. 284–326.

Foucault, M. (1967) *Madness and Civilization: A History of Insanity in the Age of Reason*. London: Tavistock.

Foucault, M. (1975) *The Birth of the Clinic: an Archaeology of Medical Perception*. New York, NY: Vintage Books.

Foucault, M. (1979) *The History of Sexuality, Volume One: An Introduction*. London: Penguin.

Foucault, M. (1984a) 'The politics of health in the eighteenth century', in P. Rabinow (ed.), *The Foucault Reader*. New York, NY: Pantheon, pp. 273–89.

Foucault, M. (1984b) 'Truth and power', in P. Rabinow (ed.), *The Foucault Reader*. New York, NY: Pantheon, pp. 51–75.

Foucault, M. (1986) *The Use of Pleasure: The History of Sexuality, Volume Two*. London: Viking.

Foucault, M. (1988) *The Care of the Self: The History of Sexuality, Volume Three*. London: Allen Lane/Penguin.

Fox, D. and Karp, D. (1988) 'Images of plague: infectious disease in the visual arts', in E. Fee and D. Fox (eds), *AIDS: the Burdens of History*. Berkeley, CA: University of California Press, pp. 172–89.

Fox, N. (1993) *Postmodernism, Sociology and Health*. Buckingham: Open University Press.

Fox, N. (1997) 'Is there life after Foucault? Texts, frames and differends', in A. Petersen and R. Bunton (eds), *Foucault, Health and Medicine*. London: Routledge, pp. 31–50.

Fox, N. (1998) 'Postmodernism and "health"', in A. Petersen and C. Waddell (eds), *Health Matters: a Sociology of Illness, Prevention and Care*. Sydney: Allen and Unwin, pp. 9–22.

Fox, N. (2002) 'Refracting "health": Deleuze, Guattari and body-self', *Health*, 6 (3), 347–64.

Frank, A. (1990) 'Bringing bodies back in: a decade review', *Theory, Culture & Society*, 7, 131–62.

Frank, A. (1991) 'For a sociology of the body: an analytical review', in M. Featherstone, M. Hepworth and B. Turner (eds), *The Body: Social Process and Cultural Theory*. London: Sage, pp. 36–102.

Frank, A. (1998) 'Just listening: narrative and deep illness', *Families, Systems & Health*, 16 (3), 197–212.

Frankenberg, R. (1988) '"Your time or mine?": an anthropological view of the tragic temporal contradictions of biomedical practice', *International Journal of Health Services*, 18 (1), 11–35.

Frankenberg, R. (1990) 'Disease, literature and the body in the era of AIDS – a preliminary exploration', *Sociology of Health & Illness*, 12 (3), 351–60.

Franklin, S. (1990) 'Deconstructing "desperateness": the social construction of infertility in popular representations of new reproductive technologies', in M. McNeil, I. Varcoe and S. Yearly (eds), *The New Reproductive Technologies*. New York, NY: St Martin's Press, pp. 200–29.

Freidson, E. (1970) *Professional Dominance: the Social Structure of Medical Care*. Chicago, IL: Aldine.

Gabe, J. and Calnan, M. (1989) 'The limits of medicine women's perception of medical technology', *Social Science & Medicine*, 28 (3), 223–31.

Gallagher, C. and Laqueur, T. (1987) 'Introduction', in C. Gallagher and T. Laqueur (eds), *The Making of the Modern Body: Sexuality and Society in the Nineteenth Century*. Berkeley, CA: University of California Press, pp. vii–xv.

Gallagher, E. (1976) 'Lines of reconstruction and extension in the Parsonian sociology of illness', *Social Science & Medicine*, 10, 207–18.

Garrett, C. (1998) *Beyond Anorexia: Narrative, Spirituality and Recovery*. Cambridge: Cambridge University Press.

Gatens, M. (1983) 'A critique of the sex/gender distinction', in J. Allen and P. Patton (eds), *Beyond Marxism? Interventions after Marx*. Sydney: Intervention Publications, pp. 143–62.

Gatens, M. (1988) 'Towards a feminist philosophy of the body', in B. Caine, E. Grosz and M. de Lepervanche (eds), *Crossing Boundaries: Feminisms and the Critique of Knowledges*. Sydney: Allen and Unwin, pp. 59–70.

Geertz, C. (1973) *The Interpretation of Cultures*. New York, NY: Basic Books.

Gerbner, G., Gross, L., Morgan, M. and Signorielli, N. (1981) 'Health and medicine on television', *New England Journal of Medicine*, 305 (15), 901–4.

Gerhardt, U. (1989) *Ideas about Illness: an Intellectual and Political History of Medical Sociology*. New York, NY: New York University Press.

Gerson, E. (1976) 'The social character of illness: deviance or politics?', *Social Science & Medicine*, 10, 219–24.

Gilman, S. (1988) *Disease and Representation: Images of Illness from Madness to AIDS*. Ithaca, NY: Cornell University Press.

Ginsburg, F. (1990) 'The "word-made" flesh: the disembodiment of gender in the abortion debate', in F. Ginsburg and A. Tsing (eds), *Uncertain Terms: Negotiating Gender in American Culture*. Boston, MA: Beacon Press, pp. 59–75.

Goldberg, D. (1993) 'My experience had a famous name', *British Medical Journal*, 306, 216.

Good, M.-J. and Good, B. (2000) 'Clinical narratives and the study of contemporary doctor–patient relationships', in G. Albrecht, R. Fitzpatrick and S. Scrimshaw (eds), *Social Studies in Health and Medicine*. London: Sage, pp. 243–58.

Good, M.-J., Good, B., Schaffer, C. and Lind, S. (1990) 'American oncology and the discourse on hope', *Culture, Medicine and Psychiatry*, 14, 59–79.

Gordon, D. (1988a) 'Tenacious assumptions in western medicine', in M. Lock and D. Gordon (eds), *Biomedicine Examined*. Dordrecht: Kluwer, pp. 19–56.

Gordon, D. (1988b) 'Clinical science and clinical expertise: changing boundaries between art and science in medicine', in M. Lock and D. Gordon (eds), *Biomedicine Examined*. Dordrecht: Kluwer, pp. 257–95.

Gordon, L. (1978) 'The politics of birth control, 1920–1940: the impact of professionals', in J. Ehrenreich (ed.), *The Cultural Crisis of Modern Medicine*. New York, NY: Monthly Review Press, pp. 144–84.

Graham, H. (1987) 'Women's smoking and family health', *Social Science & Medicine*, 25 (1), 47–56.

Green, E., Thompson, D. and Griffiths, F. (2002) 'Narratives of risk: women at midlife, medical "experts" and health technologies', *Health, Risk & Society*, 4 (3), 273–86.

Greil, A., Porter, K., Leitko, T. and Riscilli, C. (1989) 'Why me? Theodicies of infertile women and men', *Sociology of Health & Illness*, 11 (3), 213–29.

Grosz, E. (1990) 'Inscriptions and body-maps: representations and the corporeal', in T. Threadgold and A. Cranny-Francis (eds), *Feminine/Masculine and Representation*. Sydney: Allen and Unwin, pp. 62–74.

Guarnaccia, P. (2001) 'Introduction: the contribution of medical anthropology to anthropology and beyond', *Medical Anthropology Quarterly*, 15 (4), 423–8.

Gwyn, R. (2002) *Communicating Health and Illness*. London: Sage.

Hahn, R. (1985a) 'Between two worlds: physicians as patients', *Medical Anthropology Quarterly*, 16 (4), 87–98.

Hahn, R. (1985b) 'A world of internal medicine: portrait of an internist', in R. Hahn and A. Gaines (eds), *Physicians of Western Medicine: Anthropological Approaches to Theory and Practice*. Dordrecht: D. Reidel, pp. 51–111.

Hall, S. (1980) 'Cultural studies and the centre: some problematics and problems', in S. Hall, D. Hobson, A. Lowe and P. Willis (eds), *Culture, Media, Language*. London: Hutchinson, pp. 15–47.

Hallowell, N. (1999) 'Doing the right thing: genetic risk and responsibility', *Sociology of Health & Illness*, 21 (5), 597–621.

Haraway, D. (1988) 'A manifesto for cyborgs: science, technology and socialist feminism in the 1980s', in E. Weed (ed.), *Coming to Terms: Feminism, Theory and Practice*. New York, NY: Routledge, pp. 173–204.

Haraway, D. (1989) 'The biopolitics of postmodern bodies: determinations of self in immune system discourse', *Differences*, 1 (1), 3–44.

Haraway, D. (1992) 'The promises of monsters: a regenerative politics for inappropriate/d others', in L. Grossberg, C. Nelson and P. Treichler (eds), *Cultural Studies*. New York, NY: Routledge, pp. 295–337.

Hardey, M. (1999) 'Doctor in the house: the Internet as a source of lay knowledge and the challenge to expertise', *Sociology of Health & Illness*, 21 (6), 820–35.

Hardey, M. (2002) '"The story of my illness": personal accounts of illness on the Internet', *Health*, 6 (1), 31–46.

Harding, J. (1997) 'Bodies at risk: sex, surveillance and hormone replacement therapy', in A. Petersen and R. Bunton (eds), *Foucault, Health and Medicine*. London: Routledge, pp. 134–50.

Hargreaves, J. (1986) *Sport, Culture and Power*. Cambridge: Polity Press.

Hargreaves, J. (1997) 'Women's boxing and related activities: introducing images and meanings', *Body & Society*, 3 (4), 33–50.

Hart, N. (1982) 'Is capitalism bad for your health?', *British Journal of Sociology*, 33 (3), 435–43.

Hartouni, V. (1991) 'Containing women: reproductive discourse in the 1980s', in C. Penley and A. Ross (eds), *Technoculture*. Minneapolis, MN: University of Minnesota Press, pp. 27–56.

Heath, S. (1982) *The Sexual Fix*. Basingstoke: Macmillan Press.

Helman, C. (1978) '"Feed a cold, starve a fever" – folk models of infection in an English suburban community and their relation to medical treatment', *Culture, Medicine and Psychiatry*, 2, 107–37.

Helman, C. (1985) 'Disease and pseudo-disease: a case history of pseudo-angina', in R. Hahn and A. Gaines (eds), *Physicians of Western Medicine: Anthropological Approaches to Theory and Practice*. Dordrecht: D. Reidel, pp. 293–331.

Herzlich, C. and Pierret, J. (1987) *Illness and Self in Society*. Baltimore, MD: Johns Hopkins University Press.

Hodgetts, D. and Chamberlain, K. (1999) 'Medicalization and the depiction of lay people in television health documentary', *Health*, 3 (3), 317–33.

Hoffman-Goetz, L. (1999) 'Cancer experiences of African-American women as portrayed in popular mass magazines', *Pyscho-oncology*, 8 (1), 36–45.

Holland, R. and McKenna, J. (1984) 'Regaining trust', in R. Arditti, R. Klein and S. Minden (eds), *Test-tube Women: What Future for Motherhood?* London: Pandora, pp. 414–18.

Horst, S. and Daemmrich, I. (1987) *Themes and Motifs in Western Literature.* Tubingen: Francke Verlag.

Howarth, D. (2000) *Discourse.* Buckingham: Open University Press.

Howell, M.C. (1978) 'Paediatricians and mothers', in J. Ehrenreich (ed.), *The Cultural Crisis of Modern Medicine.* New York, NY: Monthly Review Press, pp. 201–11.

Hubbard, R. (1984) 'Personal courage is not enough: some hazards of childbearing in the 1980s', in R. Arditti, R. Klein and S. Minden (eds) *Test-tube Women: What Future for Motherhood?* London: Pandora, pp. 331–55.

Hyden, L.-C. (1997) 'Illness and narrative', *Sociology of Health & Illness*, 19 (1), 48–69.

Illich, I. (1976) *Limits to Medicine: Medical Nemesis: the Expropriation of Health.* London: Marion Boyars.

Jacobus, M., Keller, E. and Shuttleworth, S. (1990) 'Introduction', in M. Jacobus, E. Keller and S. Shuttleworth (eds), *Body/Politics: Women and the Discourses of Science.* New York, NY: Routledge, pp. 1–10.

Jensen, K. (1991) 'Humanistic scholarship as qualitative science: contributions to mass communication research', in K. Jensen and N. Jankowski (eds), *A Handbook of Qualitative Methodologies for Mass Communication Research.* London: Routledge, pp. 17–43.

Jewson, N. (1976) 'The disappearance of the sick-man from medical cosmology, 1770–1870', *Sociology*, 10, 225–44.

Johnson, T. (1972) *Professions and Power.* London: Macmillan.

Jordanova, L. (1983) 'The social sciences and history of science and medicine', in P. Corsi and P. Weindling (eds), *Information Sources in the History of Science and Medicine.* London: Butterworths, pp. 81–96.

Jordanova, L. (1989) *Sexual Visions: Images of Gender in Science and Medicine between the Eighteenth and Twentieth Centuries.* London: Harvester Wheatsheaf.

Kagawa-Singer, M., Kim, S., Wu, K., Adler, S., Kawanishi, Y., Wongripat, N. and Greendale, G. (2002) 'Comparison of the menopause and midlife transition between Japanese American and European American women', *Medical Anthropology Quarterly*, 16 (1), 64–92.

Karpf, A. (1988) *Doctoring the Media: the Reporting of Health and Medicine.* London: Routledge.

Katz, J. (1984) 'Why doctors don't disclose uncertainty', *Hastings Center Report*, February, 35–44.

Katz, P. (1985) 'How surgeons make decisions', in R. Hahn and A. Gaines (eds), *Physicians of Western Medicine: Anthropological Approaches to Theory and Practice.* Dordrecht: D. Reidel, pp. 155–76.

Kaufert, P. (1988) 'Menopause as process or event: the creation of definitions in biomedicine', in M. Lock and D.R. Gordon (eds), *Biomedicine Examined.* Dordrecht: Kluwer, pp. 331–49.

Kelly, M. (1992) 'Self, identity and radical surgery', *Sociology of Health & Illness*, 14 (3), 390–415.

Kirmayer, L. (1988) 'Mind and body as metaphors: hidden values in biomedicine', in M. Lock and D. Gordon (eds), *Biomedicine Examined.* Dordrecht: Kluwer, pp. 57–94.

Kleinman, A. (1988) *The Illness Narratives: Suffering, Healing and the Human Condition*. New York, NY: Basic Books.

Kleinman, A., Eisenberg, L. and Good, B. (1978) 'Culture, illness and care: clinical lessons from anthropological and cross-cultural research', *Annals of Internal Medicine*, 88, 251–8.

Koutroulis, G. (2001) 'Soiled identity: memory-work narratives of menstruation', *Health*, 5 (2), 187–205.

Krantzler, N. (1986) 'Media images of physicians and nurses in the United States', *Social Science & Medicine*, 22 (9), 933–52.

Kress, G. (1985) *Linguistic Processes in Socio-cultural Practice*. Geelong: Deakin University Press.

Kroker, A. (1992) 'Sacrificial sex', in J. Miller (ed.), *Fluid Exchanges: Artists and Critics in the AIDS Crisis*. Toronto: University of Toronto Press, pp. 321–8.

Kroker, A. and Cook, D. (1988) *The Postmodern Scene: Excremental Culture and Hyperaesthetics*. Toronto: Macmillan.

Kroker, A. and Kroker, M. (1988) 'Panic sex in America', in A. Kroker and M. Kroker (eds), *Body Invaders: Sexuality and the Postmodern Condition*. Toronto: Macmillan, pp. 10–19.

Lakoff, G. and Johnson, M. (1981) *Metaphors We Live By*. Chicago, IL: University of Chicago Press.

Laqueur, T. (1987) 'Orgasm, generation, and the politics of reproductive biology', in C. Gallagher and T. Laqueur (eds), *The Making of the Modern Body: Sexuality and Society in the Nineteenth Century*. Berkeley, CA: University of California Press, pp. 1–41.

Lasch, C. (1980) *The Culture of Narcissism: American Life in an Age of Diminishing Expectations*. New York, NY: Abacus.

Lawler, J. (1991) *Behind the Screens: Nursing, Somology and the Problem of the Body*. Melbourne: Churchill Livingstone.

Lawrence, S. and Bendixen, K. (1992) 'His and hers: male and female anatomy in anatomy texts for US medical students, 1890–1989', *Social Science & Medicine*, 35 (7), 925–34.

Laws, S. (1990) *Issues of Blood: the Politics of Menstruation*. Basingstoke: Macmillan.

Lawton, J. (1998) 'Contemporary hospice care: the sequestration of the unbounded body and dirty dying', *Sociology of Health & Illness*, 20 (2), 123–39.

Lazarus, E. (1988) 'Theoretical considerations for the study of the doctor–patient relationship: implications of a perinatal study', *Medical Anthropology Quarterly*, 2 (1), 34–58.

Lee, S. (2002) 'Health and sickness: the meaning of menstruation and premenstrual syndrome in women's lives', *Sex Roles*, 46 (1/2), 25–35.

Lehtonen, M. (2000) *The Cultural Analysis of Texts*. London: Sage.

Leiss, W., Kline, S. and Jhally, S. (1986) *Social Communication in Advertising: Persons, Products and Images of Well-being*. New York, NY: Methuen.

Leslie, C. (2001) 'Backing into the future', *Medical Anthropology Quarterly*, 15 (4), 428–40.

Lippman, A. (1992) 'Led (astray) by genetic maps: the cartography of the human genome and health care', *Social Science & Medicine*, 35 (12), 1469–76.

Little, M., Jordens, C., Paul, K., Montgomery, K. and Philipson, B. (1998) 'Liminality: a major category in the experience of cancer illness', *Social Science & Medicine*, 47 (10), 1485–94.

Littlewood, R. (1991) 'From disease to illness and back again', *Lancet*, 337, 1013–16.

Lock, M. (1985) 'Models and practice in medicine: menopause as syndrome or life transition?', in R. Hahn and A. Gaines (eds), *Physicians of Western Medicine: Anthropological Approaches to Theory and Practice.* Dordrecht: D. Reidel, pp. 115–40.

Lock, M. (1986) 'Introduction: anthropological approaches to menopause: questioning received wisdom', *Culture, Medicine and Psychiatry*, 10, 1–5.

Lonsdale, M. (1992) 'Sexual violence', *Arena*, 99/100, 80–97.

Lucie-Smith, E. (1975) *The Waking Dream: Fantasy and the Surreal in Graphic Art, 1450–1900.* New York, NY: Alfred Knopf.

Lupton, D. (1992) 'Ideology and health reporting', *Media Information Australia*, 65, 28–35.

Lupton, D. (1993a) 'AIDS risk and heterosexuality in the Australian press', *Discourse & Society*, 4 (3), 307–28.

Lupton, D. (1993b) 'The construction of patienthood in medical advertising', *International Journal of Health Services*, 23 (4), 805–19.

Lupton, D. (1993c) 'Risk as moral danger: the social and political functions of risk discourse in public health', *International Journal of Health Services*, 23 (3), 425–35.

Lupton, D. (1994a) *Moral Threats and Dangerous Desires: AIDS in the News Media.* London: Taylor and Francis.

Lupton, D. (1994b) 'Femininity, responsibility and the technological imperative: discourses on breast cancer in the Australian press', *International Journal of Health Services*, 24 (1), 73–89.

Lupton, D. (1995) *The Imperative of Health: Public Health and the Regulated Body.* London: Sage.

Lupton, D. (1996) 'Constructing the menopausal body: the discourses on hormone replacement therapy', *Body & Society*, 2 (1), 91–7.

Lupton, D. (1997a) 'Psychoanalytic sociology and the medical encounter: Parsons and beyond', *Sociology of Health & Illness*, 19 (5), 561–79.

Lupton, D. (1997b) 'Foucault and the medicalisation critique', in A. Petersen and R. Bunton (eds), *Foucault, Health and Medicine.* London: Routledge, pp. 94–110.

Lupton, D. (1999) 'Risk and the ontology of pregnant embodiment', in D. Lupton (ed.), *Risk and Sociocultural Theory: New Directions and Perspectives.* Cambridge: Cambridge University Press, pp. 59–85.

Lupton, D. and Chapman, S. (1991) 'Death of a heart surgeon: reflections on press accounts of the murder of Victor Chang', *British Medical Journal*, 303, 1583–6.

Lupton, D. and McLean, J. (1998) 'Representing doctors: discourses and images in the Australian press', *Social Science & Medicine*, 46 (8), 947–58.

Lynch, M. (1987) 'The body: thin is beautiful', *Arena*, 79, 128–45.

Lyons, A. and Willott, S. (1999) 'From suet pudding to superhero: representations of men's health for women', *Health*, 3 (3), 283–302.

McCombie, S. (1987) 'Folk flu and viral syndrome: an epidemiological perspective', *Social Science & Medicine*, 25 (9), 987–93.

McCracken, G. (1988) *Culture and Consumption: New Approaches to the Symbolic Character of Consumer Goods and Activities.* Bloomington, IN: Indiana University Press.

McKee, J. (1988) 'Holistic health and the critique of western medicine', *Social Science & Medicine*, 26 (8), 775–84.

Mackie, R. (1992) 'When the body fails, so does autonomy', *Sydney Morning Herald*, 11 May, 24.

McKinlay, J. and Stoeckle, I. (1988) 'Corporatization and the social transformation of doctoring', *International Journal of Health Services*, 18 (2), 191–205.

McLaughlin J. (1975) 'The doctor shows', *Journal of Communication*, 25 (3), 18–24.

McMahon, K. (1990) 'The *Cosmopolitan* ideology and the management of desire', *Journal of Sex Research*, 27 (3), 381–96.

Malchiodi, C. (1997) 'Invasive art: art as empowerment for women with breast cancer', in S. Hogan (ed.), *Feminist Approaches to Art Therapy*. London: Routledge, pp. 49–64.

Manderson, L. (1998) 'Health matters in developing economies', in A. Petersen and C. Waddell (eds), *Health Matters: A Sociology of Illness, Prevention and Care*. Sydney: Allen and Unwin, pp. 97–113.

Manion, E. (1988) 'A ms.-managed womb', in A. Kroker and M. Kroker (eds), *Body Invaders: Sexuality and the Postmodern Condition*. Toronto: Macmillan, pp. 183–99.

Mansfield, A. and McGinn, B. (1993) 'Pumping irony: the muscular and the feminine', in S. Scott and D. Morgan (eds), *Body Matters: Essays on the Sociology of the Body*. London: Falmer, pp. 49–68.

Marshall, S. (1990) 'Picturing deviancy', in T. Boffin and S. Gupta (eds), *Ecstatic Antibodies: Resisting the AIDS Mythology*. London: Rivers Oram Press, pp. 19–36.

Martin, E. (1987) *The Woman in the Body: a Cultural Analysis of Reproduction*. Boston, MA: Beacon Press.

Martin, E. (1990a) 'Toward an anthropology of immunology: the body as nation state', *Medical Anthropology Quarterly*, 4 (4), 410–26.

Martin, E. (1990b) 'The ideology of reproduction: the reproduction of ideology', in F. Ginsburg and A. Tsing (eds), *Uncertain Terms: Negotiating Gender in American Culture*. Boston, MA: Beacon Press, pp. 300–14.

Martin, E. (1991) 'The egg and the sperm: how science has constructed a romance based on stereotypical male–female roles', *Signs: Journal of Women in Culture and Society*, 16 (3), 485–501.

Martin, E. (1992) 'Body narratives, body boundaries', in L. Grossberg, C. Nelson and P. Treichler (eds), *Cultural Studies*. New York, NY: Routledge, pp. 409–23.

Martin, E. (2000) 'Flexible bodies: science and a new culture of health in the US', in S. Williams, J. Gabe and M. Calnan (eds), *Health, Medicine and Society: Key Theories, Future Agendas*. London: Routledge, pp. 123–45.

Martin, R. (1997) 'Looking and reflecting: returning the gaze, re-enacting memories and imagining the future through phototherapy', in S. Hogan (ed.), *Feminist Approaches to Art Therapy*. London: Routledge, pp. 150–76.

Maseide, P. (1991) 'Possibly abusive, often benign and always necessary. On power and domination in medical practice', *Sociology of Health & Illness*, 13 (4), 545–61.

May, C. (1992a) 'Individual care? Power and subjectivity in therapeutic relationships', *Sociology*, 26 (4), 589–602.

May, C. (1992b) 'Nursing work, nurse's knowledge, and the subjectification of the patient', *Sociology of Health & Illness*, 14 (4), 472–87.

Mechanic, D. (1979) *Future Issues in Health Care: Social Policy and the Rationing of Medical Services*. New York, NY: The Free Press.

Mechanic, D. (1993) 'Social research in health and the American sociopolitical context: the changing fortunes of medical sociology', *Social Science & Medicine*, 36 (2), 95–102.

Mennell, S. (1985) *All Manners of Food*. Oxford: Basil Blackwell.

Meyers, J. (1985) *Disease and the Novel, 1880–1960*. London: Macmillan.

Modell, J. (1989) 'Last chance babies: interpretations of parenthood in an in vitro fertilization programme', *Medical Anthropology Quarterly*, 3 (2), 124–38.

Montgomery, S. (1991) 'Codes and combat in biomedical discourse', *Science as Culture*, 2 (3), 341–91.

Morgan, D. (1993) 'You too can have a body like mine: reflections on the male body and masculinities', in S. Scott and D. Morgan (eds), *Body Matters: Essays on the Sociology of the Body*. London: Falmer, pp. 69–88.

Morgan, D. and Scott, S. (1993) 'Bodies in a social landscape', in S. Scott and D. Morgan (eds), *Body Matters: Essays on the Sociology of the Body*. London: Falmer, pp. 1–21.

Moscucci, O. (1990) *The Science of Woman: Gynaecology and Gender in England, 1800–1929*. Cambridge: Cambridge University Press.

Muller, J. and Koenig, B. (1988) 'On the boundary of life and death: the definition of dying by medical residents', in M. Lock and D. Gordon (eds), *Biomedicine Examined*. Dordrecht: Kluwer, pp. 351–74.

Murcott, A. (ed.) (1983) *The Sociology of Food and Eating*. Aldershot: Gower.

Murcott, A. (1993) 'Purity and pollution: body management and the social place of infancy', in S. Scott and D. Morgan (eds), *Body Matters: Essays on the Sociology of the Body*. London: Falmer, pp. 122–34.

Nash, J. (1992) 'Attack of the superbugs', *Time*, 31 August, 44–7.

Nations, M., Camino, L. and Walker, F. (1985) '"Hidden" popular illnesses in primary care: residents' recognition and clinical implications', *Culture, Medicine and Psychiatry*, 9, 223–40.

Navarro, V. (1976) *Medicine under Capitalism*. New York, NY: Prodist.

Nelkin, D. and Gilman, S. (1988) 'Placing blame for devastating disease', *Social Research*, 55 (3), 361–78.

Nelkin, D. and Tancredi, L. (1989) *Dangerous Diagnostics: the Social Power of Biological Information*. New York, NY: Basic Books.

Newman, E. (1985) 'Who controls birth control?', in W. Faulkner and E. Arnold (eds), *Smothered by Technology: Technology in Women's Lives*. London: Pluto Press, pp. 128–43.

Nicolson, M. and McLaughlin, C. (1987) 'Social constructionism and medical sociology: a reply to M.R. Bury', *Sociology of Health & Illness*, 9 (2), 107–27.

Noble, C. and Bell, P. (1992) 'Reproducing women's nature: media constructions of IVF and related issues', *Australian Journal of Social Issues*, 27 (1), 17–30.

Oakley, A. (1980) *Women Confined: Towards a Sociology of Childbirth*. Oxford: Martin Robertson.

Oakley, A. (1984) *The Captured Womb: a History of Medical Care of Pregnant Women*. Oxford: Basil Blackwell.

Oakley, A. (1987) 'From walking wombs to test-tube babies', in M. Stanworth (ed.), *Reproductive Technologies: Gender, Motherhood and Medicine*. Oxford: Polity Press, pp. 30–56.

Oakley, A. (1989) 'Smoking in pregnancy: smokescreen or risk factor? Towards a materialist analysis', *Sociology of Health & Illness*, 11 (4), 311–35.

O'Hara, L. (1989) 'The operating theatre as degradation ritual: a student nurse's view', *Science as Culture*, 6, 78–103.

Olivar, J. (1993) '"My fight for life" (interview with Olivia Newton-John)', *Australian Women's Weekly*, February, 4–9.

Orbach, S. (1988) *Fat is a Feminist Issue*. London: Arrow Books.

Outram, D. (1989) *The Body and the French Revolution: Sex, Class and Political Culture*. New Haven, CT: Yale University Press.

Park, K. (1992) 'Medicine and society in medieval Europe, 500–1500', in A. Wear (ed.), *Medicine in Society: Historical Essays*. Cambridge: Cambridge University Press, pp. 59–90.

Parker, I. (1992) *Discourse Dynamics: Critical Analysis for Social and Individual Psychology*. London: Routledge.

Parker, I. and the Bolton Discourse Network (1999) *Critical Textwork: an Introduction to Varieties of Discourse and Analysis*. Buckingham: Open University Press.

Parsons, T. (1987/1951) 'Illness and the role of the physicians: a sociological perspective', in J.D. Stoeckle (ed.), *Encounters between Patients and Doctors: an Anthology*. Cambridge, MA: MIT Press, pp. 147–56.

Patel, M. (1987) 'Evaluation of holistic medicine', *Social Science & Medicine*, 24, 169–75.

Patton, C. (1986) *Sex and Germs: the Politics of AIDS*. Montreal: Black Rose Books.

Pellegrino, E. (1980) 'Introduction: to look feelingly – the affinities of medicine and literature', in E. Peschel (ed.), *Medicine and Literature*. New York, NY: Neale Watson Academic Publications, pp. xv–xix.

Peschel, E. (ed.) (1980) *Medicine and Literature*. New York, NY: Neale Watson Academic Publications.

Petchesky, R. (1987) 'Foetal images: the power of visual culture in the politics of reproduction', in M. Stanworth (ed.), *Reproductive Technologies: Gender, Motherhood and Medicine*. Cambridge: Polity Press, pp. 57–80.

Petersen, A. (1998) 'Sexing the body: representations of sex differences in Gray's *Anatomy*, 1858 to the present', *Body & Society*, 4 (1), 1–15.

Petersen, A. and Bunton, R. (eds) (1997) *Foucault, Health and Medicine*. London: Routledge.

Petersen, A. and Lupton, D. (1997) *The New Public Health: Health and Self in the Age of Risk*. London: Sage.

Pill, R. and Stott, N. (1982) 'Concepts of illness causation and responsibility: some preliminary data from a sample of working-class mothers', *Social Science & Medicine*, 16, 43–52.

Pinell, P. (1987) 'How do cancer patients express their points of view?', *Sociology of Health & Illness*, 9 (1), 25–44.

Plummer, K. (ed.) (1981) *The Making of the Modern Homosexual*. London: Hutchinson.

Porter, M. (1990) 'Professional–client relationships and women's reproductive health care', in S. Cunningham-Burley and N.P. McKeganey (eds), *Readings in Medical Sociology*. London: Routledge, pp. 182–210.

Porter, R. (1985) 'Introduction', in R. Porter (ed.), *Patients and Practitioners: Lay Perceptions of Medicine in Pre-Industrial Society*. Cambridge: Cambridge University Press, pp. 1–22.

Porter, R. (1992) 'The patient in England, *c.* 1660–1800', in A. Wear (ed.), *Medicine in Society: Historical Essays*. Cambridge: Cambridge University Press, pp. 91–118.

Posner, T. (1991) 'What's in a smear? Cervical screening, medical signs and metaphors', *Science as Culture*, 2 (2), 160–87.

Posner, T. and Vessey, M. (1988) *Prevention of Cervical Cancer: the Patient's View*. London: King Edward's Hospital Fund for London.

Potter, J. and Wetherell, M. (1987) *Discourse and Social Psychology: Beyond Attitudes and Behaviour*. London: Sage.

Pouchelle, M.-C. (1990) *The Body and Surgery in the Middle Ages* (translated by R. Morris). Cambridge: Polity Press.

Pringle, R. (1992) 'Absolute sex? Unpacking the sexuality/gender relationship', in R. Connell and G. Dowsett (eds), *Rethinking Sex: Social Theory and Sexuality Research*. Melbourne: Melbourne University Press, pp. 76–101.

Prior, L. (2000) 'Reflections on the "mortal" body in late modernity', in S. Williams, J. Gabe and M. Calnan (eds), *Health, Medicine and Society: Key Theories, Future Agendas*. London: Routledge, pp. 186–202.

Prior, L. and Bloor, M. (1993) 'Why people die: social representations of death and its causes', *Science as Culture*, 3 (3), 346–75.

Quilliam, S. (1990) 'Positive smear: the emotional issues and what can be done', *Health Education Journal*, 49 (1), 19–20.

Rapp, R. (1985) 'XYLO: a true story', in R. Arditti, R. Klein and S. Minden (eds), *Test-tube Women: What Future for Motherhood?* London: Pandora, pp. 313–28.

Rapp, R. (1990) 'Constructing amniocentesis: maternal and medical discourses', in F. Ginsburg and A. Tsing (eds), *Uncertain Terms: Negotiating Gender in American Culture*. Boston, MA: Beacon Press, pp. 28–42.

Raymond, J., Klein, R. and Dumble, L. (1991) *RU486: Misconceptions, Myths and Morals*. Cambridge, MA: Institute on Women and Technology.

Reiger, K. (1987) 'The embodiment of resistance: reproductive struggles and feminism', *Arena*, 79, 92–107.

Renaud, M. (1978) 'On the structural constraints to state intervention in health', in J. Ehrenreich (ed.), *The Cultural Crisis of Modern Medicine*. New York, NY: Monthly Review Press, pp. 101–20.

Reynolds, T. (1987) *Your Cancer, Your Life*. Melbourne: Greenhouse Books.

Rhodes, T. and Shaughnessy, R. (1990) 'Compulsory screening: advertising AIDS in Britain, 1980–1989', *Policy and Politics*, 18 (1), 55–61.

Richardson, R. (1988) *Death, Dissection and the Destitute*. London: Penguin.

Rier, D. (2000) 'The missing voice of the critically ill: a medical sociologist's first-person account', *Sociology of Health & Illness*, 22 (1), 68–93.

Risse, G. (1988) 'Epidemics and history: ecological perspectives and social responses', in E. Fee and D. Fox (eds), *AIDS: the Burdens of History*. Berkeley, CA: University of California Press, pp. 33–66.

Risse, G. (1992) 'Medicine in the age of Enlightenment', in A. Wear (ed.), *Medicine in Society: Historical Essays*. Cambridge: Cambridge University Press, pp. 149–96.

Rittenhouse, C. (1991) 'The emergence of pre-menstrual syndrome as a social problem', *Social Problems*, 38 (3), 412–25.

Robotham, J. (2002a) 'Parents fail to get full picture on ultrasounds', *Sydney Morning Herald*, 30 September.

Robotham, J. (2002b) 'Webheads know what ails them', *Sydney Morning Herald*, 13 December.

Rodin, M. (1992) 'The social construction of pre-menstrual syndrome', *Social Science & Medicine*, 35 (1), 49–56.

Rose, H. (1987) 'Victorian values in the test-tube: the politics of reproductive science and technology', in M. Stanworth (ed.), *Reproductive Technologies: Gender, Motherhood and Medicine*. Cambridge: Polity Press, pp. 151–73.

Rosenberg, C. (1988) 'Disease and social order in America: perceptions and expectations', in E. Fee and D. Fox (eds), *AIDS: the Burdens of History*. Berkeley, CA: University of California Press, pp. 12–32.

Roth, J. (1981/1972) 'Some contingencies of the moral evaluation and control of clientele: the case of the hospital emergency service', in P. Conrad and R. Kern (eds), *The Sociology of Health and Illness: Critical Perspectives*. New York, NY: St Martin's Press, pp. 377–94.

Rothfield, P. (1992) 'Backstage in the theatre of representation', *Arena*, 99/100, 98–111.

Rowland, R. (1992) *Living Laboratories: Woman and Reproductive Technologies*. Sydney: Pan Macmillan.

Russell, C. and Schofield, T. (1986) *Where It Hurts: an Introduction to Sociology for Health Workers*. Sydney: Allen and Unwin.

Ruzek, S. (1981) 'The women's self-help movement', in P. Conrad and R. Kern (eds), *The Sociology of Health and Illness: Critical Perspectives*. New York, NY: St Martin's Press, pp. 563–70.

Sacks, O. (1984) *A Leg to Stand On*. New York, NY: Summit Books.

Saltonstall, R. (1993) 'Healthy bodies, social bodies: men's and women's concepts and practices of health in everyday life', *Social Science & Medicine*, 36 (1), 7–14.

Sandelowski, M., Holditch-Davis, D. and Harris, B. (1990) 'Living the life: explanations of infertility', *Sociology of Health & Illness*, 12 (2), 195–215.

Santalahti, P., Hemminkik, E., Latikka, A.-M. and Ryynanen, M. (1998) 'Women's decision-making in prenatal screening', *Social Science & Medicine*, 46 (8), 1067–76.

Saul, H. (1993) 'Bad timing puts babies at risk', *New Scientist*, 10 April, 12–13.

Scambler, G. (1987) 'Introduction', in G. Scambler (ed.), *Sociological Theory and Medical Sociology*. London: Tavistock, pp. 1–7.

Scheper-Hughes, N. and Lock, M. (1987) 'The mindful body: a prolegomenon to future work in medical anthropology', *Medical Anthropology Quarterly*, 1, 6–41.

Schiebinger, L. (1987) 'Skeletons in the closet: the first illustrations of the female skeleton in eighteenth-century anatomy', in C. Gallagher and T. Laqueur (eds), *The Making of the Modern Body: Sexuality and Society in the Nineteenth Century*. Berkeley, CA: University of California Press, pp. 42–82.

Scott, A. (1999) 'Paradoxes of holism: some problems in developing an anti-oppressive medical practice', *Health*, 3 (2), 131–49.

Scully, D. and Bart, P. (1981) 'A funny thing happened on the way to the orifice: women in gynaecology textbooks', in P. Conrad and R. Kern (eds), *The Sociology of Health and Illness: Critical Perspectives*. New York, NY: St Martin's Press, pp. 350–5.

Seale, C. (2001) 'Sporting cancer: struggle language in news reports of people with cancer', *Sociology of Health & Illness*, 23 (3), 308–29.

Sears, A. (1992) '"To teach them how to live": the politics of public health from tuberculosis to AIDS', *Journal of Historical Sociology*, 5 (1), 61–83.

Seddon, G. (1993) 'Imaging the mind', *Meanjin*, 52 (1), 183–94.

Seidman, S. (1991) *Romantic Longings: Love in America, 1830–1980*. New York, NY: Routledge.

Seidman, S. (1992) *Embattled Eros: Sexual Politics and Ethics in Contemporary America*. New York, NY: Routledge.

Seymour, W. (1989) *Bodily Alterations: an Introduction to a Sociology of the Body for Health Workers*. Sydney: Allen and Unwin.

Seymour, W. (1998) *Remaking the Body: Rehabilitation and Change*. London: Routledge.

Shakespeare, T. (1994) 'Cultural representations of disabled people: dustbins for disavowal?', *Disability & Society*, 9 (3), 283–99.

Shakespeare, T. (1999) '"Losing the plot?" Medical and activist discourses of contemporary genetics and disability', *Sociology of Health & Illness*, 21 (5), 669–88.

Shilling, C. (1991) 'Educating the body: physical capital and the production of social inequalities', *Sociology*, 25 (4), 653–72.

Showalter, E. (1990) *Sexual Anarchy: Gender and Culture at the Fin de Siècle*. New York, NY: Viking.

Silverman, D. (1987) *Communication and Medical Practice: Social Relations in the Clinic*. London: Sage.

Singer, L. (1993) *Erotic Welfare: Sexual Theory and Politics in the Age of Epidemic*. New York, NY: Routledge.

Singer, M. (1987) 'Cure, care and control: an ectopic encounter with biomedical obstetrics', in H.A. Baer (ed.), *Encounters with Biomedicine: Case Studies in Medical Anthropology*. New York, NY: Gordon and Breach, pp. 249–65.

Singer, M. (1990) 'Postmodernism and medical anthropology: words of caution', *Medical Anthropology*, 12, 289–304.

Skultans, V. (1988) 'Menstrual symbolism in South Wales', in T. Buckley and A. Gottlieb (eds), *Blood Magic: the Anthropology of Menstruation*. Berkeley, CA: University of California Press, pp. 137–60.

Smart, B. (1985) *Michel Foucault*. London: Ellis Horwood.

Smith, G. (1985) 'Prescribing the rules of health: self-help and advice in the late eighteenth century', in R. Porter (ed.), *Patients and Practitioners: Lay Perceptions of Medicine in Pre-Industrial Society*. Cambridge: Cambridge University Press, pp. 249–82.

Sontag, S. (1989) *Illness as Metaphor/AIDS and Its Metaphors*. New York, NY: Anchor.

Spence, J. (1986) *Putting Myself in the Picture: a Political, Personal and Photographic Autobiography*. London: Camden Press.

Stanworth, M. (1987) 'The Deconstruction of Motherhood', in M. Stanworth (ed.), *Reproductive Technologies: Gender, Motherhood and Medicine*. Cambridge: Polity Press, pp. 10–35.

Starr, P. (1982) *The Social Transformation of American Medicine*. New York, NY: Basic Books.

Stein, H. (1990) *American Medicine as Culture*. Boulder, CO: Westview.

Steinberg, D. (1990) 'The depersonalization of women through the administration of "*in vitro* fertilization"', in M. McNeil, I. Varcoe and S. Yearly (eds), *The New Reproductive Technologies*. New York, NY: St Martin's Press, pp. 74–122.

Stoeckle, J. and Barsky, A. (1981) 'Attributions: uses of social science knowledge in the "doctoring" of primary care', in L. Eisenberg and A. Kleinman (eds), *The Relevance of Social Science for Medicine*. Dordrecht: D. Reidel, pp. 223–40.

Strickler, J. (1992) 'The new reproductive technology: problem or solution?', *Sociology of Health & Illness*, 14 (1), 111–32.

Strong, P. (1979) *The Ceremonial Order of the Clinic: Patients, Doctors and Medical Bureaucracies*. London: Routledge and Kegan Paul.

Strong, P. (1990) 'Epidemic psychology: a model', *Sociology of Health & Illness*, 12 (3), 249–59.

Syme, S. and Alcalay, R. (1982) 'Control of cigarette smoking from a social perspective', *Annual Review of Public Health*, 3, 179–99.

Taleporos, G. and McCabe, M. (2002) 'Body image and physical disability – personal perspectives', *Social Science & Medicine*, 54, 971–80.

Taylor, K. (1988) 'Physicians and the disclosure of undesirable information', in M. Lock and D. Gordon (eds), *Biomedicine Examined*. Dordrecht: Kluwer, pp. 441–63.

Tesh, S. (1988) *Hidden Arguments: Political Ideology and Disease Prevention Policy.* New Brunswick, NJ: Rutgers University Press.

Treichler, P. (1990) 'Feminism, medicine, and the meaning of childbirth', in M. Jacobus, E. Keller and S. Shuttleworth (eds), *Body/Politics: Women and the Discourses of Science.* New York, NY: Routledge, pp. 113–38.

Tsing, A. (1990) 'Monster stories: women charged with perinatal endangerment', in F. Ginsburg and A. Tsing (eds), *Uncertain Terms: Negotiating Gender in American Culture.* Boston, MA: Beacon Press, pp. 282–99.

Turner, B. (1991a) 'Recent developments in the theory of the body', in M. Featherstone, M. Hepworth and B. Turner (eds), *The Body: Social Process and Cultural Theory.* London: Sage, pp. 1–35.

Turner, B. (1991b) 'The discourse of diet', in M. Featherstone, M. Hepworth and B. Turner (eds), *The Body: Social Process and Cultural Theory.* London: Sage, pp. 157–69.

Turner, B. (1992) *Regulating Bodies: Essays in Medical Sociology.* London: Routledge.

Turner, B. (1995) *Medical Power and Social Knowledge* (2nd edn). London: Sage.

Turner, B. (1996) *The Body and Society: Explorations in Social Theory* (2nd edn). London: Sage.

Turner, G. (1990) *British Cultural Studies: an Introduction.* Boston, MA: Unwin Hyman.

Turow, J. (1989) *Playing Doctor: Television, Storytelling and Medical Power.* New York, NY: Oxford University Press.

Turow, J. and Coe, L. (1985) 'Curing television's ills: the portrayal of health care', *Journal of Communication,* 35 (4), 36–51.

van der Geest, S. and Whyte, S. (1989) 'The charm of medicines: metaphors and metonyms', *Medical Anthropology Quarterly,* 3 (4), 345–67.

Vasseleu, C. (1991) 'Life itself', in R. Diprose and R. Ferrell (eds), *Cartographies: Poststructuralism and the Mapping of Bodies and Spaces.* Sydney: Allen and Unwin, pp. 55–64.

Vigarello, G. (1988) *Concepts of Cleanliness: Changing Attitudes in France since the Middle Ages* (translated by J. Birrell). Cambridge: Cambridge University Press.

Wadler, J. (1992) 'My left breast: part two', *HQ,* Summer, 122–34.

Waitzkin, H. (1981) 'A Marxist analysis of the health care systems of advanced capitalist societies', in L. Eisenberg and A. Kleinman (eds), *The Relevance of Social Science for Medicine.* Dordrecht: D. Reidel, pp. 333–70.

Waitzkin, H. (1984) 'The micropolitics of medicine: a contextual analysis', *International Journal of Health Services,* 14 (3), 339–78.

Waitzkin, H. and Stoeckle, J. (1972) 'The communication of information about illness', *Advances in Psychosomatic Medicine,* 8, 180–215.

Wajcman, J. (1991) *Feminism Confronts Technology.* Sydney: Allen and Unwin.

Walsh, V. (1980) 'Contraception: the growth of a technology', in The Brighton Women and Science Group (ed.), *Alice through the Microscope: the Power of Science over Women's Lives.* London: Virago, pp. 182–207.

Watney, S. (1987) *Policing Desire: Pornography, AIDS and the Media.* London: Comedia.

Watson, J. (2000) *Male Bodies: Health, Culture and Identity.* Buckingham: Open University Press.

Wear, A. (1985) 'Puritan perceptions of illness in seventeenth-century England', in R. Porter (ed.), *Patients and Practitioners: Lay Perceptions of Medicine in Pre-Industrial Society.* Cambridge: Cambridge University Press, pp. 55–99.

Wear, A. (1992) 'Making sense of health and the environment in early modern England', in A. Wear (ed.), *Medicine in Society: Historical Essays.* Cambridge: Cambridge University Press, pp. 119–48.

Weeks, J. (1986) *Sexuality.* London: Tavistock.

Weeks, J. (1987) 'Questions of identity', in P. Caplan (ed.), *The Cultural Construction of Sexuality.* London: Tavistock, pp. 31–51.

Weeks, J. (1991) *Against Nature: Essays on History, Sexuality and Identity.* London: Rivers Oram Press.

Wellings, K. (1985) 'Help or hype: an analysis of media coverage of the 1983 "pill scare"', in D. Leathar, G. Hastings, K. O'Reilly and J. Davies (eds), *Health Education and the Media II.* Oxford: Pergamon, pp. 109–15.

Wertz, R. and Wertz, D. (1981) 'Notes on the decline of midwives and the rise of medical obstetricians', in P. Conrad and R. Kern (eds), *The Sociology of Health and Illness: Critical Perspectives.* New York, NY: St Martin's Press, pp. 165–83.

White, R. (2002) 'Social and political aspects of men's health', *Health,* 6 (3), 267–86.

Wiener, A. (1993) 'Problems on the other side of the fence', *British Medical Journal,* 306, 661.

Williams, G. and Busby, H. (2000) 'The politics of "disabled" bodies', in S. Williams, J. Gabe and M. Calnan (eds), *Health, Medicine and Society: Key Theories, Future Agendas.* London: Routledge, pp. 169–87.

Williams, R. (1976) 'Developments in the sociology of culture', *Sociology,* 19, 497–506.

Williams, R. (1990) *A Protestant Legacy: Attitudes to Death and Illness among Older Aberdonians.* Oxford: Oxford University Press.

Williams, S. (2001) 'Sociological imperialism and the profession of medicine revisited: where are we now?', *Sociology of Health & Illness,* 23 (2), 135–58.

Williamson, J. (1989) 'Every virus tells a story', in E. Carter and S. Watney (eds), *Taking Liberties: AIDS and Cultural Politics.* London: Serpent's Tail, pp. 69–80.

Willis, E. (1978) 'Alternative medicine and the struggle for legitimacy', *New Doctor,* 9, 15–18.

Willis, E. (1989) *Medical Dominance: the Division of Labour in Australian Health Care* (revised edition). Sydney: Allen and Unwin.

Willis, S. (1991) *A Primer for Daily Life.* London: Routledge.

Wilson, A. (1985) 'Participant or patient? Seventeenth century childbirth from the mother's point of view', in R. Porter (ed.), *Patients and Practitioners: Lay Perceptions of Medicine in Pre-Industrial Society.* Cambridge: Cambridge University Press, pp. 129–44.

Wiltshire, J. and Parker, J. (1996) 'Containing abjection in nursing: the end of shift handover as a site of containment', *Nursing Inquiry,* 3, 23–9.

Winship, J. (1987) *Inside Women's Magazines.* London: Pandora.

Wright, P. (1988) 'Babyhood: the social construction of infant care as a medical problem in England in the years around 1900', in M. Lock and D. Gordon (eds), *Biomedicine Examined.* Dordrecht: Kluwer, pp. 299–330.

Wright, P. and Treacher, A. (1982) 'Introduction', in P. Wright and A. Treacher (eds), *The Problem of Medical Knowledge: Examining the Social Construction of Medicine.* Edinburgh: Edinburgh University Press, pp. 1–22.

Young, S. and Concar, D. (1992) 'These cells were made for learning', *New Scientist Supplement,* 21 November.

Zola, I. (1981) 'Medicine as an institution of social control', in P. Conrad and R. Kern (eds), *The Sociology of Health and Illness: Critical Perspectives.* New York, NY: St Martin's Press, pp. 511–27.

Index